MCSE Windows® 2000 Directory Services Administration Lab Manual

MCSE Windows® 2000 Directory Services Administration Lab Manual

Lee Cottrell

McGraw-Hill/Osborne
New York Chicago San Francisco
Lisbon London Madrid Mexico City Milan
New Delhi San Juan Seoul Singapore Sydney Toronto

McGraw-Hill/Osborne
2600 Tenth Street
Berkeley, California 94710
U.S.A.

To arrange bulk purchase discounts for sales promotions, premiums, or fund-raisers, please contact McGraw-Hill/Osborne at the above address. For information on translations or book distributors outside the U.S.A., please see the International Contact Information page immediately following the index of this book.

MCSE Windows® 2000 Directory Services Administration Lab Manual

1234567890 FGR FGR 01987654321

ISBN 0-07-222303-0

Publisher
Brandon A. Nordin

Vice President & Associate Publisher
Scott Rogers

Acquisitions Editor
Chris Johnson

Senior Project Editor
Betsy Manini

Acquisitions Coordinator
Athena Honore

Technical Editor
Fred Shimmin

Production and Editorial Services
Anzai!, Inc.

Series Designer
Roberta Steele

Cover Series Designer
Greg Scott

This book was composed with Corel VENTURA™ Publisher.

This book is for my wife Laurie and my daughter Elizabeth. They are the glue that holds my life together. Without their support I could not have achieved anything. Thank you.

ABOUT THE AUTHOR

Lee M. Cottrell has been teaching networking, hardware, and computer programming at the Bradford School in Pittsburgh for seven years. In addition to teaching, Mr. Cottrell advises students, maintains some of the school's networks and computer equipment, and writes curricula for ten Bradford Schools.

Mr. Cottrell also runs a small computer consulting business in Pittsburgh. His work has included building networks for several offices, writing database-driven Visual Basic programs, designing and maintaining web sites, and building and maintaining computers. The primary goal of the business is to allow Mr. Cottrell to keep a hand in the field.

Mr. Cottrell's educational background is quite varied. He graduated *magna cum laude* from the University of Pittsburgh with a Bachelor of Science in Pure Mathematics. Afterward, he enrolled in the Pitt Graduate School of Education and received a Professional Certificate and certification to teach mathematics in state of Pennsylvania high schools. Most recently, he completed a Master of Science in Information Science from the University of Pittsburgh.

Mr. Cottrell can be reached at lee_cottrell@hotmail.com.

CONTENTS

ACKNOWLEDGMENTS

I would like to thank the following people for all their help in preparing this book for publication:

- Chris Johnson, Athena Honore, and all of the hard-working people at Osborne Media Group for getting me started and believing in me
- Fred Shimmin for finding all of my technical mistakes
- Ann Fothergill-Brown for converting my text into readable English and for teaching me some big words
- The students, staff, and faculty at Bradford School for putting up with my moods during this project

INTRODUCTION

The *MCSE Windows 2000 Directory Services Lab Manual* is designed to accompany the *MCSE Windows 2000 Directory Services Administration Study Guide (Exam 70-217)* (McGraw-Hill/Osborne, 2000). The lab exercises in this manual complement and extend the topics in the Study Guide, and are designed to help you practice important Active Directory skills.

Despite being designed to complement the study guide, the manual can stand well on its own. It presents all of the skills needed to succeed in the working world. In addition, the manual can serve as a "how to" guide for an administrator in the field.

Lab Exercises

Understanding the theory behind networking and the principles behind Windows 2000 directory service is important for a network administrator. The question is can you transfer that knowledge to a system situation? Each exercise allows you to apply and practice a particular concept or skill in a real-world scenario.

Case Studies Each certification objective is presented as a case study. The case studies provide a conceptual opportunity to apply your newly developed knowledge.

Learning Objectives Working hand-in-hand with the study guide, one objective is to help you pass the certification exam. The second objective is to have you develop critical thinking. In networking, not all installations, re-installations, or network and system problems present themselves in the same fashion each time. You need to be able to analyze the situation, to consider your options and the results of each option, and to select and implement an option. If your first choice works, great; if it doesn't, you start over again.

Lab Materials and Setup To fully accomplish each lab, the hardware and software requirements below must be met. If meeting the requirements is not possible, then read through the steps and become familiar with the procedures as best you can.

Windows 2000 Professional workstation:

- 64MB RAM
- Pentium 133 MHz or higher
- VGA monitor or better
- Mouse or other pointing device
- 12× or faster CD-ROM
- One or more hard drives with a minimum of 4GB free space
- Network card with either a BNC (coaxial cable) or cat5 connection
- Dial-up or LAN connection (optional)

Windows 2000 server:

- 128MB RAM
- Pentium 133 MHz or higher
- VGA monitor or better
- Mouse or other pointing device
- 12× or faster CD-ROM
- One or more hard drives with a minimum of 4GB free space
- Network card with either a BNC (coaxial cable) or cat5 connection
- Dial-up or LAN connection (optional)

The computers can be connected using a small network hub.

Getting Down to Business The hands-on portion of each lab is step-by-step, not click-by-click. The steps provide explanations and instructions, walking you through each task relevant to the certification exam.

Lab Analysis Test

The lab analysis test questions demand short-to-medium answers that quickly assess your comprehension of the material in the study guide and in each lab in the chapter. The answers should be given in your own words. They show that you've synthesized the information and that you've gained a comprehensive understanding of the key concepts.

Key Term Quiz

The key terms are technical words that you should recognize. Knowing their definitions and purposes will help you with the exam and on the job.

Solutions

Each chapter provides solutions for the lab exercises, the lab analysis test, and the key term quiz. You should compare your lab procedures, test answers, and key term definitions with the lab procedure solutions, the lab test answers, and the given definitions. Readers who may be familiar with Windows 2000 will find that, in certain parts of the lab exercises, a step can be accomplished in more than one way. The end result, and your understanding of the process to reach that end result, is the main objective.

Good luck with the text and in your future career as a network administrator!

MCSE
MICROSOFT CERTIFIED SYSTEMS ENGINEER

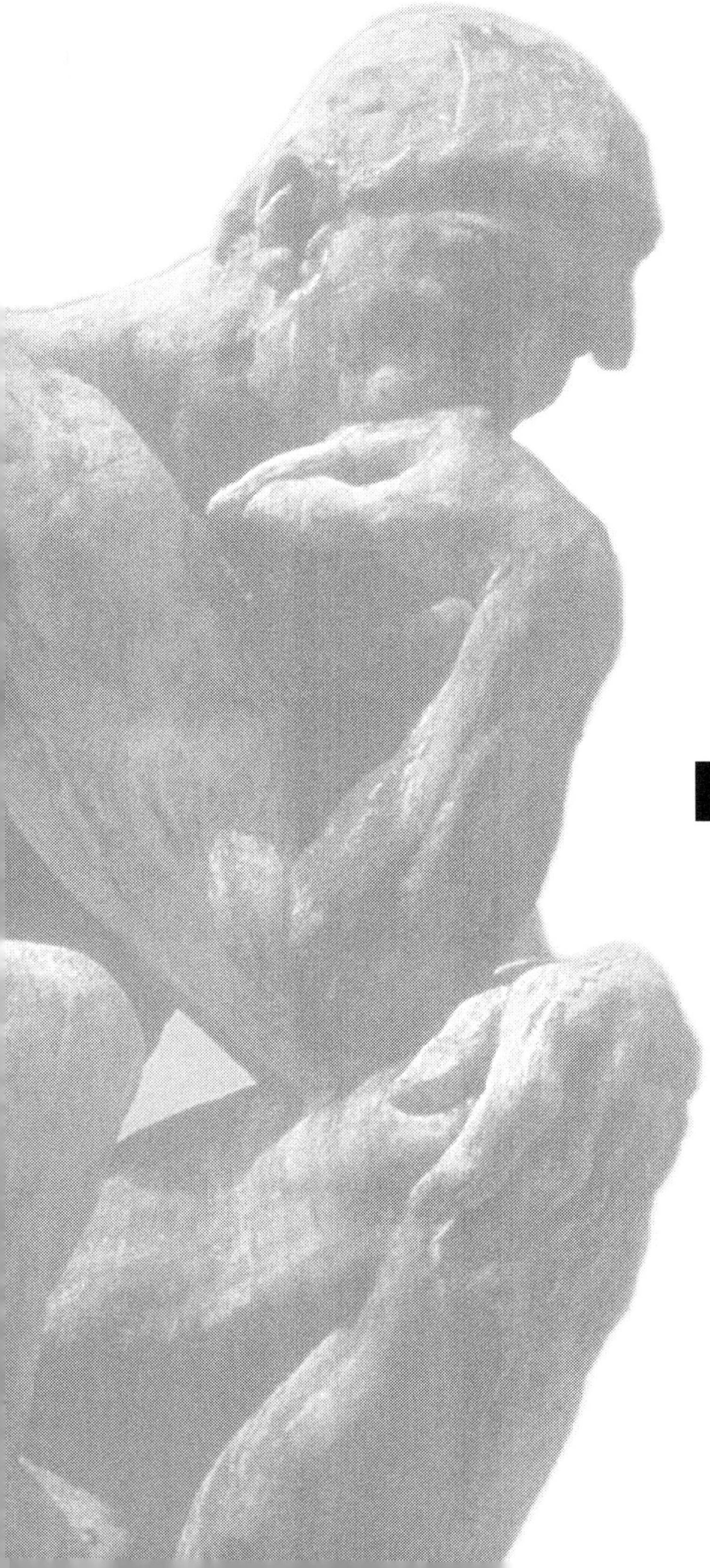

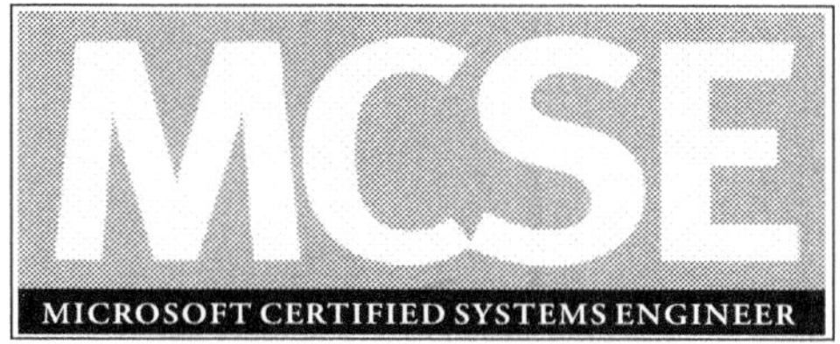

1

Introducing Windows 2000 Directory Services Administration

LAB EXERCISES

1.01 Explaining the Benefits of Windows 2000 Directory Services Administration

1.02 Installing and Configuring Domain Name Service

- Lab Analysis Test
- Key Term Quiz
- Lab Wrap-Up
- Lab Solutions

You have been hired as a network consultant for C&C Services. C&C is a non-profit organization specializing in job training and placement. C&C has several sites in the city and numerous network resources. Your job is to make the administration of these resources easier.

Part of your overall strategy is to use the Active Directory to organize and coordinate the existing networks. Active directory is new to the C&C organization. You will have to set up Active Directory and train the current network administrators in its use.

To prepare for Active Directory, you have to do things. First, you have to sell the bosses at C&C on the technology. Second, you have to install a DNS server at C&C's main site. Both of these are discussed below.

The labs that follow are designed to help you to tie together what you learned in Chapter 1 of* MCSE Windows 2000 Directory Services Administration Study Guide *and to think of those skills within the context of on-the-job experiences.

LAB EXERCISE 1.01

30 Minutes

Explaining the Benefits of Windows 2000 Directory Services Administration

On your first day, the network administrator of C&C, Joanne Tinsley, calls you into her office for a meeting. After the usual pleasantries, Joanne describes a problem in the organization. Employees in the South Side branch are writing documents that the Hill branch needs. Unfortunately, the employees in the Hill are having a hard time finding the documents. South Side's solution has been to e-mail the documents to the Hill. This approach works until South Side changes the original document. The Hill employees then have the wrong document. Joanne asks how the Active Directory can help solve this problem.

Learning Objectives

In this lab, you learn the basic terminology and features of Active Directory. At the end of the lab, you'll be able to

- Define directory services
- List and describe the features of Active Directory

Lab Materials and Setup

Before Joanne will allow you to work on her servers, you'll have to sell her on what Active Directory does. Because Joanne is a network administrator, you can speak the lingo to her. To properly address the topic, you decide to start with the definitions and properties of directory services. Once you cover those items, a brief list of the things that Active Directory can do is appropriate.

No materials are needed for this lab.

Management is usually the hardest group of people to convince that a new technology is good. In dealing with management, do your best to be honest, and try to show how the new technology can enhance the business.

Getting Down to Business

In this lab, you will convince Joanne of the need for directory services. You should stick to the benefits of Active Directory and stay away from possible limitations.

Step 1. Briefly define directory services.

Step 2. List and describe the benefits of Active Directory. Be sure to use C&C as the basis for all examples.

LAB EXERCISE 1.02

15 Minutes

Installing and Configuring Domain Name Service

You are visiting the South Side branch, one of C&C's biggest sites. Dave Jones, South Side's administrator, mentions that Domain Name Service (DNS) is not installed at the organization. They have been relying on their Internet service provider for DNS services. You convince him that they should install DNS, which will save them considerable expense in the long run. You decide that installing DNS is the first task that you will perform for C&C Services.

Learning Objectives

In this lab, you install DNS and build lookup zones for one server. At the end of the lab, you'll be able to

- Install DNS
- Configure DNS for forward and reverse lookups

Lab Materials and Setup

Installing DNS is simply a matter of running Add/Remove Windows Components and adding the DNS network service. Configuring DNS requires you to answer a few questions. The wizard asks for a zone name, the type of DNS, and if reverse lookup is required.

You need administrative access to the server. You may need a copy of the Windows 2000 Server CD, depending on your network.

Getting Down to Business

DNS must be installed before Active Directory can work. Here is what you need to do.

Step 1. Go to control panel. Add the Windows component DNS.

Step 2. Select DNS from the Administrative Tools group on the Start button. Right-click the name of your server, and select Next to begin the configuration of DNS.

Step 3. Create a forward lookup zone named **CandC.com**.

Step 4. Name the DNS zone **dns.CandC.com**.

lab Warning

Try to avoid using a name that is the same as the World Wide Web (WWW) name of your company or another company. A name like that will confuse both your DNS server and your employees. Use a name similar to, but different from, the WWW name.

Step 5. Create a reverse lookup zone. Select Standard Primary for the type and add 169 as the network ID. Keep the default reverse DNS name.

lab hint

Reverse lookups provide the ability to get a web address from an IP address. Web servers and web programs running on the web servers primarily use them. For example, the Apache web server allows Perl scripts to access the actual name of a referring web site. This feature can be used for security or tracking purposes. On one Perl site, the reverse lookup names are used to ensure that visitors enter the site from the appropriate page.

LAB ANALYSIS TEST

The following questions will help you to apply your knowledge in a business setting.

1. How do Organizational Units (OU) help a business with organization and delegation of network responsibilities?

2. How could a transitive trust introduce a security hole into an organization?

3. You notice that a network's performance is less efficient after an upgrade to Active Directory. What are the possible causes of this problem?

4. Your web server's performance is less efficient after creating a reverse lookup zone. Why?

5. You are trying to install Windows 2000 Professional on a client machine using the remote installation service (RIS). The wizard keeps crashing. What could be causing the crash?

KEY TERM QUIZ

Use the following vocabulary terms to complete the sentences below. Not all of the terms will be used.

Active Directory Services Interface (ADSI)

delegation

distinguished name

global catalog

relative distinguished name

replication

schema

trusts

1. Identifying an object by its entire position in a tree is accomplished using the ____________________.
2. ____________________ is the process of copying a file to remote servers.
3. Giving network administration duties to other users is said to be a ____________________ of one's duties.
4. All of the files and objects tracked in a network are kept in the ____________________.
5. Rules (also called ____________________) define the constraints and limitations placed on objects.

LAB WRAP-UP

Congratulations on completing the first lab! You are on your way to learning how to use Active Directory. In this chapter you described the features of Active Directory and installed DNS on a Windows 2000 server.

In the next chapter you will install and begin to configure Active Directory. DNS is a required element in the Active Directory step. By installing DNS here, you have saved yourself a step in the next lab.

The skills applied in this lab are very common in a networked organization. As servers are installed, DNS often must be installed to speed local network operations. As new technologies are introduced to the network, management needs to be sold on their usefulness. It is unlikely that you will work in an organization that gives you a completely free hand regarding network purchases and changes.

LAB SOLUTIONS FOR CHAPTER 1

Lab Exercise 1.01

Joanne needs to be convinced of the need to use Active Directory as the directory service. You could start by describing what a directory service is and where it came from.

cross Reference

Directory structures are discussed in Certification Objective 1.01 in the text.

Once Joanne is clear about what a directory structure does, you should discuss the limitations of a typical older directory service. Try to address the directory structure used currently or in the past at the organization. Talking about a directory structure that the organization understands allows you to address known limitations of the structure and still keep the attention of your audience. C&C has migrated from Windows NT to Windows 2000. Given that situation, you should attack the domain model used in NT.

After breaking down the existing data structure, you then describe the benefits of Active Directory. Start by listing the major features. Then, go into detail. Describe exactly how each feature of Active Directory will benefit C&C. Be explicit: use the business structure to drive the discussion. For example, describe how the South Side and Hill documents can be replicated using Active Directory.

The features of Active Directory form the basis of most of Certification Objectives 1.01 and 1.02.

You should conclude with the argument that Active Directory is one of the best features of Windows 2000, and a reason to upgrade. Active Directory is a combination of the best features from several directory services into a single, well-designed product. Not using Active Directory in the C&C network is like not using oil in a car. Eventually the network will become too congested to run properly.

Lab Exercise 1.02

The first step is to install DNS. Go to the Control Panel, and select the Add/Remove icon. Click the Add/Remove Windows Components button to see the list of services available on Windows 2000. Scroll down and select Networking Services as shown in Figure 1-1. Select Details to see a list of available network services. Select Domain Name System (DNS), then click OK. You are returned to the Components Screen.

FIGURE 1-1

Selecting Networking Services

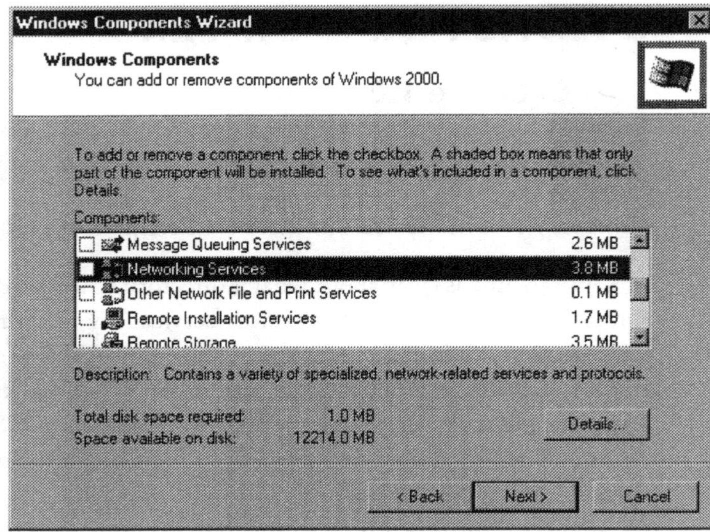

Select Next to start installing DNS. When prompted, insert the Windows 2000 Server CD into the CD drive and select OK. If the Windows 2000 CD starts, click the window close button to close the start-up box. When the installation is done, select Finish.

lab hint

To stop a CD from auto playing on insertion into the CD drive, hold down the SHIFT button until the CD stops spinning. SHIFT overrides the auto-play feature of Windows.

Once installed, DNS needs to be configured. Go to Start | Programs | Administrative Tools. Select the new DNS shortcut. The first screen shows the servers in your network.

Right-click the name of the local server and select Configure. Select Next when the wizard starts. Figure 1-2 shows the next screen.

Because this is the first DNS server to be installed in C&C's organization, select the first radio button, then select Next. The screen shown in Figure 1-3 appears next, giving you the option of installing a forward lookup zone.

Most DNS servers need this zone. Ensure that it is selected and then select Next. You'll use a standard primary zone as shown in Figure 1-4.

In the next screen you provide a name for the DNS zone. Nearly anything can be used, although it is suggested that you avoid the name of an existing server.

FIGURE 1-2

Selecting the root server

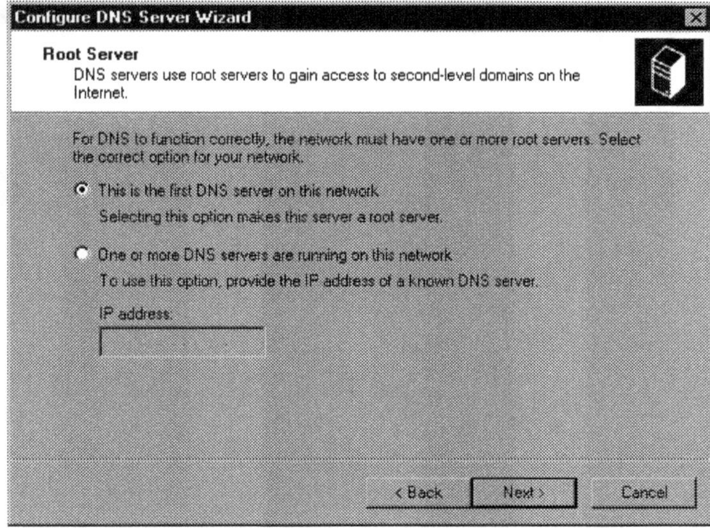

Name the zone **CandC**, then select Next. Figure 1-5 shows the name of the local file in which the DNS information will be stored.

Keep the default name and select Next.

FIGURE 1-3

Creating a forward lookup zone

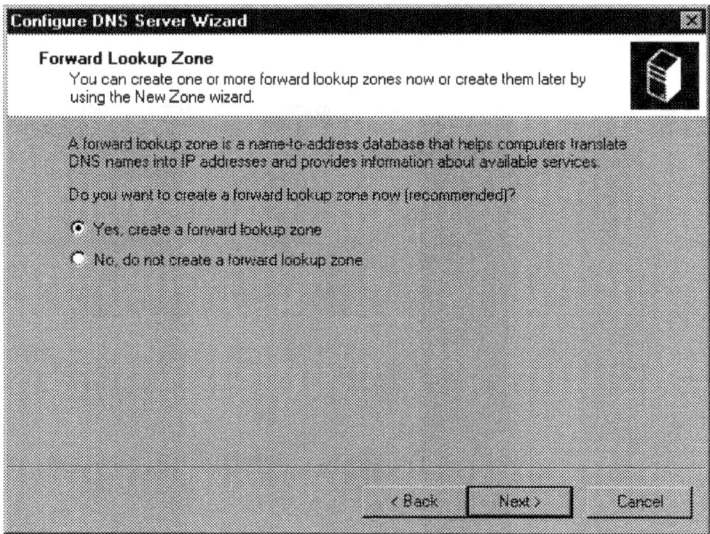

FIGURE 1-4

Choosing a zone type

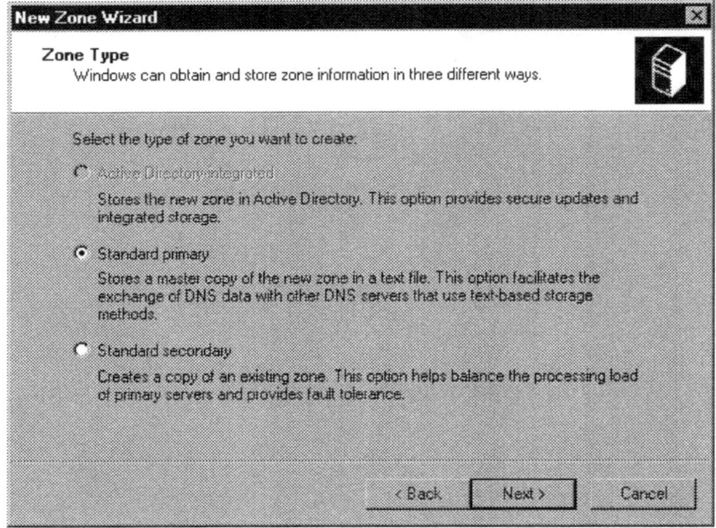

The webmasters at C&C want to get the actual names of visitors to the web site. That requires you to create a reverse lookup zone. Because a reverse lookup zone is the default, ensure that Yes is selected and then select Next.

The next screen might look familiar. Each zone must have a type. As before, you will create a standard primary zone for C&C. For reverse lookup to work, a reverse

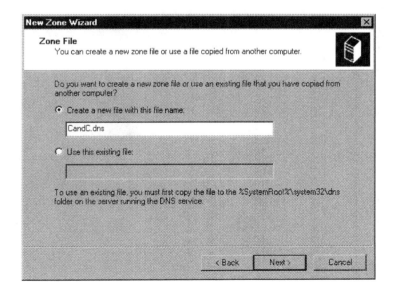

FIGURE 1-5

Naming the file in which DNS information will be stored

New Zone Wizard
Zone File
You can create a new zone file or use a file copied from another computer.
Do you want to create a new zone file or use an existing file that you have copied from another computer?
Create a new file with this file name:
CandC.dns
Use this existing file:
To use an existing file, you must first copy the file to the %SystemRoot%\system32\dns folder on the server running the DNS service.
< Back
Next >
Cancel

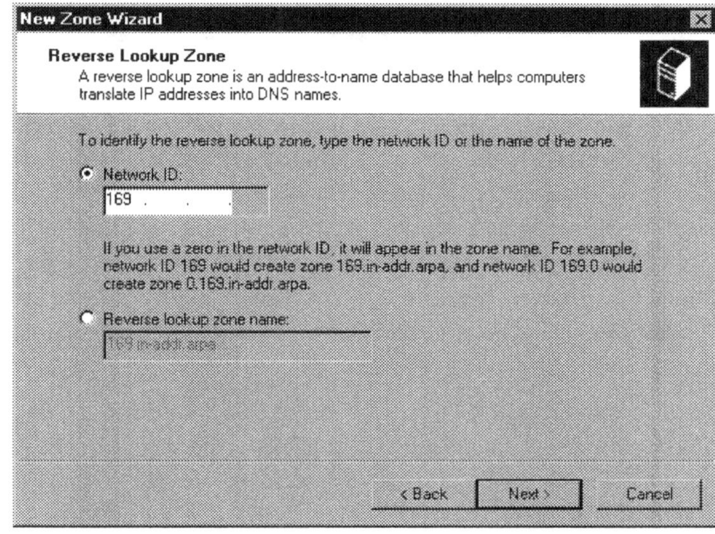

FIGURE 1-6 Identifying the reverse DNS server

DNS server must be provided. The World Wide Web Consortium (W3C) maintains a reverse lookup server at IP address 169. Enter that address as shown in Figure 1-6.

The next screen asks for a file. Accept the default and select Next.

The final screen summarizes what you did. Please review it to ensure that it looks like Figure 1-7. When the screens match, hit finish. DNS is now configured.

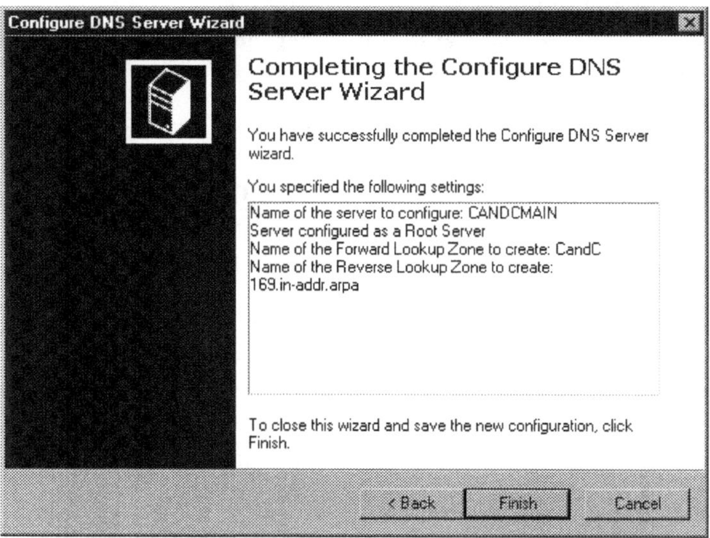

FIGURE 1-7 Reviewing the DNS installation summary

ANSWERS TO LAB ANALYSIS TEST

1. Organizational units (OUs) help to organize a network by allowing the network administrator to group users and objects. As an example, most organizations have reasonably well-defined roles. A school has teachers, students, staff, and administrators. Each has a specified set of network requirements. By assigning the rights to perform the requirements to an OU, and then by assigning the users to the appropriate OU, the rights are automatically assigned to the users. OU structures can be nested. In the school example, administrators have all of the rights teachers have, with a few additions. Rather than rebuild the rights for administrator, you can nest the administration OU under the teacher OU. The teacher rights will be assigned to the administrators, and additional rights can be assigned to the administrators.

   Delegation occurs if users in an OU are given permission to maintain certain network services. A common example is the delegation of print server management. In the school, the people who work most with the printers are the staff and teachers. By giving members of these OUs control over the printers, the network administrators do not have to kill every wayward print job, or clear every paper jam. When properly used, delegation empowers employees to fix problems near at hand and frees the network administrator to work on the "hard stuff."

2. Transitive trusts automatically apply trusts to certain domains. For example, if domain X trusts domain Y, and domain Y trusts domain Z, then the transitive trust of domain X trusting domain Z is set up. Consider this example: Domain X is the staff of a school. Domain Y represents the teachers, and domain Z represents the students. It makes sense that staff can work with teacher objects. The staff might need to see attendance records or grades at any time. It also makes sense that teachers are able to see and work with student objects. It may not make sense that the staff members are able to work with student objects. The transitive trust allows staff to work with student objects.

3. Many possibilities for solving this problem exist. Two likely problems are Dynamic Domain Name Service (DDNS) and the replication of the global catalog. DDNS updates remote servers when changes are made to the main DNS catalog. Replication ensures that each remote server has a current copy of the global catalog. Either type of update, if done often enough, will cause excessive network traffic. Too much traffic and a network can crash.

4. Reverse lookups are very costly in terms of network performance. Most web servers automatically store the IP address of the requestor of a page. The reverse lookup function converts the IP address to a URL. Getting the URL requires the web server to ask a DNS server to whom the IP address belongs. At the minimum, one additional request per web transaction is needed. That one request doesn't seem too bad until you consider that most

web pages require several transactions to download the HTML, pictures, and other files to the client. Thus, a page with 5 pictures and a sound would require at least 7 transactions to display the page for the client. Each would cause the reverse lookup to get the name of the requestor. Some local caching can be done, but disk space constraints usually limit it.

5. Remote installation service (RIS) often fails for hardware reasons. Before installing, you should ensure that your network meets all of the conditions. Be sure that the servers are at least 166 MHz Pentiums having 128MB of RAM and 2GB of disk space free. Clients must be 166 MHz or higher Pentiums with 32MB of RAM and an 800MB disk. By default, the RIS installation process creates a single partition on the client system, overwriting existing partitions. This behavior can be modified by using the answer files.

ANSWERS TO KEY TERM QUIZ

1. distinguished name
2. replication
3. delegation
4. global catalog
5. schema

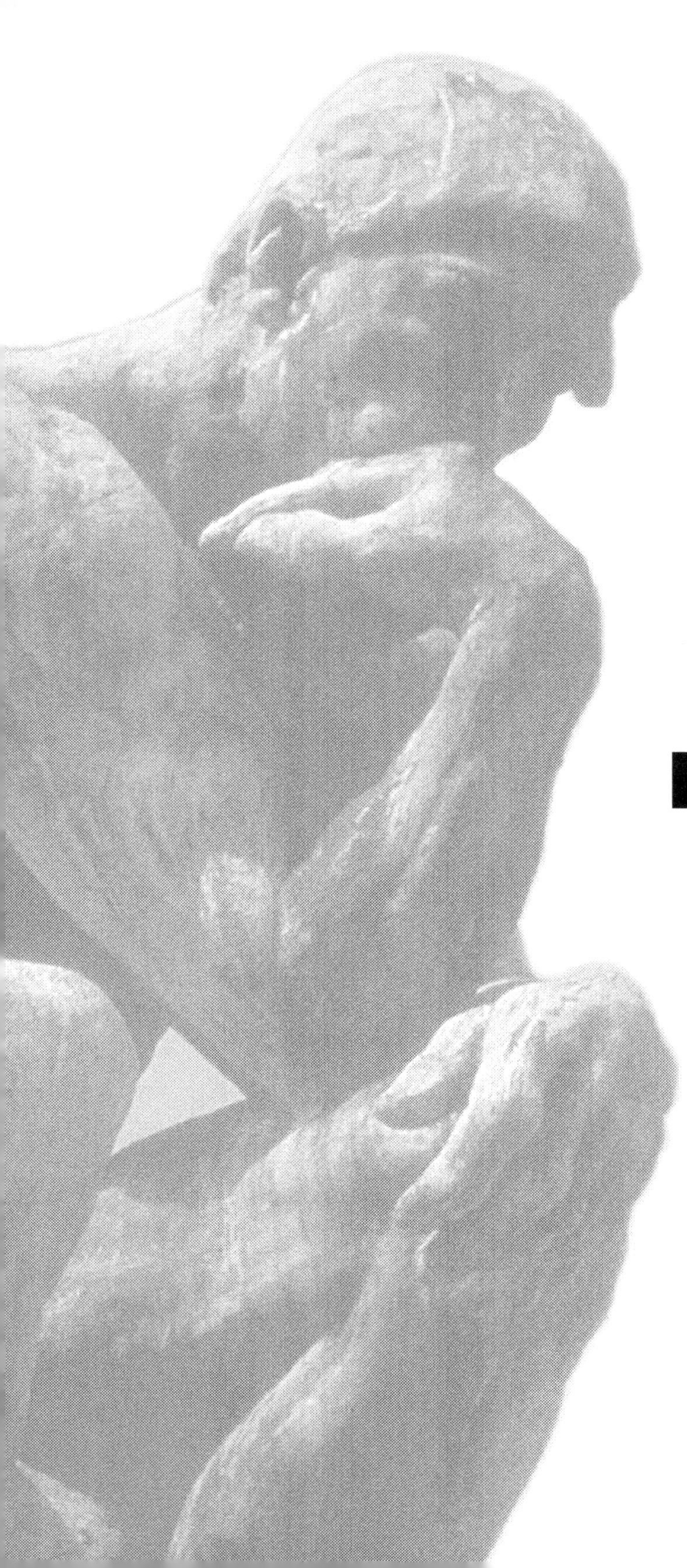

2

Installing the Components of Active Directory

LAB EXERCISES

To bring order to C&C's network resources, you need to install Active Directory. Active Directory installs easily, but it takes some time to set up properly. Many steps must be completed before Active Directory will work properly.

To install Active Directory at C&C, you need to install the software and to create a site for each branch. To install it properly, you have to partition and format a hard drive. Site links, a bridgehead server, and a global catalog server are also required to improve the network's performance. When you are done with those tasks, the Active Directory servers will be installed and working properly.

LAB EXERCISE 2.01

15 Minutes

Formatting a Drive for Use with Active Directory (optional)

While examining the C&C main servers, you notice two unused partitions on a secondary hard drive. Joanne is aware of the problem and suggests that you use that space for the Active Directory database and logs. You know that those objects should be located on NTFS drives formatted in a non-standard manner.

This lab is based on the first "On the Job Comment" after Figure 2-7 in the Study Guide. The format command, while simple, is not intuitive. This lab can be skipped if your network already contains NTFS partitions.

Learning Objectives

In this lab, you learn how to configure two partitions for optimal Active Directory performance. At the end of the lab, you'll be able to

- Get help for command-line operations
- Use the Format command on the command line
- Verify partition status

Lab Materials and Setup

The space you will format is unused space. You have no need to back up any data. All that you need for this lab is an administrative account and password.

Getting Down to Business

Step 1. Go to the command prompt.

Step 2. Get help for the Format command.

Step 3. Format the first partition for the Active Directory database. Use the NTFS file system with the 4096 cluster size. Name the partition **ADDatabase**.

Step 4. Format the second partition for the Active Directory log. Use the NTFS file system with the 8192 cluster size. Name the partition **ADLog**.

Step 5. Run the disk manager, and verify that the drives are formatted and healthy.

LAB EXERCISE 2.02

Installing Active Directory in a New Domain

15 Minutes

On your first day, Joanne discussed the need for the various sites to be able to find each other's files and resources. In that case, the best approach is to run Active Directory with several sites and a global catalog. You need to perform several tasks before Active Directory will work. Installing Active Directory is the first step in the process.

You know that Domain Name Service (DNS) is installed on the server. That makes the Active Directory setup a little easier. The DNS server is called **dns.CandC.com** and has forward and reverse lookup zones both activated.

Learning Objectives

In this lab, you install Active Directory for C&C. At the end of the lab, you'll be able to:

- Promote a server to domain controller
- Install Active Directory
- Create a new domain

Lab Materials and Setup

Installing Active Directory is simply a matter of following the wizard. Some pre-planning is suggested, though. Read through the steps before you begin to install Active Directory. You need these materials:

- Windows 2000 CD
- Administrator account and password
- At least one NTFS volume in the server (two are preferable, but the second one is optional)
- A DNS server installed on the network
- A network card in the server, connected to a hub

Getting Down to Business

Step 1. Verify that DNS is installed and updateable.

Step 2. Start the Active Directory wizard by running DCPROMO. Recall that DCPROMO promotes the member server to domain controller.

Step 3. Create a new domain tree and forest.

Step 4. Name the domain **CandCmain.com**. Avoid using punctuation in the name; it's not compatible with Microsoft DNS.

lab hint

If your organization is registered with InterNIC, you can use the registered domain name here.

Step 5. Give the machine the NetBIOS name **CANDCMAIN**.

Step 6. Specify the database and log locations. Place the database in the folder **D:\win2000\NTDS**. Place the log in the folder **E:\win2000\NTDS**.

Step 7. Specify the location of the shared system volume. For C&C, place the shared system volume in the folder **D:\win2000\sysvol**.

lab hint

In your network, the paths for steps 6 and 7 may vary. It is suggested (but not required) that the database and log folders reside on separate drives or in separate partitions. It is suggested (but not required) that the drives be NTSF formatted. Step 7 requires a NTFS partition. See Lab Exercise 2.01 for a discussion of how to format the drives.

Step 8. Select the default permission types for accounts on the server. Because C&C uses Windows 2000 servers only, select the second option. If your network has Windows NT servers, select the first option.

Step 9. Create a Directory Services Restore Mode Administrator password. The password is used to restore the Active Directory from a backup location. The password does not need to coordinate with any other account. Use **ADRestore** for the password, or enter any other password that you will not forget.

Step 10. Review the installation options, and fix any problems. For future reference, copy the summarized data into a text file. Store that file in the same location as the database created in step 6.

Step 11. Verify that the installation was successful.

lab hint

The subsequent labs all use the Microsoft Management Console (MMC) snap-in tool. The labs direct you to open and close the tool at the start and end of each lab. If you prefer, you can keep MMC open and simply save between labs.

LAB EXERCISE 2.03

10 Minutes

Creating Sites for Active Directory

Remember that you are trying to simplify the task of finding resources within C&C's network. Each branch has files and resources that the other branches need. The simplest way to organize the network is to create a site for each branch. C&C has four branches and a library extension. The branches are Main, South Side, North Side, and Hill. The local library has contracted for some access to C&C data through a server installed at the main library. You will therefore create five sites for the C&C network.

Learning Objectives

In this lab, you create sites for the C&C network. At the end of the lab, you'll be able to:

- Create a site
- Name a site
- Use the default site link

Lab Materials and Setup

Creating a site is simply a matter of defining its name and the domain to which it belongs. Typically, a site corresponds to a WAN border in an organization. You need these materials:

- Windows 2000 CD
- Administrator account and password

Getting Down to Business

Step 1. Start an empty Microsoft management console.

Step 2. Select the Add/Remove menu.

Step 3. Add the Active Directory Sites and Services snap-in.

Step 4. Expand the Active Directory sites.

Step 5. To add a site, right-click Sites, and select New Site.

Step 6. Create the main site first. Give the site the name **mainsite**.

Step 7. Select the site link to use. If no site links have been created, use **DEFAULTIPSITELINK**, as provided by the wizard.

Step 8. Select the domain controller in which the site will reside. For C&C, select **CandC.com**.

Step 9. Repeat steps 5 through 8 until you have built all five sites. Name the other sites **north**, **south**, **library**, and **hill**.

Step 10. Save the MMC screen as **candc.msc**.

LAB EXERCISE 2.04

10 Minutes

Creating Subnets

Joanne, the network administrator at C&C, wants to use the private IP addresses for the machines at each site. She would like to be able to easily track the IP addresses that belong to each site. You propose to set up an IP scheme that provides both a site reference and a machine reference. As an example, you propose using the private IP address range **192.168.1.*machine***. Machines at each site would have an IP address of the form **192.168.1.*x***, where *x* is a number from 0 to 255.

For your proposal to work, you need to set up a subnet mask for each site. Your goal is to have the subnet masks work, and to allow the branch machines to access each other. You propose using **255.255.255.0** as the subnet. That selection provides room in the organization for 256 computers.

Joanne wonders how she will understand which IP addresses belong with which sites. You describe how the masks distribute the IP addresses using Classless Inter-Domain Routing (CIDR) rules. The first 128 addresses can go to Main, the next 64 can go to South Side, and so on. That scheme provides unique IP addresses to all the sites and permits easy tracing of IP addresses.

Learning Objectives

In this lab, you learn to define subnetworks in Windows 2000. At the end of the lab, you'll be able to:

- Create subnet masks
- Assign network ranges to subnetworks

Lab Materials and Setup

Typically, a subnetwork is defined on WAN boundaries. Because South Side and North Side are distinct entities connected by a WAN link, they make logical subnetworks. You need these materials:

- Administrator account and password
- The candc.msc file created in Lab Exercise 2.03

Getting Down to Business

Step 1. Start MMC, and open the candc.msc file.

Step 2. Open the Subnet folder found inside the Sites folder.

Step 3. Right-click the folder and select New Subnet.

Step 4. Assign an address of **192.168.1.0** with a subnet of **255.255.255.0** to Main.

Step 5. Set up each of the other sites. Use the address **192.168.1.0** for each site. Assign a different mask to each branch: **255.255.255.128** to South Side, **.192** to North Side, **.224** to Hill, and **.240** to Library.

The suggested masks are based on the Classless Inter-Domain Routing (CIDR) scheme. Each mask describes how many hosts are possible on the network. For a reasonably clear description of how CIDR works, visit public.pacbell.net/dedicated/cidr.html.

LAB EXERCISE 2.05

10 Minutes

Creating Site Links

After the subnet discussion, Joanne reminds you that the branches need to share data among themselves. In particular, users in South Side, North Side, and Hill have to be able to share data. How can Active Directory make the process faster?

You decide to create site links between the sites.

Learning Objectives

In this lab, you learn how to create links between sites. At the end of the lab, you'll be able to:

- Create a site link
- Assign costs to the site link
- Assign replication times to the site link

Lab Materials and Setup

C&C's branch offices are networked using high-speed dedicated connections. You can therefore use the IP replication method. You need these materials:

- Administrator account and password
- The candc.msc file modified in Lab Exercise 2.04

Getting Down to Business

Step 1. Run MMC, and open the candc.msc file.

Step 2. Expand Inter Site Transport under the Sites folder.

Step 3. Add a new site link to the IP folder.

Step 4. Create a site link between South Side and North Side. Give the link the name **SouthNorth** (or use an appropriate name of your choice).

Step 5. Repeat the process to create links **SouthHill** and **HillNorth**.

Step 6. Assign costs and replication times to the links. Set all replication times to **210 minutes**. Assign a cost of **25** to SouthHill. Assign a cost of **35** to HillNorth. Assign a cost of **20** to SouthNorth.

LAB EXERCISE 2.06

Creating a Bridgehead Server

5 Minutes

Joanne is excited about the site links. She clearly sees their positive impact on network performance. But she's bothered by the issue of which server controls the replication of sites. Does South maintain South replication and North maintain North? Or does some central server handle things?

You reply that bridgehead servers control the replication of data. If each site tried to handle the replication, occasionally North and South would replicate at the same time, causing enormous WAN traffic. The bridgehead server receives all incoming traffic from the sites and replicates it to the sites. If two sites have the same file, the bridgehead server replicates to only one of the sites. Because the CANDCMAIN server is the most powerful server in the organization, you and Joanne decide that it is the best candidate for bridgehead status.

Learning Objectives

In this lab, you make CANDCMAIN the bridgehead server for the C&C network. At the end of the lab, you'll be able to designate a bridgehead server.

Lab Materials and Setup

CANDCMAIN is the logical choice for the assignment as bridgehead. Because the site links use the IP transport method, you'll use IP for the bridgehead server. You need these materials:

- Administrator account and password
- The candc.msc file modified in Lab Exercise 2.05

Getting Down to Business

Step 1. Run MMC, and open the candc.msc file.

Step 2. Expand until you reach the Server folder under the Main site.

Step 3. Get the properties of the CANDCMAIN server.

Step 4. Select and add IP for the transport method.

Step 5. Save the file, and exit MMC.

LAB EXERCISE 2.07

Creating a Site Link Bridge

5 Minutes

Joanne approaches you with a worried look on her face. She tells you that one of the costs for the site link is occasionally wrong. The HillNorth link shares its WAN line with a large university. Every November, December, March, and April (finals time), the WAN traffic increases dramatically. The cost then goes to about 100. She suggests that it would be faster to go from North to South, and then from South to Hill.

You tell her that a site link bridge is the answer to the problem. A site link bridge will force the traffic to avoid the HillNorth link when replicating from Hill to North. Creating the link is fairly easy. You suggest that Joanne could switch the link bridge off and on as needed throughout the year. You offer to demonstrate.

Learning Objectives

In this lab, you demonstrate how to switch on a site link bridge for the C& C network. At the end of the lab, you'll be able to create a site link bridge.

Lab Materials and Setup

Because you created the site links in an earlier exercise in this chapter, all you need to do now is to group the links. You need these materials:

- Administrator account and password
- The candc.msc file modified in Lab Exercise 2.06

Getting Down to Business

Step 1. Run MMC, and open the candc.msc file.

Step 2. Expand Inter Site Transport under the Sites folder.

Step 3. Right-click the IP folder, and select New Site Link Bridge.

Step 4. Add the SouthNorth and SouthHill links to the bridge.

Step 5. Save the file, and exit MMC.

LAB EXERCISE 2.08

Creating Connection Objects

5 Minutes

Joanne has been reviewing your work and is very pleased. She found one item that may cause a problem in the near future, though. Occasionally, the sites need to replicate more often than the 3.5-hour period currently specified. The need arises occasionally when one site creates a document that the other sites need immediately.

You realize that the situation can be handled by using a manual connection object. You proceed to show Joanne how the connection is made.

Learning Objectives

In this lab, you set up a connection object for the C&C network. At the end of the lab, you'll be able to:

- Create a connection object
- Set the properties of a connection object

Lab Materials and Setup

As was the case with the previous links, you'll use the IP replication protocol over C&C's high-speed links. You need these materials:

- Administrator account and password
- The candc.msc file modified in Lab Exercise 2.07

Getting Down to Business

Step 1. Run MMC, and open the candc.msc file.

Step 2. Expand to view the CANDCMAIN server.

Step 3. Right-click the NTDS setting, and add a connection object. Select the server that will use the connection object.

Step 4. Right-click the connection object, and set the replication schedule.

LAB EXERCISE 2.09

10 Minutes

Creating a Global Catalog

Joanne asks two very good questions. How will one site find files on the other sites? Where is the main database stored?

You reply that the global catalog can be kept on any server, but that it is usually kept on the main server.

In fact, you know that the global catalog was automatically created when the first server was added to Active Directory. Thus, CANDCMAIN holds the global catalog.

Learning Objectives

In this lab, you create a global catalog for C&C's network. At the end of the lab, you'll be able to:

- Turn on the global catalog
- Describe the global catalog
- Set the default query policy

Lab Materials and Setup

Because the global catalog is already created, your task is to verify its existence and to add a few properties. You need these materials:

- Administrator account and password
- The candc.msc file modified in Lab Exercise 2.07

Getting Down to Business

Step 1. Run MMC, and open the candc.msc file.

Step 2. Expand to the CANDCMAIN server.

Step 3. Right-click the NTDS setting, and select Properties.

Step 4. Verify that the check box for global catalog is selected. Create a description for the global catalog and set the default query policy.

LAB ANALYSIS TEST

The following questions will help you to apply your knowledge in a business setting.

1. You are trying to install Active Directory with FAT32 volumes. The setup program will not go past the placement of the SYSVOL file. What is the problem, and how can you fix it?

2. How many hosts will the subnet mask 255.255.255.252 control?

3. Your network has three sites, each connected through a site link. The cost to go from A to B is dramatically faster than the cost to go from A to C and then C to B. How can you force the network to use the faster link?

4. In a network with 12 servers, you need to decide where to build sites. Five of the servers are in one building and are directly connected using 100 Base T network cable. Another two servers are located in a different building and are directly connected using 100 Base T network cable. The remaining five servers are connected by dialup line. How many sites should such a network use? Which machines are in each site?

5. In the scenario in question 4, which replication protocol should be used to link the sites?

KEY TERM QUIZ

Use the following vocabulary terms to complete the sentences below. Not all of the terms will be used.

bridgehead server

connection object

DCPROMO

global catalog

IP

KCC

site link bridge

site links

subnet masks

SYSVOL

1. The ____________________ stores a copy or a partial copy of files and resources belonging to each site.
2. To set a replication schedule manually or to override an existing schedule, an administrator should use a(n) ____________________.
3. To begin installing Active Directory, the administrator must run the ____________________ command.
4. In the case of congestion on a WAN link, the ____________________ can tell the network a faster way to travel.
5. Using a ____________________ is one way to balance the load on a Windows 2000 network.

LAB WRAP-UP

The lab exercises in Chapter 2 laid the foundation for the remaining labs in the book. You installed Active Directory and configured it to work properly. You set up site links, site bridges, and manual connection objects. The setup of Active Directory now allows C&C's various sites to effectively start sharing files.

LAB SOLUTIONS FOR CHAPTER 2

The sections that follow walk you through the steps to solve the lab exercises. You should avoid looking at these sections unless you are stuck on a particular exercise.

Lab Exercise 2.01

Open the command prompt by selecting Start | Programs | Accessories | Command Prompt. Get help on the Format command by entering:

```
format /? | more
```

If you read the resulting display, you should be able to figure out the appropriate parameters.

C&C has three partitions on its secondary drive. You will use drive F: for the database and drive G: for the log. To format the first drive, enter this command:

```
format f: /fs:NTFS /a:4096
```

For example:

lab Warning

When you use the Format command, replace the D: with the letter of the actual drive to be formatted. Be careful to select the right drive. Recovering an accidentally formatted drive is very difficult.

When prompted, name the drive **ADDatabase**.

To format the second drive, enter this command:

```
format g: /fs:NTFS /a:8192
```

Here's a sample completed format operation:

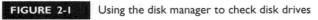

```
Command Prompt
Microsoft Windows 2000 [Version 5.00.2195]
(C) Copyright 1985-1999 Microsoft Corp.

C:\>format f: /fs:NTFS /a:4096
The type of the file system is NTFS.
Enter current volume label for drive F: ADdatabase

WARNING, ALL DATA ON NON-REMOVABLE DISK
DRIVE F: WILL BE LOST!
Proceed with Format (Y/N)? y
Verifying 2045M
Volume label (ENTER for none)? ADDatabase
Creating file system structures.
Format complete.
    2094088 KB total disk space.
    2081296 KB are available.

C:\>
```

Type **exit** to leave the command prompt.

Now, run the disk manager to verify that the drives are formatted and healthy. To run disk manager, right-click the My Computer icon and select Manage. When the Computer Management window opens, select Disk Management. Verify that drives F: and G: are formatted and healthy, as shown in Figure 2-1.

FIGURE 2-1 Using the disk manager to check disk drives

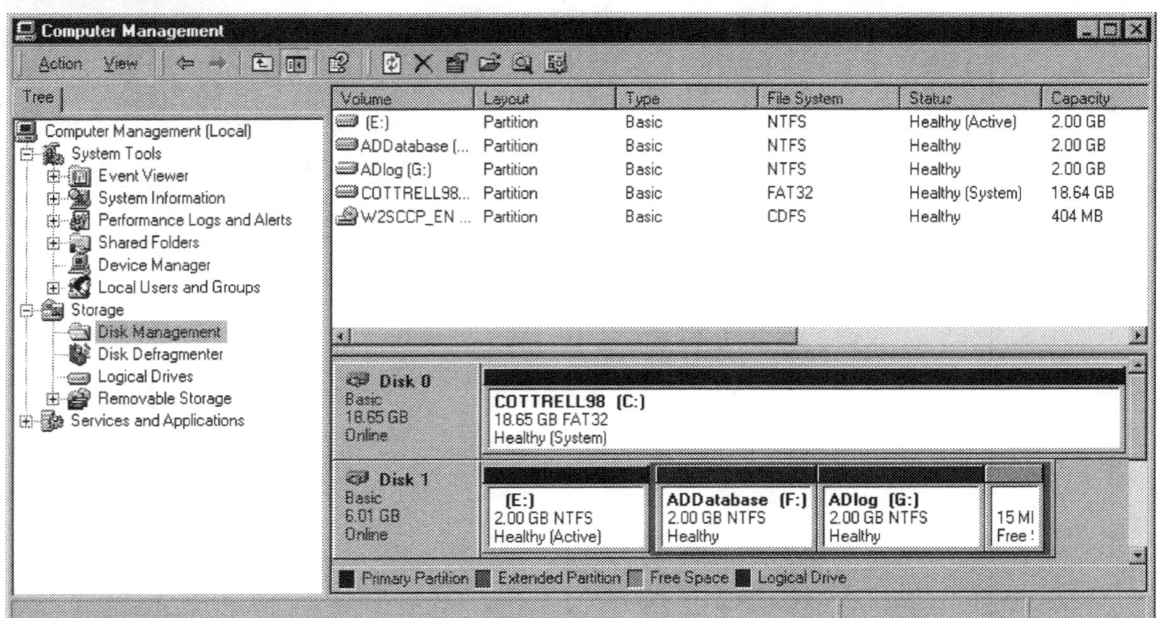

Lab Exercise 2.02

Active Directory installs best when a Microsoft DNS server is present. To verify that DNS is running on the server, select Start | Administrative Tools | DNS. Verify that forward and reverse lookup zones are both running:

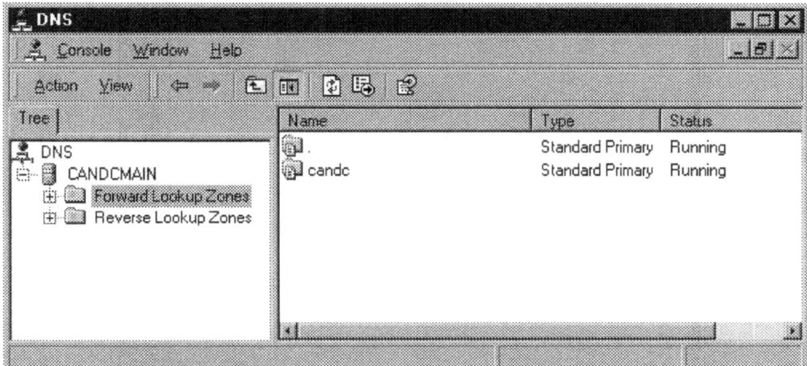

Once DNS is up, start the Active Directory installation wizard: Select Start | Run, and then type **DCPROMO** into the run box. When the wizard starts, click Next.

You are installing a new controller for the C&C domain, and so you select the first option (Figure 2-2), and select Next.

Again, because this domain is the first, select "Create a new domain tree" as shown in Figure 2-3, and select Next.

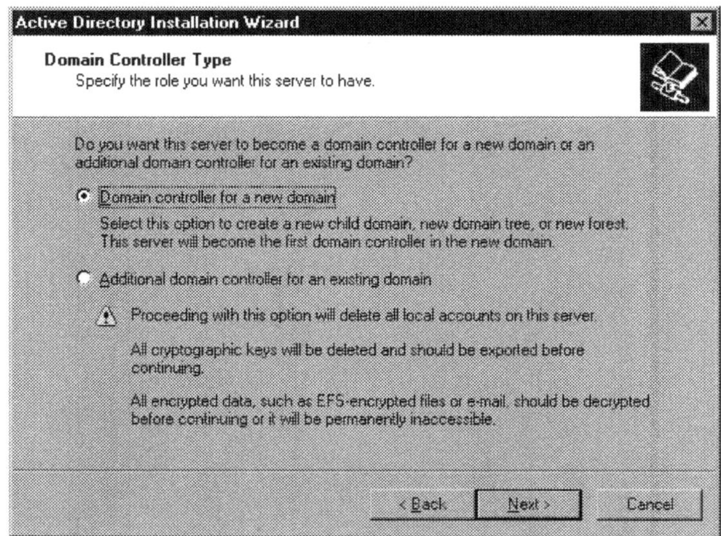

FIGURE 2-2 Choosing to install a new controller

FIGURE 2-3

Creating a new domain tree

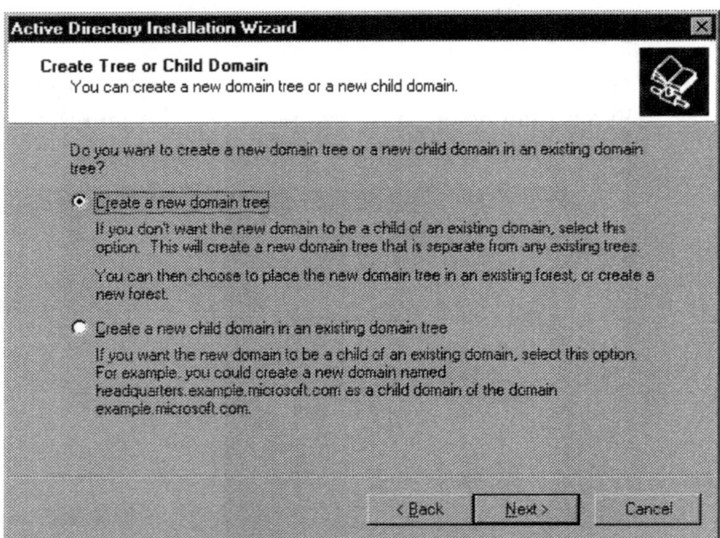

Because the network is also new, select "Create a new forest of domain trees" and select Next.

After the forest has been created, you need to give the domain the name **CandCmain.com** as shown in Figure 2-4. Select Next.

Name the machine CANDCMAIN as shown in Figure 2-5, and select Next.

FIGURE 2-4

Naming a new domain

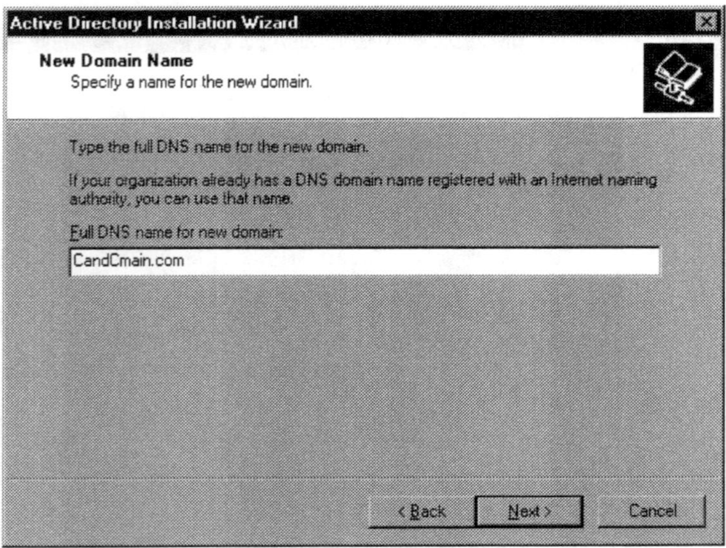

FIGURE 2-5

Identifying the machine to the NetBIOS

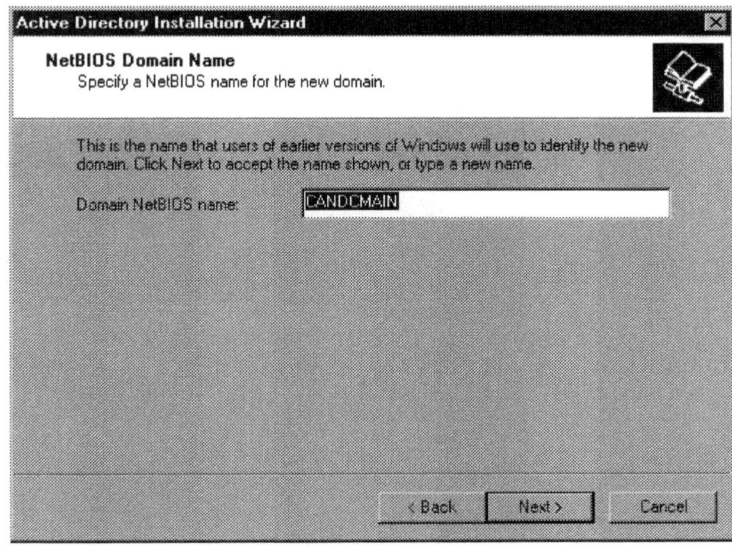

The next screen gives the locations in which to place the Active Directory database and log files. For C&C, use the locations shown in Figure 2-6. You may have to enter the folder names. Afterward, select Next.

The next screen gives the location in which to place the SYSVOL folder. For C&C, use the drive where the database was placed (Figure 2-7).

FIGURE 2-6

Placing the database and log files

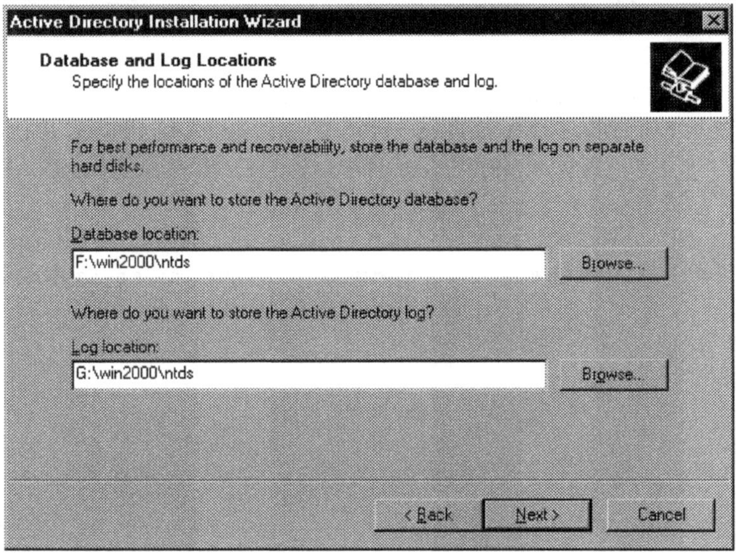

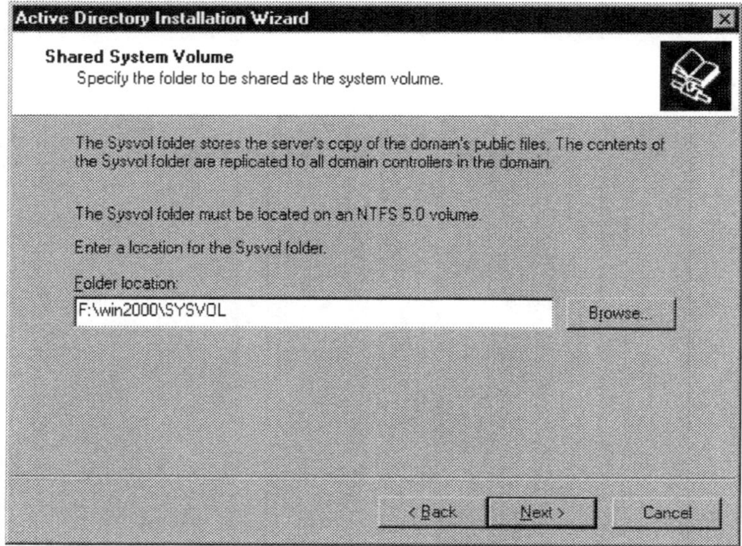

FIGURE 2-7

Placing the SYSVOL folder

Select Next. At this point, the following DNS error may occur:

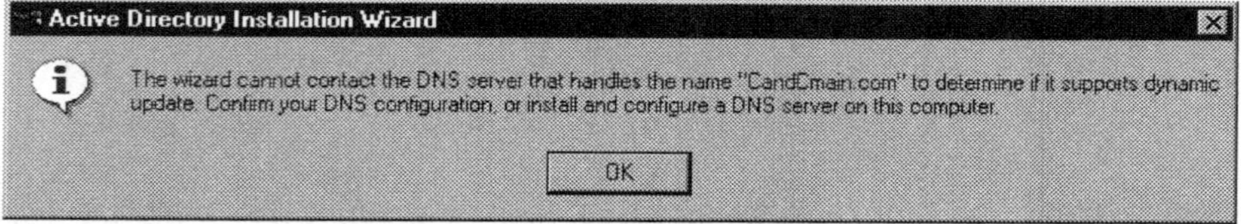

Click OK, and then continue with the installation. The next screen will fix any DNS problems that you may have.

Select "Yes" to install DNS, and then select Next. Because C&C uses only Windows 2000 servers, the default DNS permissions are set as shown in Figure 2-8. Afterward, select Next.

You now have to create a password to permit data restoration. Use the password **ADRestore**. Type the password into both boxes as shown in Figure 2-9 and select next.

FIGURE 2-8

Setting the default DNS permissions for a Windows 2000 –only network

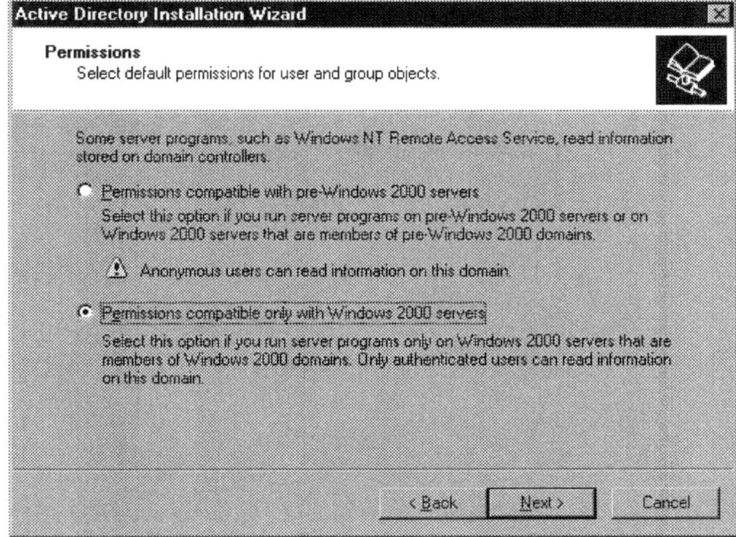

FIGURE 2-9

Specifying the restore password

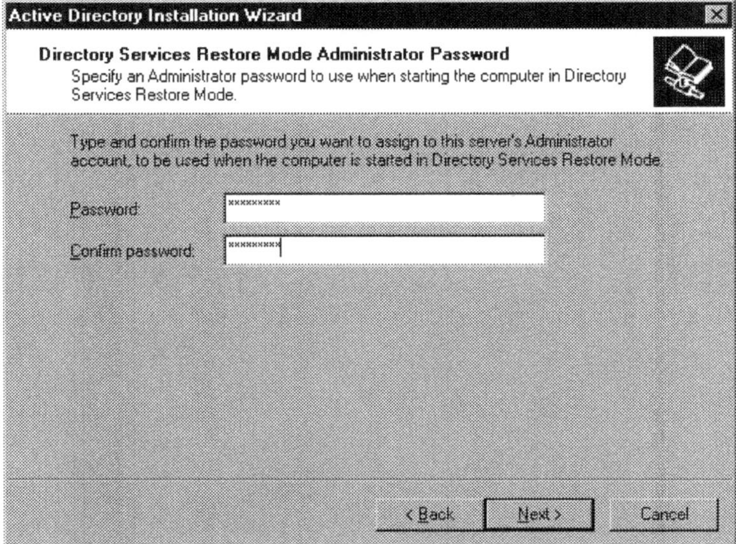

FIGURE 2-10

Reviewing the settings summary

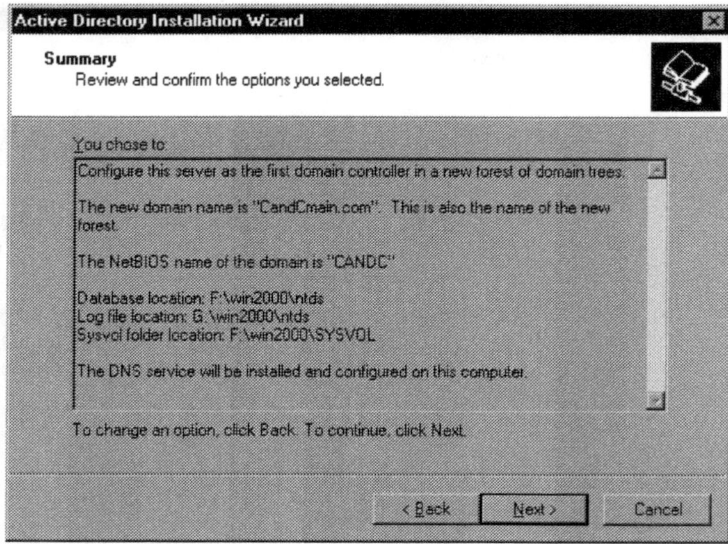

Finally you're finished. Compare your screen with Figure 2-10, and fix any discrepancies.

Select Next to see the progress monitor screen depicted in Figure 2-11 as Active Directory is configured.

When you see the screen depicted in Figure 2-12, Active Directory is installed. Select Finish, and reboot your machine to finalize the changes.

FIGURE 2-11

Monitoring the configuration of Active Directory

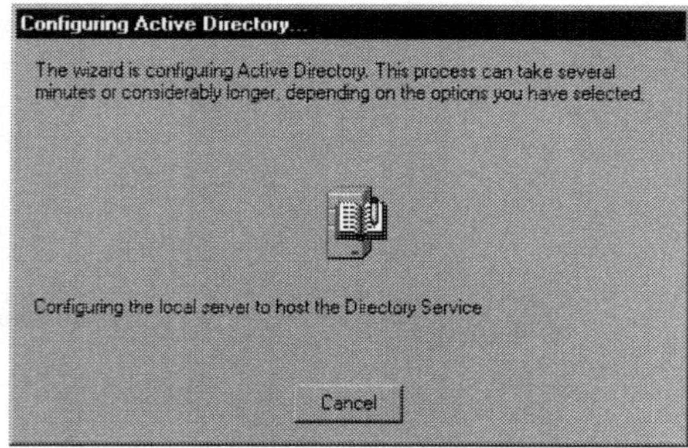

FIGURE 2-12

Finishing the installation of Active Directory

Lab Exercise 2.03

Start an empty MMC console by choosing Start | Run and entering MMC in the run box.

On the Console menu, select Add/Remove.

At the Add/Remove screen, select the Add button to see the list of standalone snap-ins (Figure 2-13).

FIGURE 2-13

Selecting from the list of standalone snap-ins

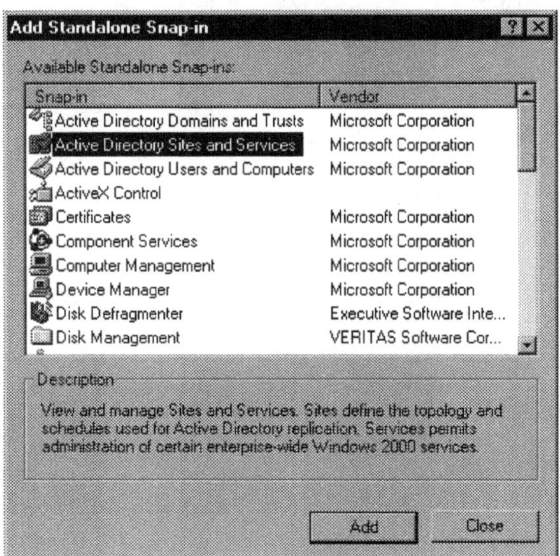

Select Active Directory Sites and Services, and select Add. Close the Add Standalone window, and click OK in the Add/Remove dialog box.

Expand Active Directory to see the Sites folder. Expand the Sites folder to see the next part of the tree:

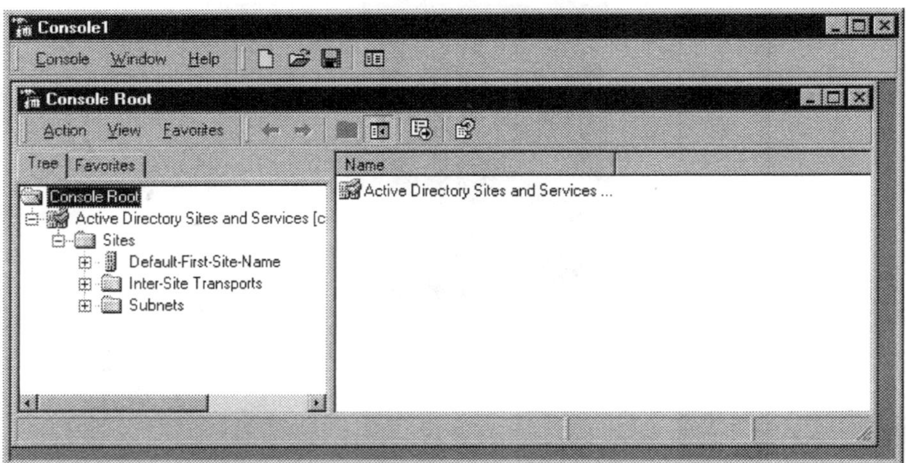

Create the Main site by right-clicking the Sites folder and selecting New Site:

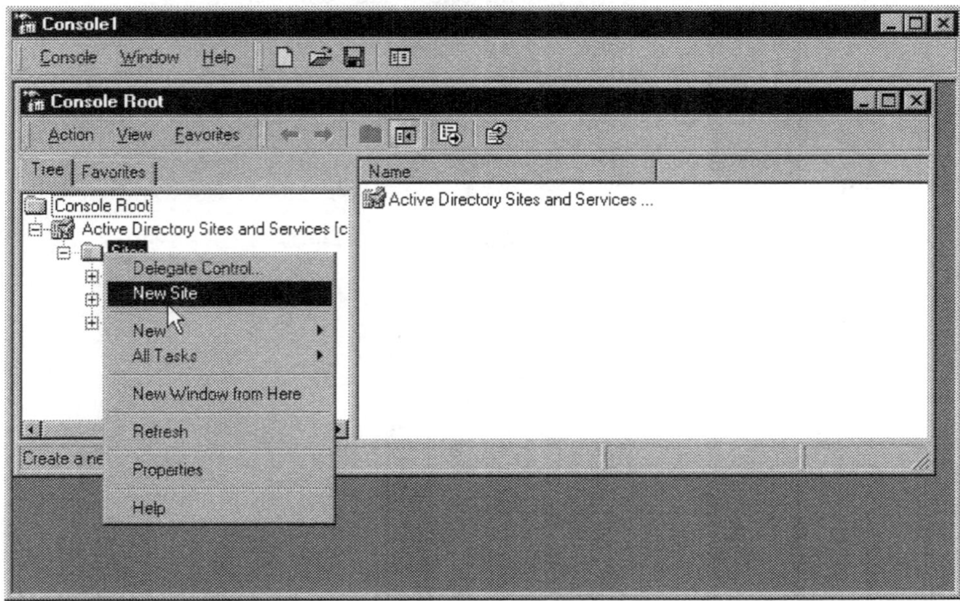

Name the first site **main** as shown in Figure 2-14. Be sure to select DEFAULTIPSITELINK as the container for the Main site. Continue creating sites until you have created **main**, **south**, **north**, **hill**, and **library**.

Figure 2-15 shows the completed group of sites. The Main site should contain the CANDCMAIN server. Expand Default-First-Site-Name and the server folder that it contains, as shown in Figure 2-15.

Right-click the CANDCMAIN server object, and select Move to. In the Move Server window, select the Main site. When the screen refreshes, the Main site contains the server. Exit the window, saving as **candc.msc**.

Lab Exercise 2.04

Start MMC, and open the candc.msc file.

Expand the Sites folder to see the Subnets folder. Right-click the Subnets folder, and select New Subnet.

In the New Object Subnet dialog box, select the Main site. Set the address and mask as shown in Figure 2-16.

Continue for the remaining sites, using the same address (**192.168.1.0**) for each site. Assign the mask **255.255.255.128** to South Side, **255.255.255.192** to North Side, **255.255.255.224** to Hill, and **255.255.255.240** to Library.

The Subnet folder should now look like Figure 2-17. Save and exit the MMC.

FIGURE 2-14

Giving a name to a new site

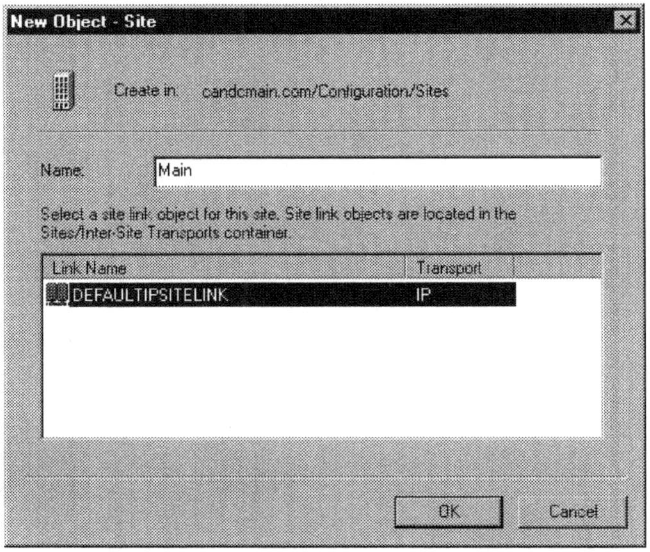

FIGURE 2-15

Reviewing the complete list of C&C sites

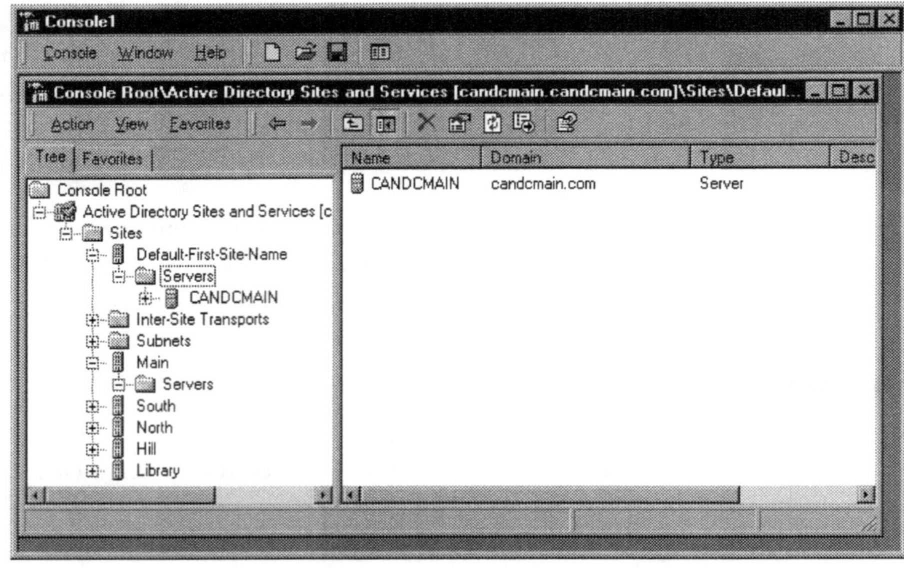

FIGURE 2-16

Setting the address and mask for a new subnet

New Object - Subnet

Create in: candcmain.com/Configuration/Sites/Subnets

Address: 192 . 168 . 1 . 0

Mask: 255 . 255 . 255 . 0

Name: 192.168.1.0/24

Enter the subnet address and mask. This will be automatically translated into a subnet name in the form network/bits-masked.
Example: address 10.14.209.14 mask 255.255.240.0 becomes subnet 10.14.208.0/20.

Select a site object for this subnet.

Site Name
Hill
Library
Main
North

OK Cancel

FIGURE 2-17

Final Settings

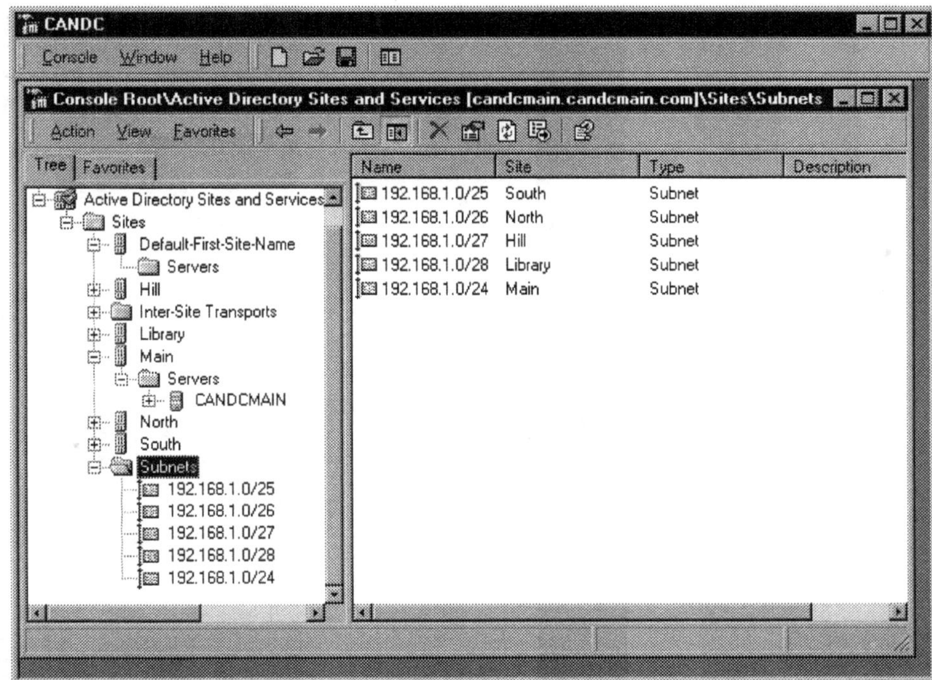

Lab Exercise 2.05

Run MMC as before, and open the candc.msc file.

Expand the Sites and the Inter Site Transport folders. Right-click the IP folder, and select New Site Link. Set up the SouthNorth link as shown in Figure 2-18, and click OK.

Repeat the process for each link.

To assign costs, start by right-clicking the SouthNorth link. Select the cost box, and type **25** into it. Set the replication time to **210** (Figure 2-19).

Set the cost and replication time for each remaining link.

When you are finished, the screen should look like Figure 2-20.

Save, and exit MMC.

FIGURE 2-18

Setting up a site link

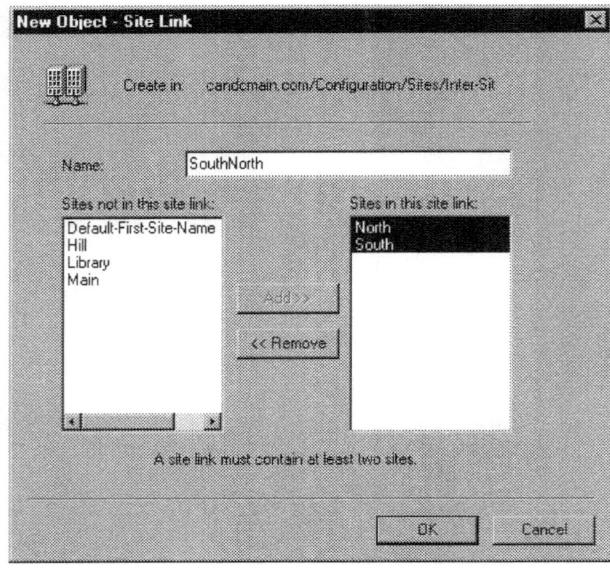

FIGURE 2-19

Assigning cost and replication properties to links

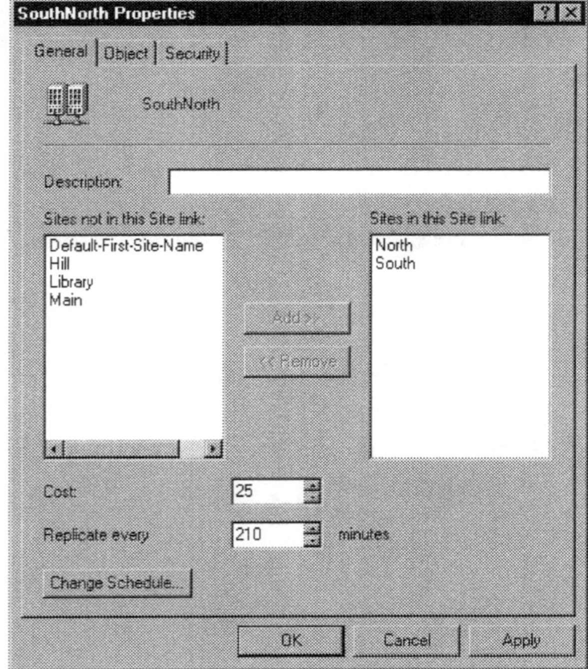

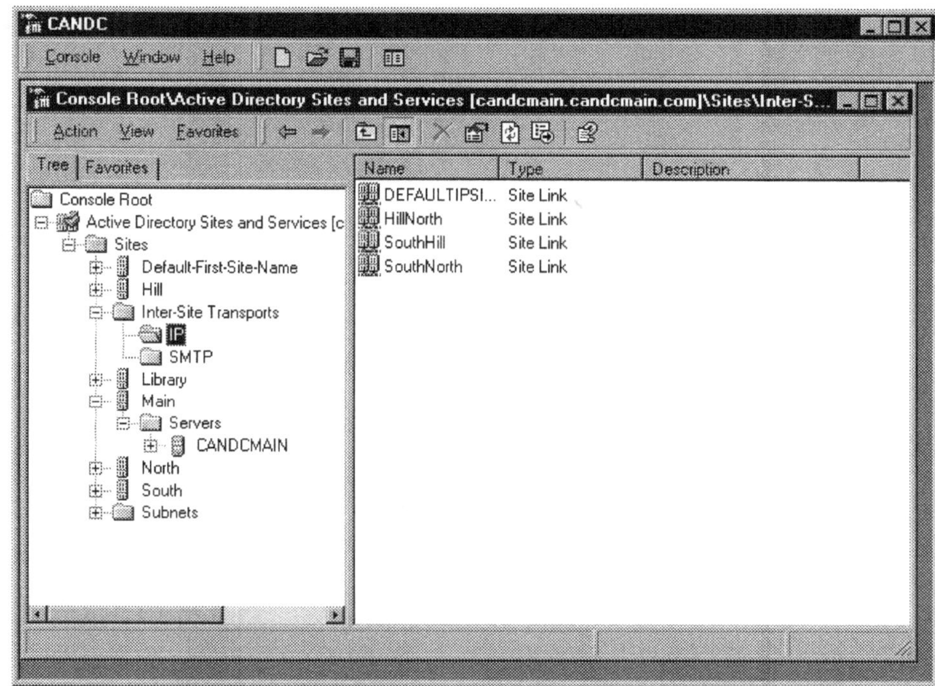

FIGURE 2-20 Verifying the new site links

Lab Exercise 2.06

Run MMC as before, and open the candc.msc file. Expand the Sites folder, the Main site, and the Server folder under Main. Right-click CANDCMAIN, and select Properties. Add the IP transport method as shown in Figure 2-21.

Select Apply, and then OK. Save, and exit MMC.

Lab Exercise 2.07

Run MMC as before, and open the candc.msc file.

Expand the Sites folder, and then the Inter-Site Transports folder.

Right-click the IP folder and select New Site Link Bridge. Add the SouthNorth and SouthHill links to the site link bridge as shown in Figure 2-22.

Click OK to close the Site Link dialog.

Your screen should look like Figure 2-23.

Save, and exit MMC.

FIGURE 2-21

Specifying the server's transport method

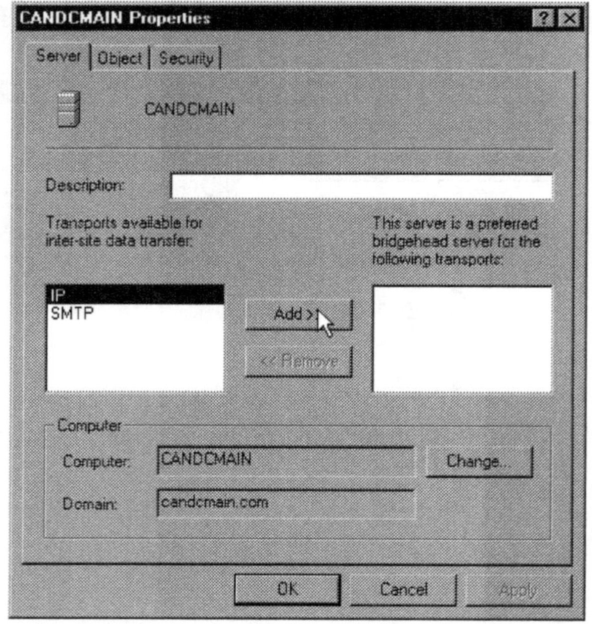

FIGURE 2-22

Adding links to the site link bridge

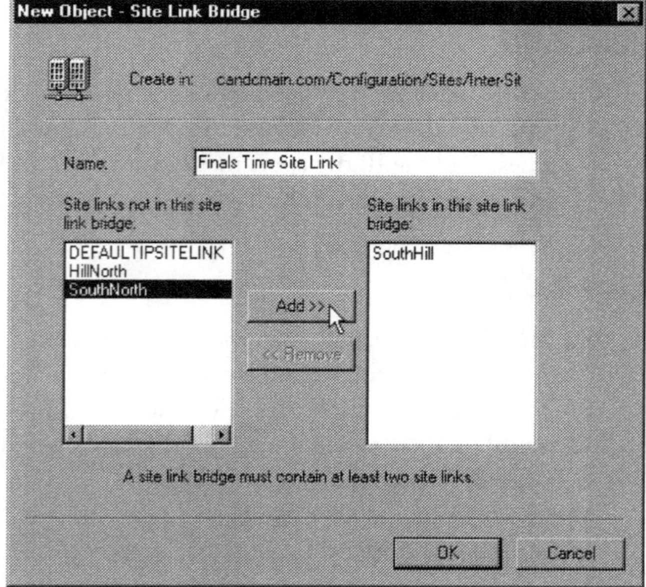

FIGURE 2-23

Verifying the addition of a new site link bridge

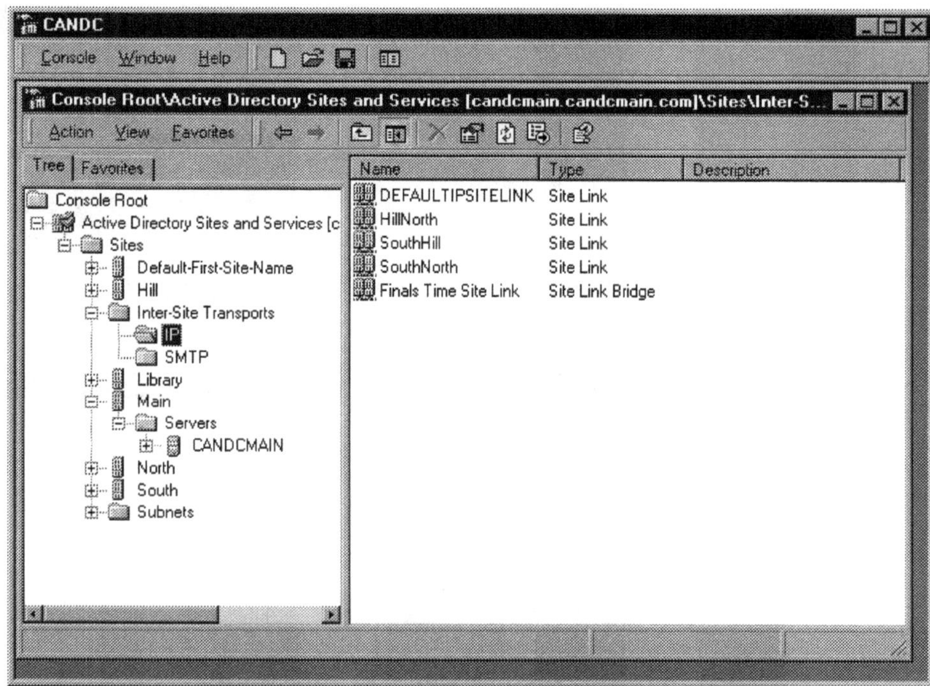

Lab Exercise 2.08

Run MMC as before, and open the candc.msc file.

Expand the Sites folder, and then the Main folder. Open the Servers folder, and expand the CANDCMAIN server.

Right-click NTDS Settings, and select New Active Directory Connection. As shown in Figure 2-24, select the CANDCMAIN server (which is also the domain controller).

Click OK.

Keep the default name and click OK again.

Right-click the new connection object shown in the right pane, and select Properties.

Click the Change Schedule button to open the schedule screen. Choose the "Four times per hour" option as shown in Figure 2-25.

Click OK to exit the schedule screen. Select Apply and click OK to exit the Properties dialog.

FIGURE 2-24

Selecting the domain controller for a new connection object

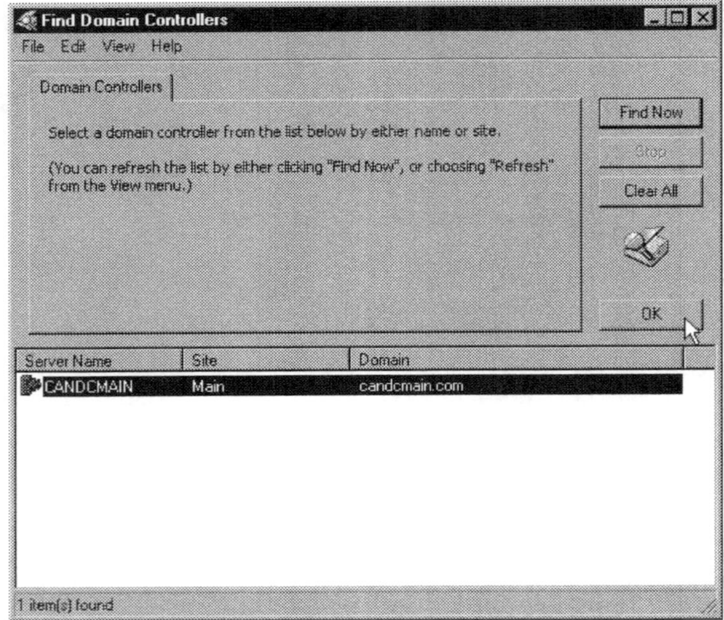

The MMC screen now looks like Figure 2-26. Save, and exit MMC.

FIGURE 2-25

Setting the schedule for a connection object

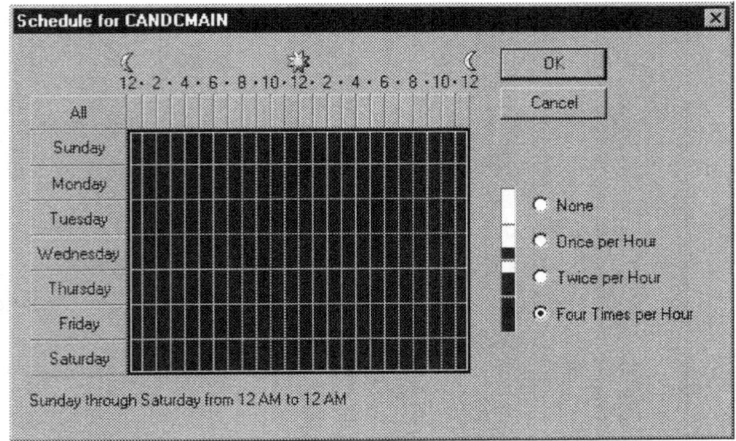

FIGURE 2-26 Reviewing the finalized MMC settings

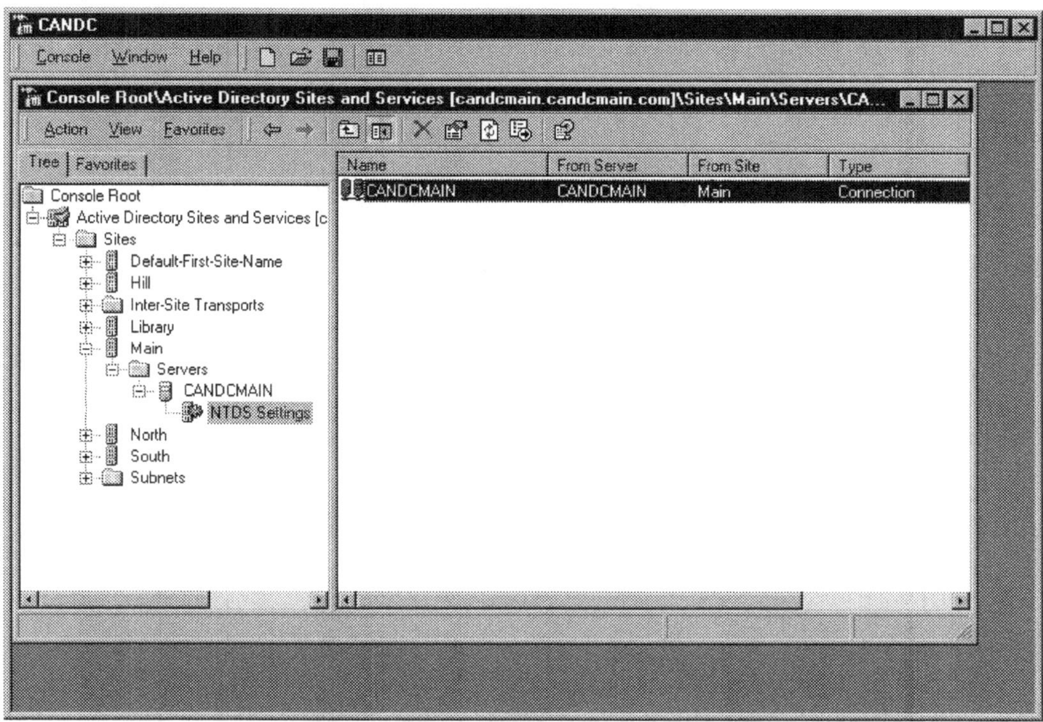

Lab Exercise 2.09

Run MMC as before, and open the candc.msc file.

Expand the Sites folder, and then the Main folder. Open the Servers folder, and expand the CANDCMAIN server.

Right-click NTDS Settings, and select Properties. Verify that the Global Catalog check box is selected. Set the other properties as shown in Figure 2-27.

Select Apply, and then click OK.

FIGURE 2-27

Editing the Global Catalog settings for the domain

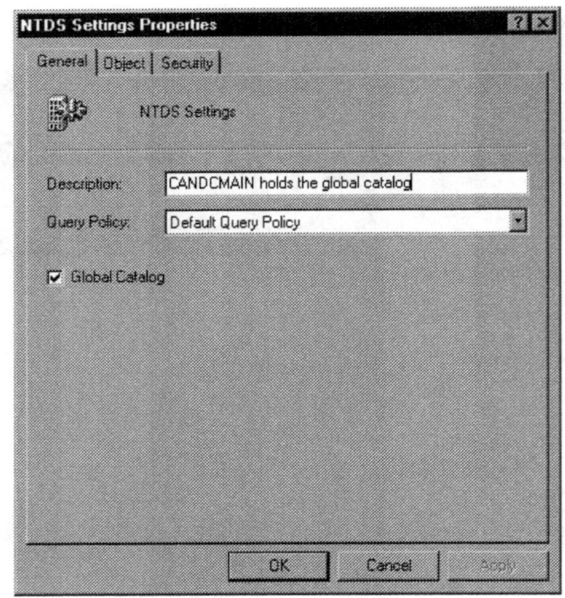

ANSWERS TO LAB ANALYSIS TEST

1. The problem is in the FAT32 partitions. SYSVOL must reside on an NTFS partition. The solution is to convert one of the drives to NTFS by using the Convert command.
2. The specified subnet mask controls up to four machines.
3. A site bridge from A to C, and then C to B instructs the network to find the faster path. The Knowledge Consistency Checker (KCC) also helps with the task by automatically finding the fastest path through the network.
4. The specified network will have seven sites. Remember that sites are best defined using WAN links as boundaries. Thus, five sites will each have one server. One site has five machines, and another site has the two-machine network.
5. Because the remote machines are using a dialup line, they can be considered to have a slow connection speed. That scenario suggests the use of the Simple Mail Transport Protocol (SMTP).

ANSWERS TO KEY TERM QUIZ

1. global catalog
2. connection object
3. DCPROMO
4. site links
5. bridgehead server

3

Configuring Active Directory

LAB EXERCISES

3.01 Verifying Active Directory

3.02 Creating a Server Object for Each Site

3.03 Assigning Roles to Servers

3.04 Seizing the PDC Role from South Side

3.05 Creating an OU Structure for C&C

- Lab Analysis Test
- Key Term Quiz
- Lab Wrap-Up
- Lab Solutions

The Active Directory server is now installed and working at C&C. Active Directory (AD) now needs to be configured to work correctly. You need to place C&C's organizational structure on the Active Directory layout. Servers need to be created and configured. Finally, the server workloads need to be optimized. You'll start by verifying that the Active Directory and the domain controller are working properly.

LAB EXERCISE 3.01

10 Minutes

Verifying Active Directory

Joanne is discussing the changes in C&C's network and brings up Active Directory. For future reference, she wants to know how to determine if Active Directory is running properly. You agree because you know that one of the worst things a network administrator can do is assume that something is working simply because it is installed.

Learning Objectives

In this lab, you learn how to verify from several sources that Active Directory is up and running properly. At the end of this lab, you'll be able to

- Verify Active Directory on startup
- Verify Active Directory from Start button entries
- Verify Active Directory from the event viewer
- Verify that the domain controller is present in network places
- Verify that remote computers can see the domain controller

Lab Materials and Setup

You will verify for Joanne that C&C's Active Directory is correctly set up. You need the administrative account to complete this lab.

Getting Down to Business

Step 1. Log in as Administrator. Select the Active Directory entry in the Configure Your Server dialog box. You should see a message indicating Active Directory's status.

Step 2. From the Start button, run Administrative Tools.

Step 3. Start the Event Viewer. Explore the information tags until you see a message indicating that Active Directory has started.

Step 4. Open network places. Expand the entire network until you see the CANDCMAIN server.

Step 5. Open Network Places or Network Neighborhood on a remote computer. Verify that CANDCMAIN can be seen.

lab hint

Steps 4 and 5 can fail owing to problems other than a failure in Active Directory.

LAB EXERCISE 3.02

20 Minutes

Creating a Server Object for Each Site

To make the C&C network run as smoothly as possible, several servers will be installed. Each site will have its own server, with a defined role. To prepare for those roles, a server must be established at every site in the Active Directory structure.

Learning Objectives

In this lab, you create a server for each site. At the end of the lab, you'll know how to add a server to the Active Directory structure.

Lab Materials and Setup

When you're done, each site will have its own server. You'll use the naming schema CANDC*sitename*. You need these materials:

- Administrator account
- LAN connection for your 2000 Server

Getting Down to Business

Step 1. Start Active Directory Sites and Services from the Start button.

Step 2. Expand the Hill site to see the Servers folder.

Step 3. Under the Hill object, create a server object named **CANDCHILL**.

Step 4. Repeat steps 2 and 3 for each site.

LAB EXERCISE 3.03

Assigning Roles to Servers

20 Minutes

Joanne is concerned that the main server will become overloaded with work. She does not want a bottleneck degrading the performance of her network. You assure Joanne that bottlenecks won't happen. You'll balance the load among the servers by assigning each server a role. Work will be spread among the sites.

Learning Objectives

In this lab, you transfer roles from the main server to remote servers. At the end of the lab, you'll be able to transfer roles from server to server.

Lab Materials and Setup

Active Directory servers can be assigned any of five roles. You decide that the Schema and Domain-Naming master roles will reside on the CANDCMAIN server. South Side, being the largest site, will host the Primary Domain Controller (PDC) role. Hill will host the Infrastructure master role and North Side will host the Relative ID (RID) master role. You will need these materials:

- Administrative account for the domain controller
- Servers created in the Active Directory for each site

Getting Down to Business

Step 1. Run Active Directory Users and Computers from the Start button.

Step 2. Connect to the domain.

Step 3. Right-click Active Directory Users, and select Operations Masters.

Step 4. Using the Change button, assign the RID role to North Side, PDC to South Side, and Infrastructure to Hill.

Step 5. Verify that the roles were changed.

LAB EXERCISE 3.04

Seizing the PDC Role from South Side

10 Minutes

It's Sunday afternoon, and you're watching your favorite football team beat their division rivals. Your cell phone rings. You answer, hoping that the pizza delivery is calling, but you hear Joanne's frantic voice on the phone instead. It seems that an accident happened in the South Side server room. A minor fire broke out. The cleaning crew, trying to be helpful, used water to put out the fire, destroying the CANDCSOUTH server. Joanne is concerned about the impact the incident will have on the network.

You tell Joanne that she did the right thing in calling. You'll go into the office and ensure that no problems occur on Monday. After hanging up, you remember that South Side is the PDC controller. That role now needs to be moved to a different server.

Learning Objectives

In this lab, you seize the PDC role from South Side and assign it to the CANDCMAIN server. At the end of this lab, you'll be able to

- Run the NTDSUTIL program
- Connect to a domain in NTDSUTIL
- Seize control of an operations role

Lab Materials and Setup

The PDC controller must be seized as soon as possible. You need the administrative account to complete this lab.

Getting Down to Business

Step 1. Run NTDSUTIL from Run on the Start button.

Step 2. View the Help screen.

Step 3. Call up the Roles menu.

Step 4. Connect to the domain.

Step 5. Seize the PDC role.

LAB EXERCISE 3.05

15 Minutes

Creating an Organizational Unit Structure for C&C

Joanne would like both central control over the network and the ability for local administrators to handle their servers as they see fit. Joanne asks if there is a way to make this scenario work. You reply that Organizational Units (OUs) allow administrators to create groups of users. Rights and permissions can be applied to the groups. When OUs are properly set up, the administrators can set basic rights for all users, and then set individual rights for groups of users. Joanne will be able to set global network rights, and her local administrators will be able to assign rights as needed to their users.

Learning Objectives

In this lab, you set up an OU structure for C&C's network. At the end of the lab, you'll be able to

- Create Organizational Units
- Nest Organizational Units
- Create a user

Lab Materials and Setup

You will build a function- and location-based OU model. That model gives Joanne central control and local administrators rights over their users. You need the administrator account to complete this lab.

Getting Down to Business

Step 1. Start Active Directory Users and Computers.

Step 2. Right-click the CANDCMAIN server, and add a new organizational unit. Create one OU per site, naming the OU after the site. (That is, create Hill, South Side, North Side, and Library OUs.)

Step 3. Create new, nested organizational units under each site OU. Create **netadmin**, **manager**, **counselor**, **staff**, and **client** OUs.

Step 4. Create an account for yourself under the netadmin OU at the main site.

LAB ANALYSIS TEST

The following questions will help you to apply your knowledge in a business setting.

1. When servers are being assigned roles, why should only one server house the Schema master role and the Domain-Naming master role?

2. Other than a server crash, what are some scenarios in which a role should be transferred?

3. When a server crashes, why should you not remove it from the Active Directory list?

4. Which is better: a location-based OU structure, or a function-based OU schema? Why?

5. Load balancing can improve the efficiency of servers. How could it reduce efficiency in a network?

KEY TERM QUIZ

Use the following vocabulary terms to complete the sentences below. Not all of the terms will be used.

- Domain-Naming
- function-based
- group policies
- load balancing
- NTDSUTIL
- Organizational Unit
- password
- PDC
- role
- schema master

1. The ____________________ acts as a Windows NT primary domain controller for computers not running Windows 2000.
2. The process of transferring roles to other servers implements ____________________ on your network.
3. The ____________________ role is in charge of all changes and modifications to the forest schema.
4. The ____________________ role is in charge of additions or deletions of domains in the forest.
5. The ____________________ command allows the administrator to seize a role from a user.

LAB WRAP-UP

In this lab, you set up Active Directory to address C&C's needs. You built organizational units for each site. You balanced the network load by transferring roles to individual servers. Finally, you saw how to seize a role.

LAB SOLUTIONS FOR CHAPTER 3

The sections that follow walk you through the steps to solve the lab exercises. You should avoid looking at these sections unless you are stuck on a particular exercise.

Lab Exercise 3.01

Log in as administrator. If the Configure Your Server dialog appears, select Active Directory in the left pane. You should see the screen in Figure 3-1.

Select Start | Programs | Administrative Tools. You should see three Active Directory entries. These entries merely indicate that the service was installed.

For proof that the service actually started, you need to check a couple of items. Select Start | Programs | Administrative Tools | Event Viewer. Open the Directory Service tab. Continue opening information items with an NTDS general source until you see the message in Figure 3-2.

Once you have verified that the service has started, you need to ensure that the domain controller is visible to users on the network. Start by checking that the server can see itself. Open My Network Places and expand the network. In the Entire Network box, select Search for Computer. Enter the name of your server as shown in the left pane of Figure 3-3. Select the Search Now button to

FIGURE 3-1

Configuring Active Directory

FIGURE 3-2

Checking the event message

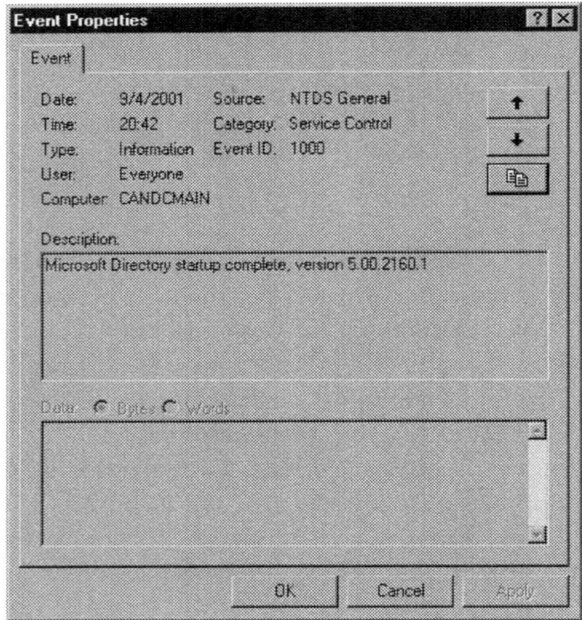

FIGURE 3-3

Finding the domain controller

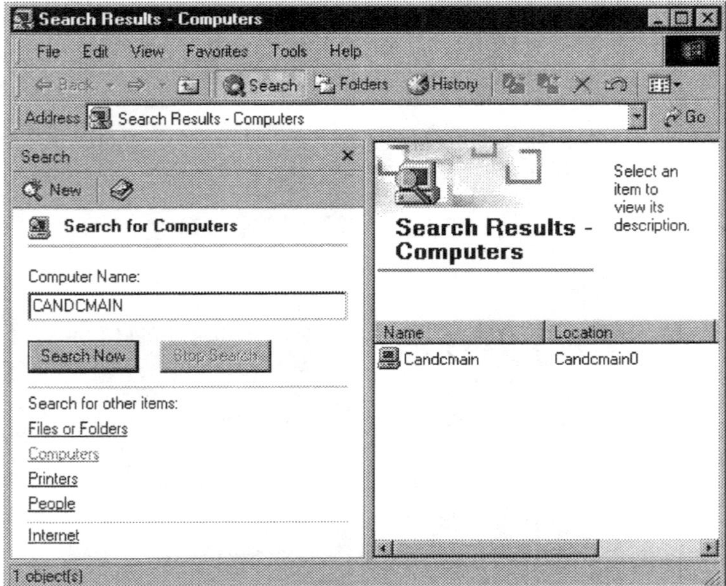

reveal the servers found, also as shown in Figure 3-3. Finally, log into a remote computer and repeat the above process. CANDCMAIN should be visible as in Figure 3-3.

lab hint

On older operating systems, the easiest way to search for a computer is to select Start | Find Computer. Type the name. The matching computer appears.

Lab Exercise 3.02

Start MMC and open the CANDC.MSC file. Expand the sites folder, and then expand each site object. Right-click the Hill server folder. Select New | Server. Give the server the name CANDCHILL. Repeat the process for the Library, North Side, and South Side branches. Name the servers CANDCLIBRARY, CANDCNORTH, CANDCSOUTH respectively. When you are finished, the MMC screen will look like the one in Figure 3-4.

FIGURE 3-4 Adding C&C's servers to Active Directory

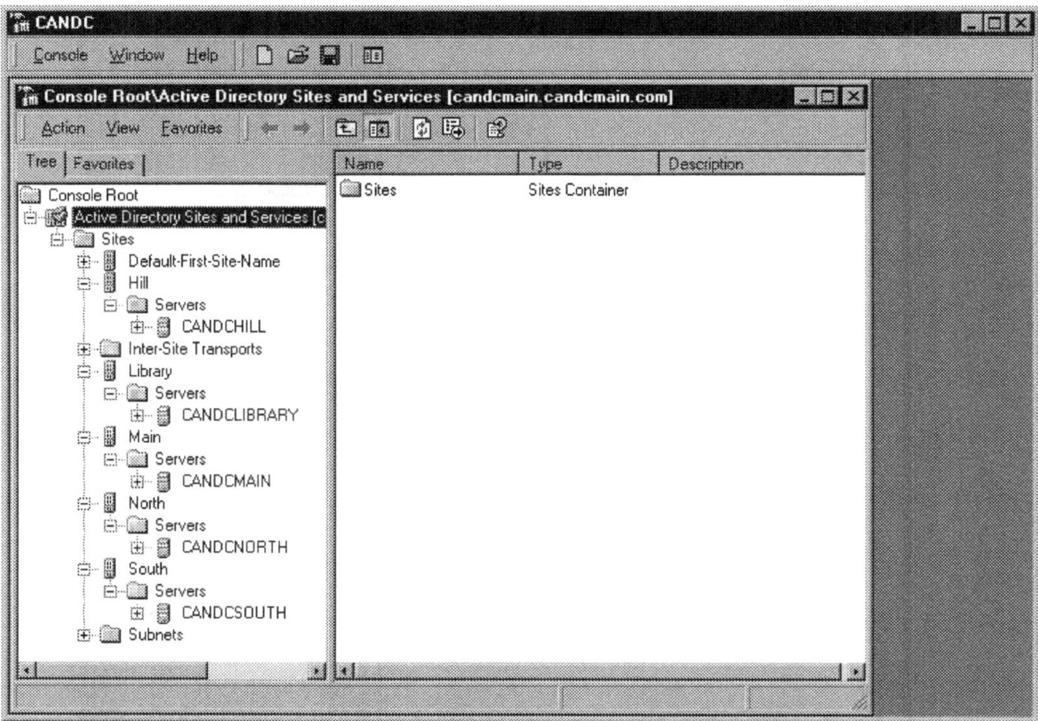

Lab Exercise 3.03

Select Start | Programs | Administrative Tools | Active Directory Users and Computers. Select the Action menu and choose Connect to Domain. As shown here, select the appropriate domain and click OK.

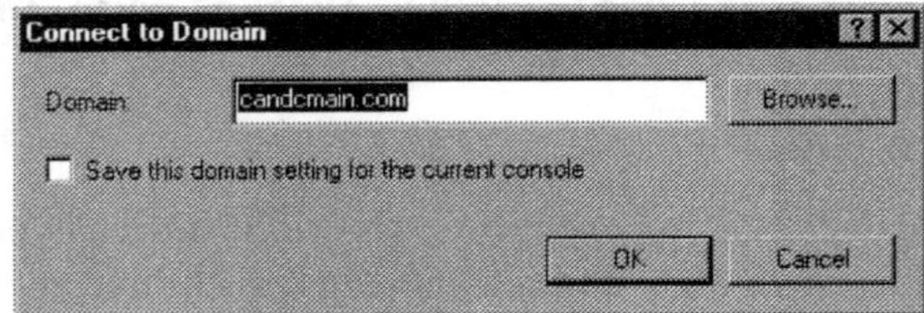

Right-click the Active Directory Users object in the left pane, and select Operations Masters. The dialog shown in Figure 3-5 opens. With the RID tab selected, use the Change button to enter **candcnorth.candcmain.com**. Repeat the process for the other two sites, using **candcsouth.candcmain.com** for PDC and **candchill.candcmain.com** for Infrastructure.

FIGURE 3-5

Assigning operations master roles

Lab Exercise 3.04

Select Start | Run. Type **NTDSUTIL**. The NTDSUTIL window opens:

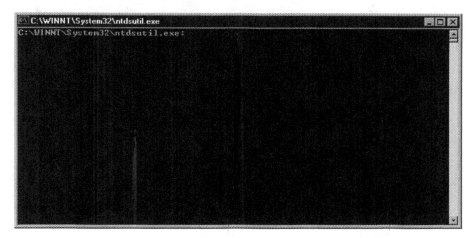

Enter a **?** to see the help screen. Enter **Roles**, and then enter a **?**. This display appears:

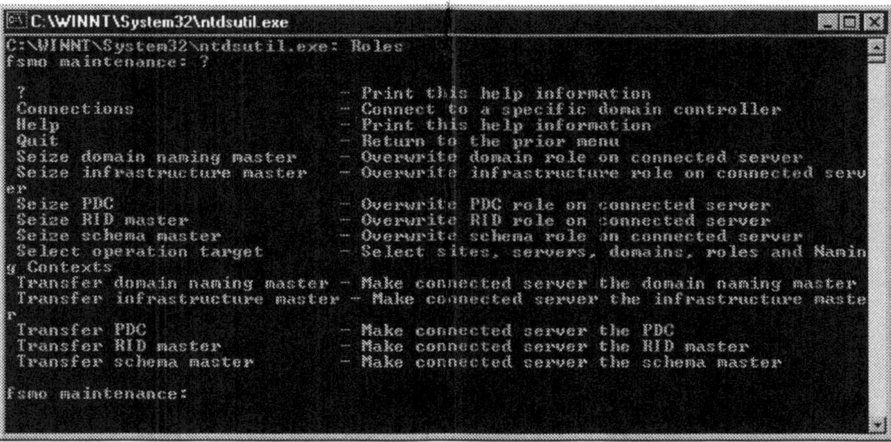

Enter **Connections**, and then enter a ? to see the options for connecting to a domain. Enter this connect command:

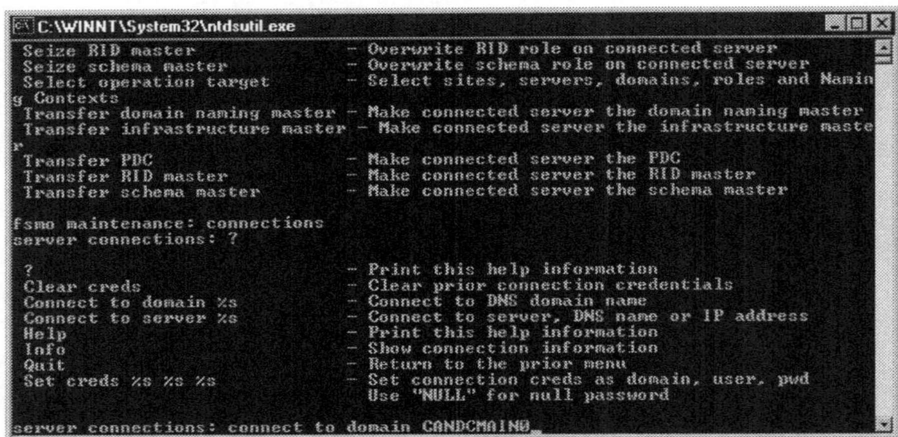

Enter **quit** to return to the Roles screen. Enter **seize pdc** as shown to take over the PDC role:

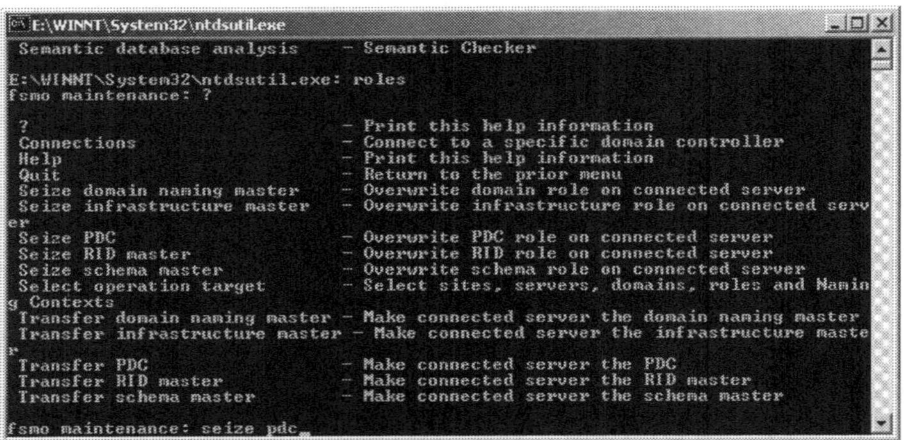

Lab Exercise 3.05

Select Start | Programs | Administrative Tools | Active Directory Users and Computers. Right-click the CANDCMAIN server. Select the new entry, and then select Organizational Unit to see the dialog box shown in Figure 3-6.

Type **Hill** and click OK. Repeat the process for South Side, North Side, Main, and Library.

Right-click Hill. Select the new entry, and then select Organizational Unit. Create OUs for **netadmin**, **manager**, **counselor**, **staff**, and **client**. Create the same OUs for each site. When you are finished, expand all sites to see Figure 3-7.

To create a user under the main.netadmin OU, right-click the netadmin OU. Select New, and then select User. Complete the fields in the New Object—User dialog as shown in Figure 3-8, but substitute your personal information. Notice that Active Directory automatically generates the full name for you.

Select Next to create a password as shown in Figure 3-9. Leave the check boxes unchecked.

Select Next to see the summary, and then select Finish. Select the netadmin group under Main to see that the user has been created (Figure 3-10).

FIGURE 3-6

Naming a new organizational unit

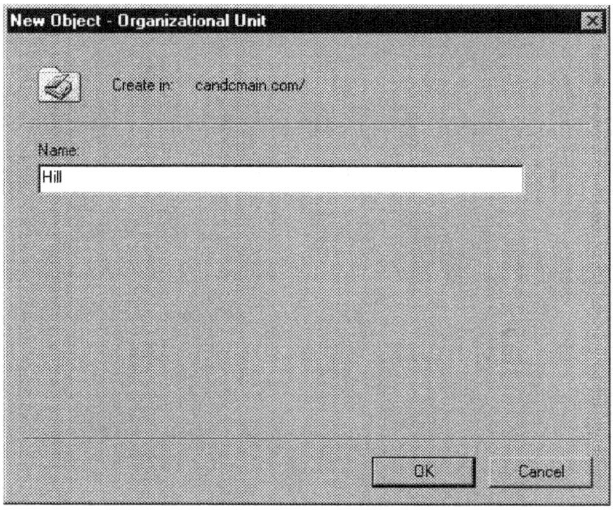

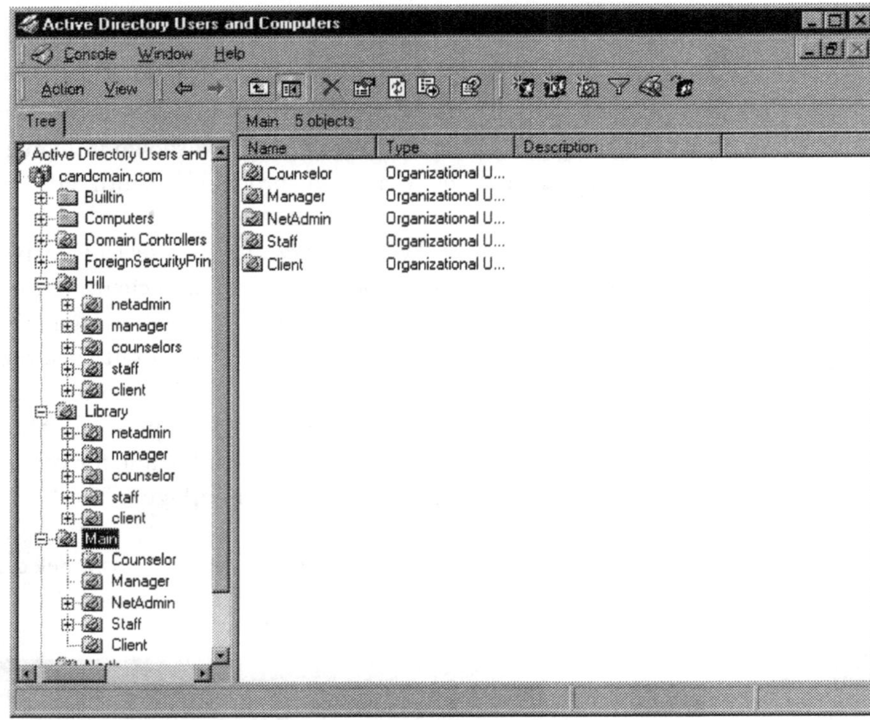

FIGURE 3-7 Viewing organizational units on the Active Directory tree

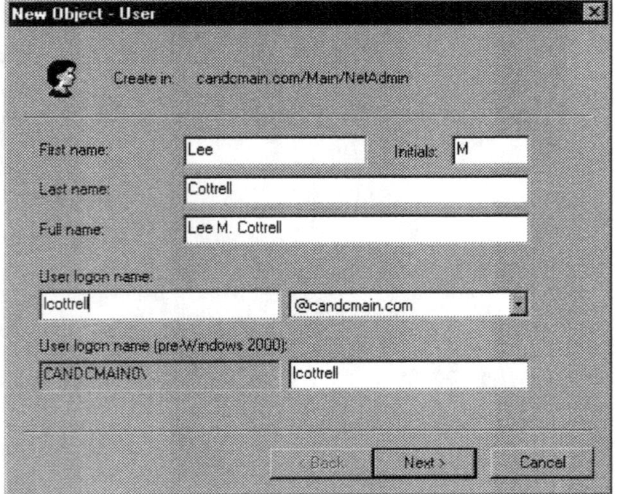

FIGURE 3-8 Entering details about a new user

FIGURE 3-9

Entering and confirming a user's password

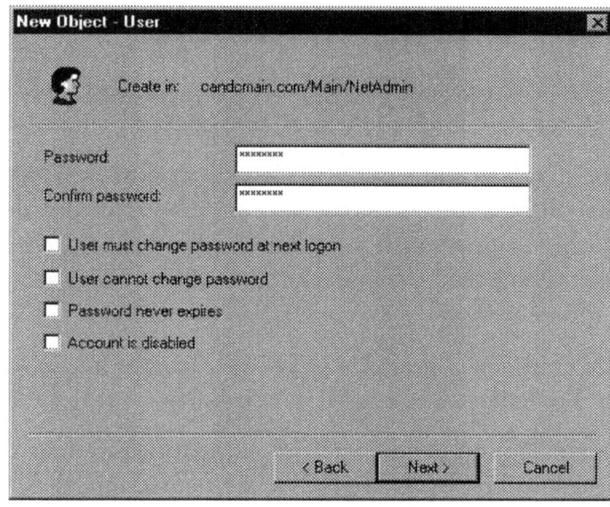

FIGURE 3-10

Viewing the users in an organizational unit

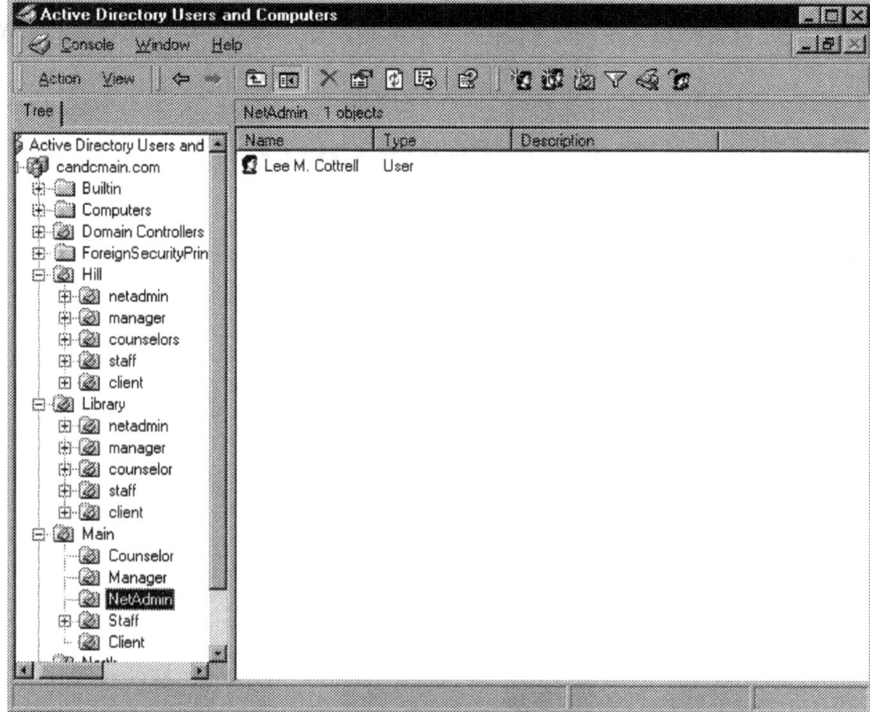

ANSWERS TO LAB ANALYSIS

1. The Schema master role and the Domain-Naming master role should live on one server. Because both roles are forest-wide roles, they must be unique to a particular domain forest.
2. Roles can be transferred to balance the load in a network. Servers that are underutilized can take the load off busy servers. As the network grows, the distribution of the server roles may need to change. Transferring a role is one way to make the change. Hardware also needs to be maintained and upgraded. As a server comes offline, another server can be set up to handle the role of the offline server.
3. A server that crashes will probably be brought back online in the near future. If you remove the server from the Active Directory list, you will have to recreate it in the near future.
4. The answer depends on the organization. Large organizations that are spread over a large geographic area will probably use the location-based model. Organizations with a number of similar users will often use the function-based model.
5. With roles spread over a network, WAN traffic may increase. Increased WAN traffic can slow a network.

ANSWERS TO KEY TERM QUIZ

1. PDC
2. load balancing
3. schema master
4. Domain-Naming
5. NTDSUTIL

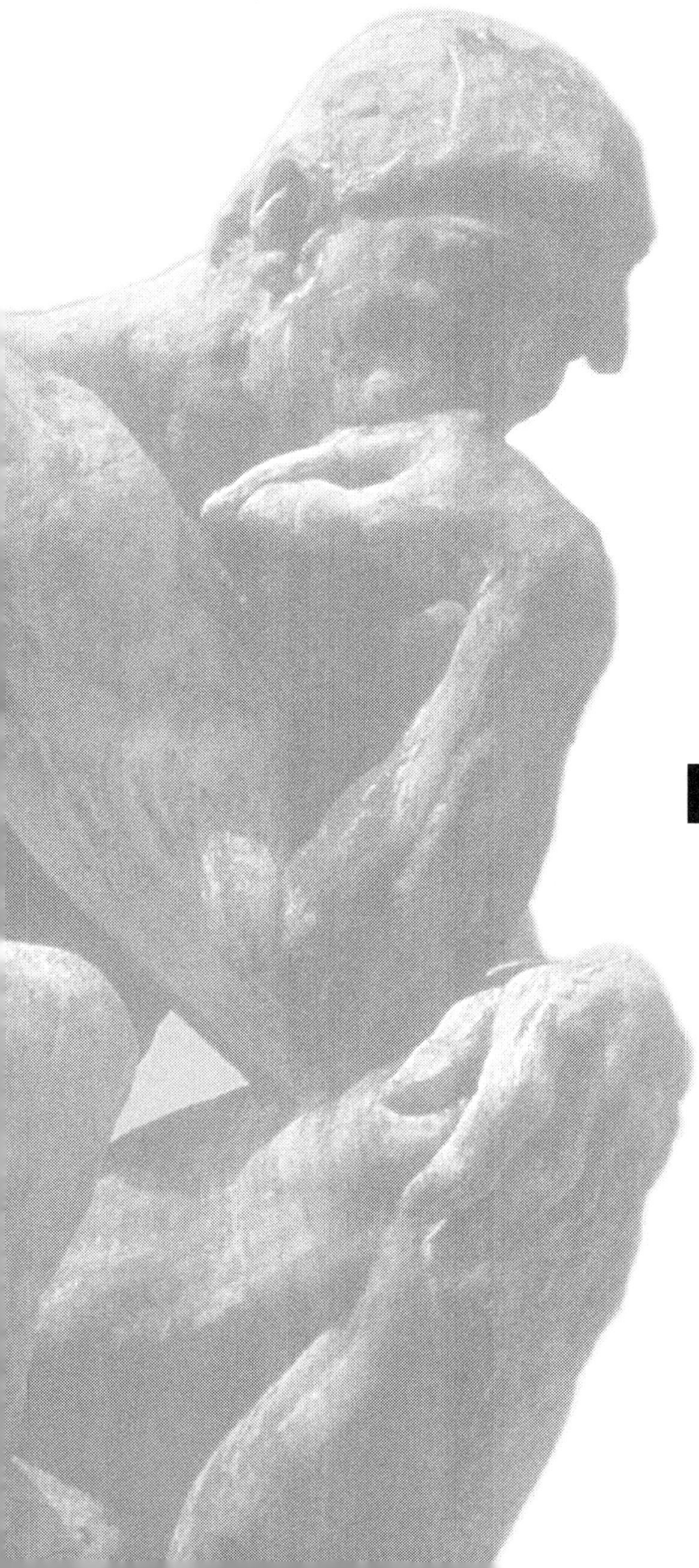

4

Backing Up and Restoring Active Directory

LAB EXERCISES

After the fire in the South Side server room, the C&C directors are worried about data loss. Reproducing the data from each site is nearly impossible. They call you into a meeting specifically to discuss what can be done, right now, about the problem.

You completely understand their fears. Data loss is an issue facing almost every company on the planet. You know that regular backups are the simplest way to ensure the continued existence of critical data. To alleviate management's fears, you create a backup routine that will ensure data reliability and not be burdensome for the computer staff and the equipment.

LAB EXERCISE 4.01

20 Minutes

Using the Wizard to Back Up Active Directory

You proceed directly to the main server room after leaving the meeting. Joanne meets you there. She congratulates you on your poise in the directors' meeting and explains that she has decided to take on the backup responsibilities personally. She wants you to show her how to perform a backup, but to keep it simple so that she won't be spending hours in the server room.

You show Joanne how to use the Windows 2000 Backup Wizard to create a backup job. That job will back up everything on the server that is crucial to the needs of the organization.

Learning Objectives

In this lab, you learn how to use the Backup Wizard to create a backup job. By the end of this lab you'll be able to:

- Start the Backup Wizard
- Create a backup job
- Schedule the backup job

Lab Materials and Setup

To create a backup job to protect the Active Directory and other data, you need these materials:

- An administrative account, or an account with backup privileges
- A backup device of some kind

lab hint

Backup devices are often tape drives. In place of a tape drive, you could use a CD burner or a file on the hard drive. Be warned that, in any scenario, a floppy drive is impractical, given the number of files that will have to be backed up.

Getting Down to Business

You proceed to show Joanne how to create a backup job to protect the server data.

Step 1. Start the backup/restore tool from System Tools on the Start button.

Step 2. Select the things that need to be backed up. Make sure that you select System State in addition to critical files.

Step 3. Decide where to store the backup.

Step 4. Select the type of backup.

Step 5. Name the backup.

Step 6. Schedule the backup.

Step 7. Exit the wizard, saving the changes.

LAB EXERCISE 4.02

Creating an Incremental Backup Script

20 Minutes

Joanne is amazed by the simplicity of the Backup Wizard. Despite the many options, the process is easy. She does wonder if the backup job needs to run every day. You know that a full backup does not need to run daily—an incremental backup will do. The incremental backup backs up only the files that have changed. You decide to use NTBACKUP to create a batch file that will run the incremental backup.

See the NTBACKUP section in Chapter 4 of the text for a full description of NTBACKUP and its switches.

Learning Objectives

In this lab, you use the command line program NTBACKUP to create an incremental backup. When you are finished, you'll have a batch file that runs from the desktop. At the end of the lab, you'll be able to:

- Start NTBACKUP from the command line
- Automate a backup job using the NTBACKUP switches
- Create a batch file.

Lab Materials and Setup

To create a backup job using NTBACKUP, you need these materials:

- An administrative account, or an account with backup privileges
- A backup device of some kind

Getting Down to Business

You create a batch file to run the NTBACKUP utility. The batch file has all the options needed to successfully run an incremental backup.

Step 1. Start the backup/restore tool. Use the backup file selection screen to create a selection information file.

Step 2. Start your favorite text editor. Notepad will work for this lab.

Step 3. The only line in the script is the NTBACKUP command. Write the NTBACKUP command. Include switches for the system state, selection information file, media name, file name, description, verification, and backup type.

Step 4. Save your script as **dailybackup.bat** on the desktop. Make sure that you use the BAT extension.

LAB EXERCISE 4.03

Restoring a File

10 Minutes

Joanne is pleased with your work, but asks a most important question: In the event of a problem, how do I get the data back? You reply that the Backup Wizard is the tool to restore the data. Restoring data is as easy as backing it up was. You show Joanne how to restore a file to the server.

Avoid letting the ease of restoring a file lull you into a feeling of security. Typically, a file needs to be restored because of some emergency. Emotions and stress are often running high. If you try to restore a file for the first time under those conditions you will likely fail—losing the data and possibly your job. Spend some time practicing the restoration of non-critical files. The more often you perform the restore task, the easier it will be when an emergency occurs.

Learning Objectives

In this lab, you restore a file to its original location. At the end of the lab, you'll be able to restore a file.

Lab Materials and Setup

To practice the restore steps for Windows 2000, you need these materials:

- An administrative account, or an account with backup privileges
- A backup device of some kind
- A completed backup on appropriate media
- A nonessential file with which to practice

Pick a nonessential file that you have created. Practicing with files created by other users is a recipe for disaster.

Getting Down to Business

To practice the steps of a restore, you're going to perform a non-authoritative file restore for C&C.

Step 1. Choose a file that is both nonessential and easy to reproduce if you make a mistake. Make sure that your chosen file is in the backup set.

Step 2. Make a copy of the file, just in case you make a mistake.

Step 3. Start the Backup Wizard.

Step 4. Select Restore

Step 5. Choose the file to restore.

Step 6. Select the location where the file is to be restored.

Step 7. Finish the Backup Wizard.

Step 8. Open the file to verify its contents.

LAB ANALYSIS TEST

The following questions will help you to apply your knowledge in a business setting.

1. When should an authoritative restore be performed?

2. You used NTBACKUP to create the daily backup as a batch file. Could you have used a different method?

3. Banks and financial institutions often back up their daily transactions to Write Once, Read Many (WORM) media. CD-ROMs are an example of a WORM medium. What legal advantages do WORM media have over a traditional magnetic media that allow many writes?

4. Why is it important for any organization to designate a backup operator?

5. Severe system crashes that result in lost data are relatively rare. What could cause a large-scale system crash, and what steps could be taken to prevent the crash?

KEY TERM QUIZ

Use the following vocabulary terms to complete the sentences below. Not all of the terms will be used.

append

authoritative

backup

differential

incremental

non-authoritative

NTBACKUP

NTDSUTIL

replace

system state

1. The ____________________ restore restores system data but doesn't change the update sequence number.
2. The ____________________ command creates a backup job in a batch file.
3. The ____________________ type of backup backs up only changed files and resets the archive bit for those files.
4. When choosing files to back up, selecting ____________________ ensures that the SYSVOL folder is included.
5. When adding on to a backup, the administrator selects "____________________ this backup to the media."

LAB WRAP-UP

Congratulations, you have protected the C&C servers!

In this chapter, you created backup jobs that allow the C&C administrators to regularly back up the servers. You also demonstrated the steps to restore a file to a server.

Both of those skills are crucial to every organization that uses a network. The data stored on a network is usually the information that runs the organization. If that data goes unprotected, the organization will eventually lose critical information and possibly go out of business.

LAB SOLUTIONS FOR CHAPTER 4

The sections that follow walk you through the steps to solve the lab exercises. You should avoid looking at these sections unless you are stuck on a particular exercise.

Lab Exercise 4.01

Start the backup/restore tool by selecting Start | Programs | Accessories | System Tools | Backup. As shown in Figure 4-1, select the Backup Wizard.

When the wizard starts, it brings up a splash screen. Select Next to begin the backup.

Choose "Back up selected files, drives, or network data" (Figure 4-2).

Expand My Computer to see the available drives. Select System State as shown in Figure 4-3 to capture the Active Directory data.

FIGURE 4-1 Starting the Backup Wizard

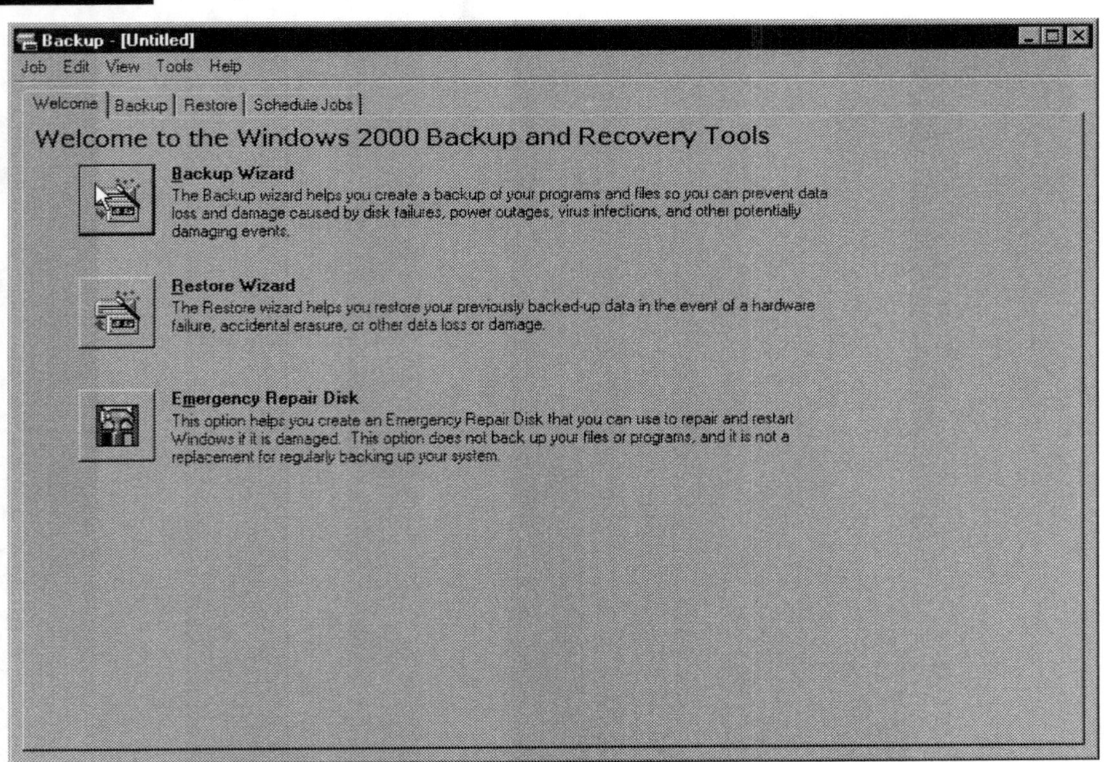

FIGURE 4-2

Determining the file inclusion level

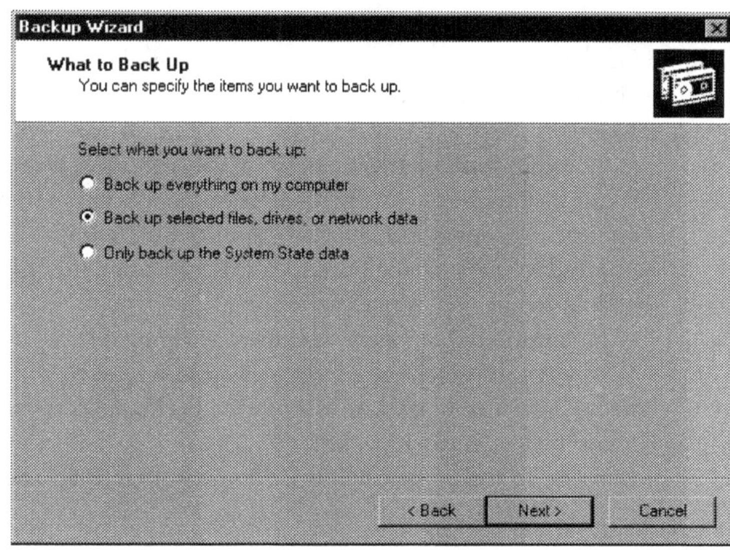

FIGURE 4-3

Selecting System State captures the Active Directory data

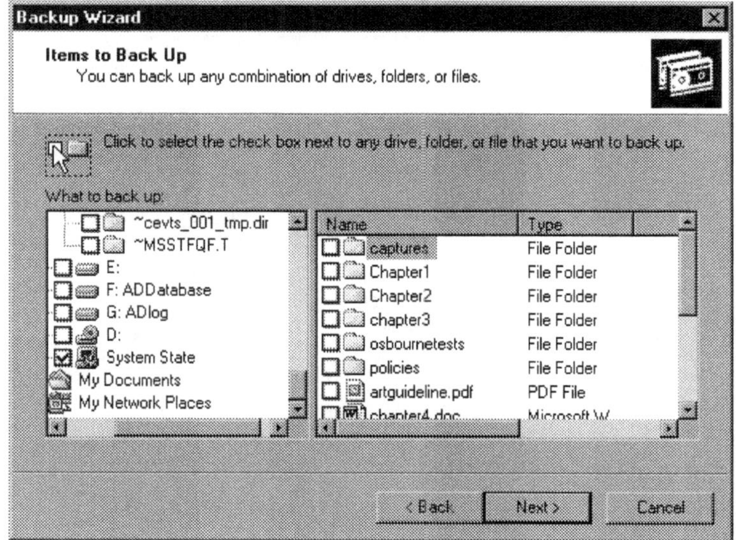

Now, expand the drives to find the data that you want to back up. Be sure to select a file that you can use to practice restoring files. Figure 4-4 shows my selection.

Notice how selected information is blue, while folders with selections inside are gray. Select Next to continue.

Once your backup selections are made, you must write the backup onto the backup medium. For the purposes of this lab, backing up to a hard drive is sufficient. As shown in Figure 4-5, specify the backup medium type and give the name and location of the backup file. If necessary, use the Browse button to find a location for the file. Select Next to continue.

The Summary box opens as shown in Figure 4-6.

You want to switch on a couple of options, and so you select the Advanced button. The current backup is a normal backup. Accept the defaults in the Type of Backup dialog, and select Next.

Choose to verify the backup as shown in Figure 4-7. Select Next.

FIGURE 4-4

Selecting individual files

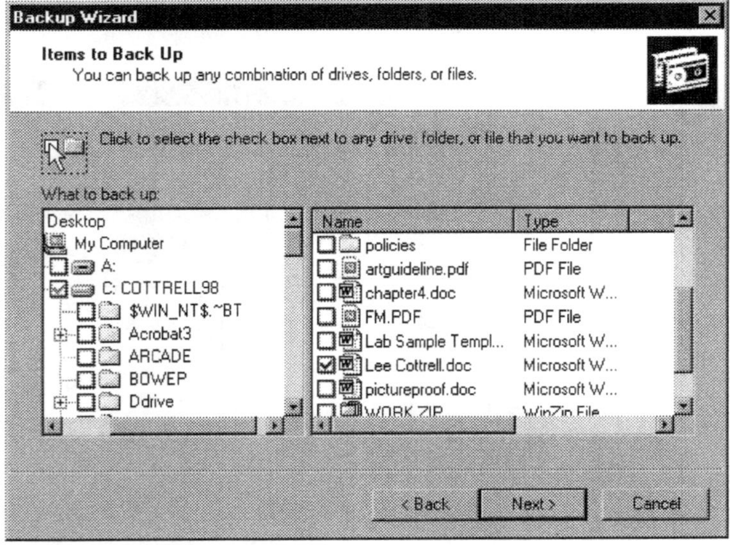

FIGURE 4-5

Specifying the details of the backup medium and the backup file

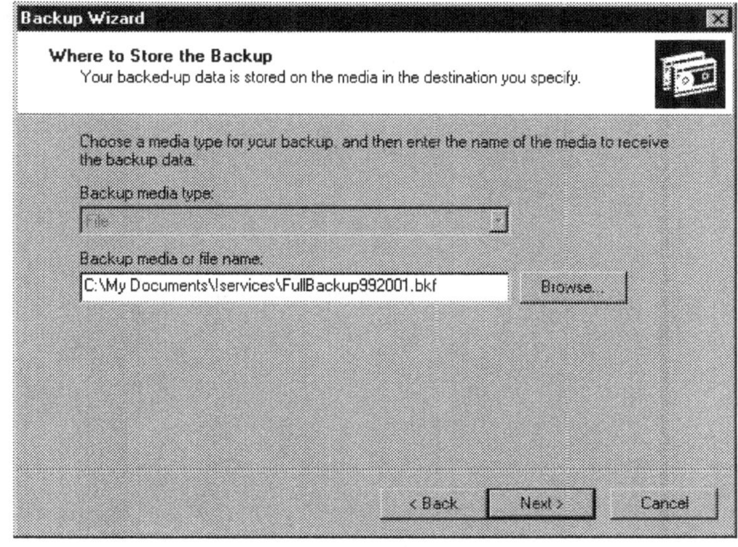

FIGURE 4-6

Reviewing the backup summary

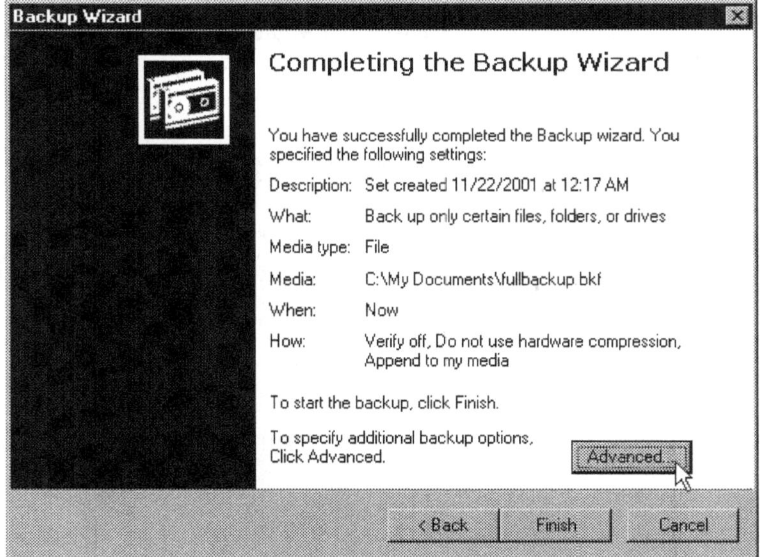

FIGURE 4-7

Setting the Verify option

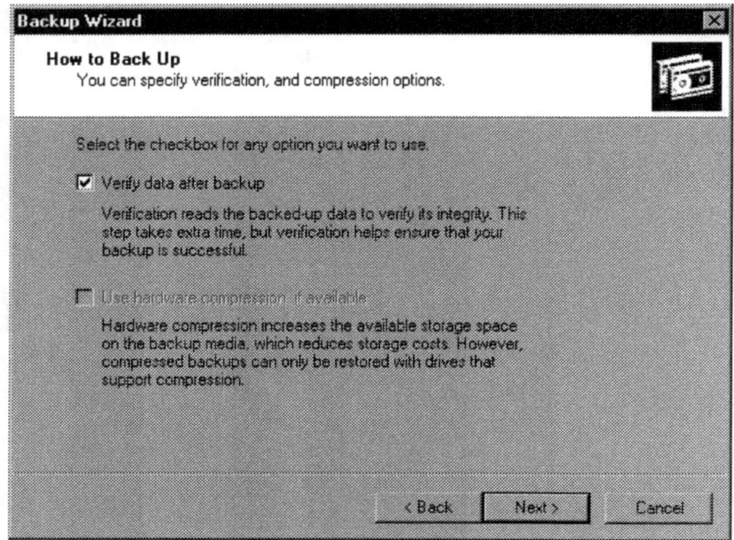

As shown in Figure 4-8, tell Windows 2000 to overwrite existing data on the media. Select Next.

Give the backup set a name similar to the one shown in Figure 4-9. Select Next.

FIGURE 4-8

Choosing to replace the existing data on the media

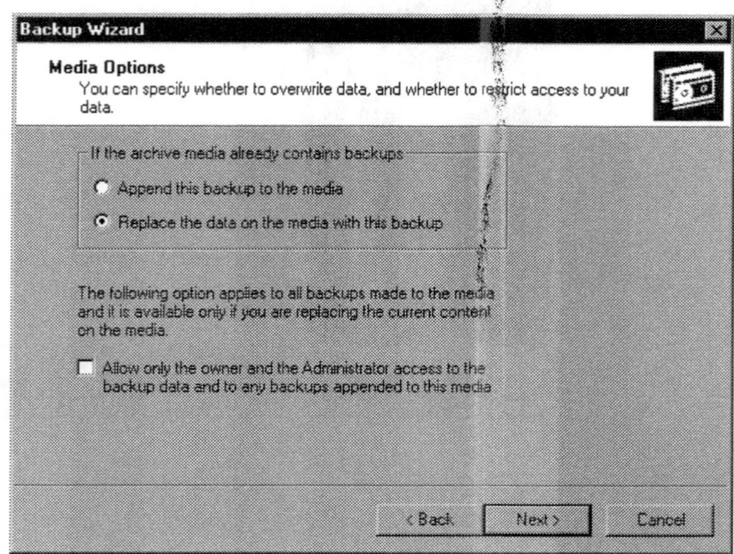

FIGURE 4-9

Labelling the backup set

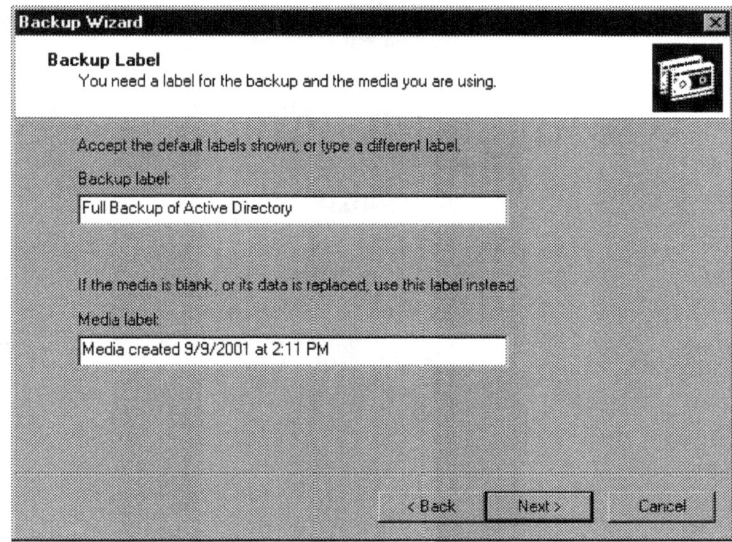

You want the job to be scheduled for every Friday. Select the Later button. You are prompted for the administrator password.

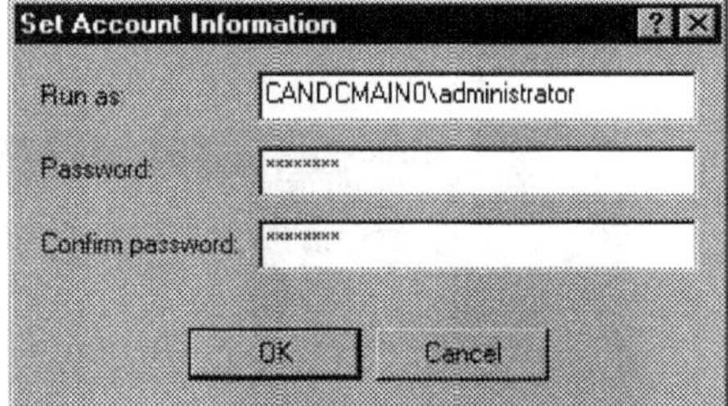

Enter and confirm the password. Give the job a name, and select Set Schedule.

You want the backup to run every Friday at 5:30 P.M. The Schedule Job dialog box should look like Figure 4-10.

Select Ok, and then Next to be brought back to the backup summary (Figure 4-11).

Notice how the summary has changed from how it looked in Figure 4-6.

FIGURE 4-10

Scheduling the backup job

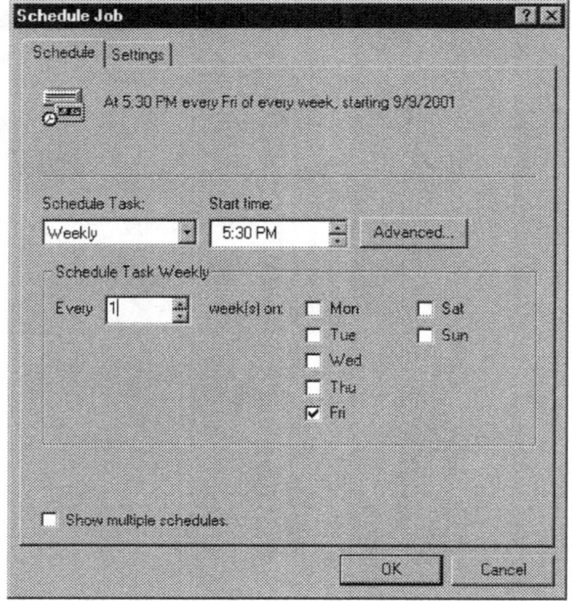

Select Finish to start the backup. You can watch the progress as the files are backed up (Figure 4-12).

FIGURE 4-11

Checking the changes in the backup summary

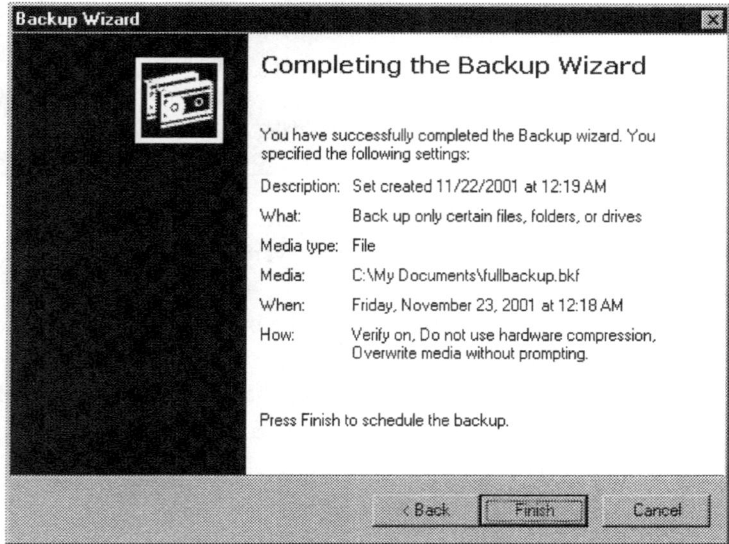

FIGURE 4-12

Viewing the progress of the backup

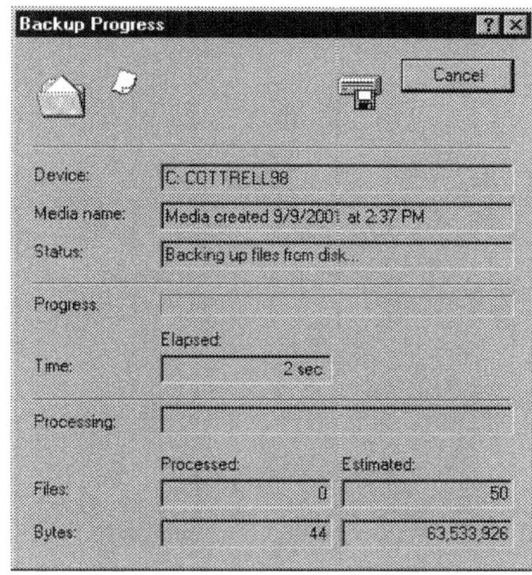

When the backup is done, the progress dialog changes to show the backup completion details.

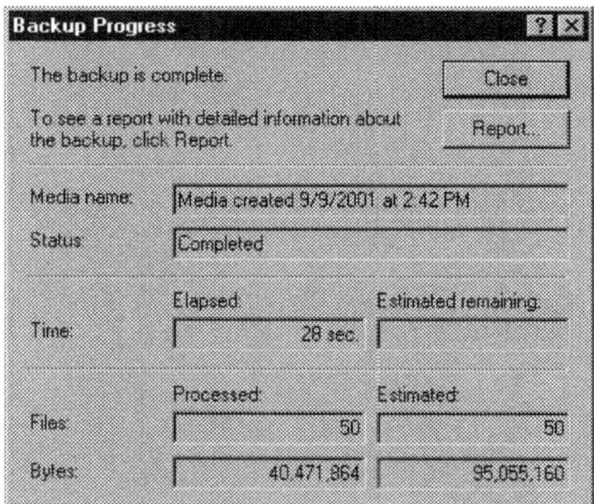

Lab Exercise 4.02

Start the backup/restore tool. Do not run the wizard. Instead, select the Backup tab.

As shown in Figure 4-13, select the files to be backed up, including the System State information.

Once the files are selected, save those selections by choosing the Schedule Job tab and then Save Selections As. Name the file **incremental.bks** and place it in the root drive, C:\. Close the backup/restore tool.

Start Notepad (notepad.exe) or another text editor. Type the command line that follows into Notepad as *one line of code.*

```
NTBACKUP backup systemstate "@c:\incremental.bks" /f
   "c:\my documents\incremental.bkf" /j "Incremental Backup" /n
   "Incremental backup" /v:Yes /m incremental
```

Save the file as **dailybackup.bat** on the desktop.

FIGURE 4-13 Selecting files for a scheduled backup

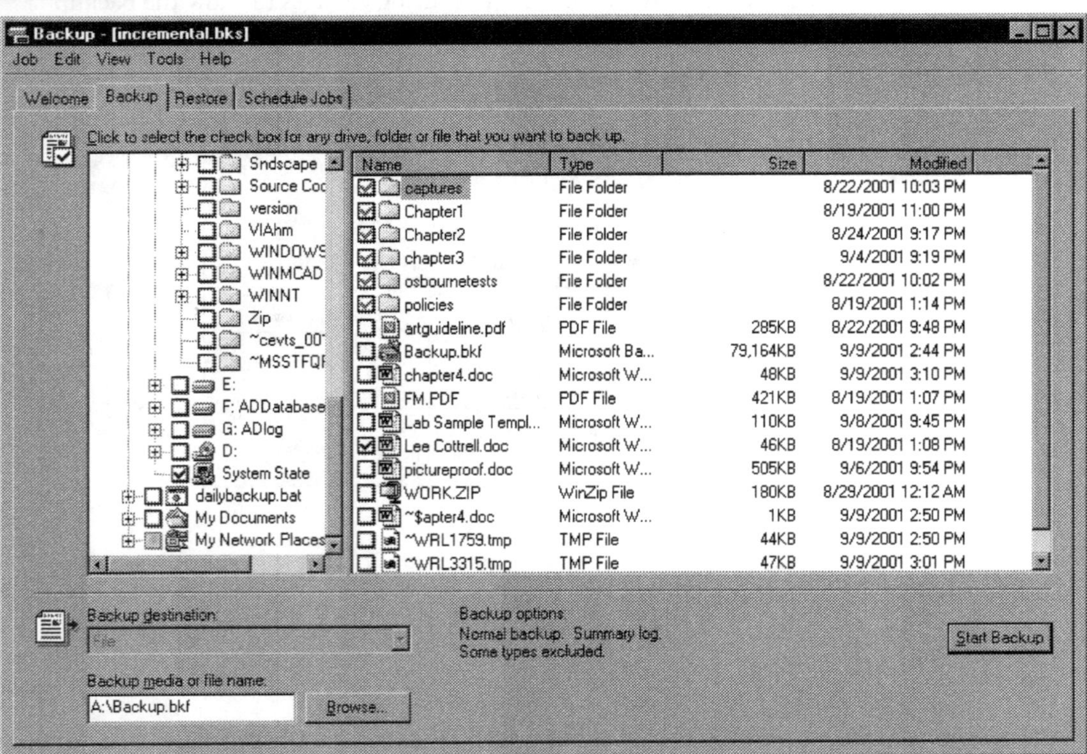

Run the script. If you have made no mistakes, then the backup routine will run. If you have made a mistake, then the backup will stop and tell you which parameter is wrong. For example:

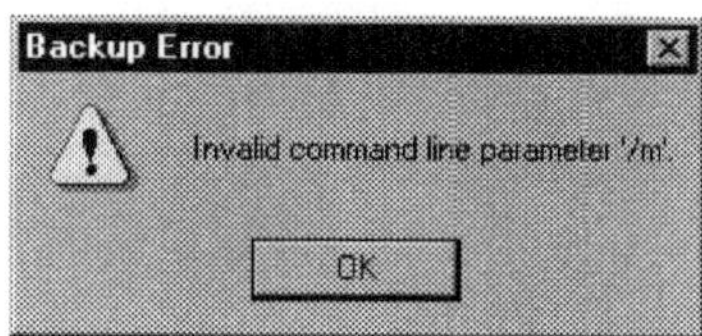

Lab Exercise 4.03

Start the backup/restore tool. Select the Restore tab.

In the left-hand pane, select the most recent option to restore.

Start expanding the folders. If prompted for the media set (as shown in the illustration) then browse to the location of the backup file.

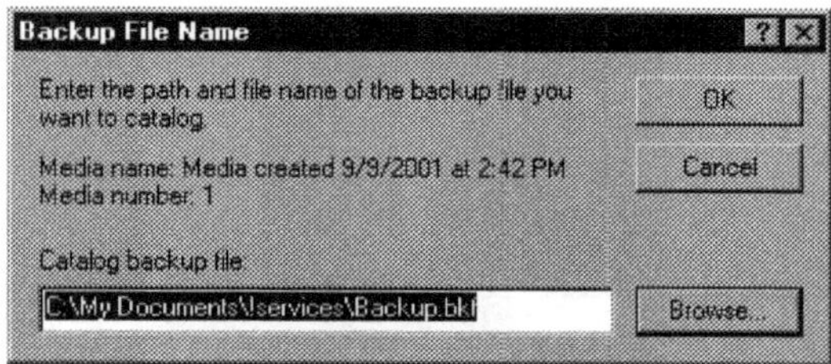

Once the backup file has been processed, select a file to restore as shown in Figure 4-14.

Select Start Restore, and then OK in the subsequent dialog boxes.

When the restore is finished, the progress dialog looks something like this:

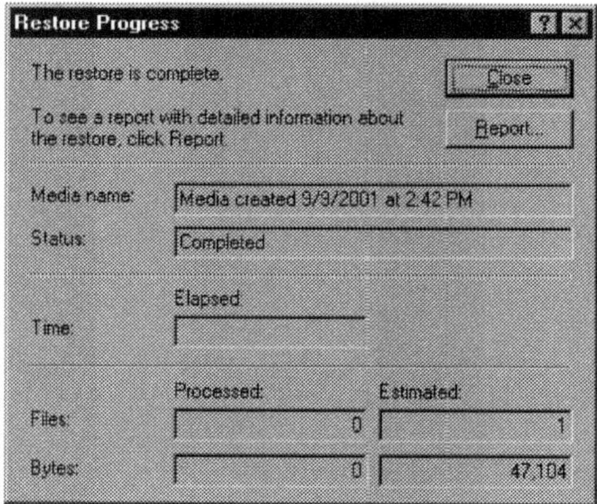

Open the file to ensure that it was correctly restored.

FIGURE 4-14 Selecting a file to restore

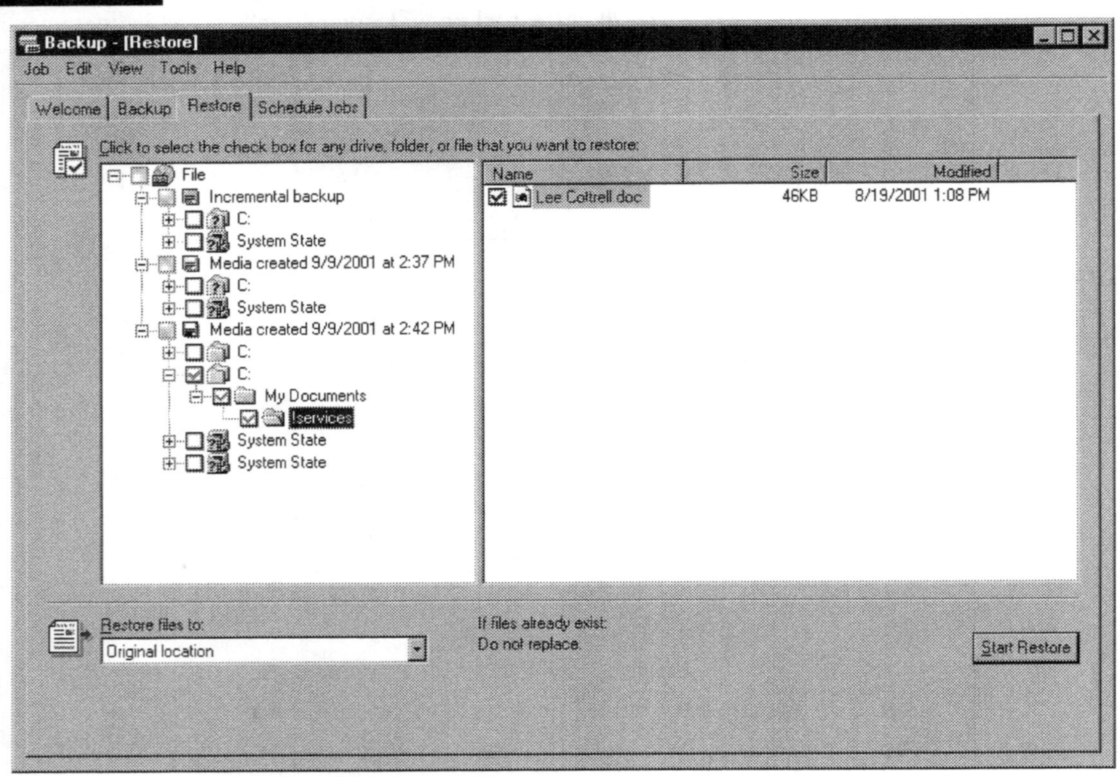

ANSWERS TO LAB ANALYSIS TEST

1. An authoritative restore should be performed when the Active Directory becomes corrupt. Active Directory can become corrupt when an employee deletes Active Directory objects or when a virus is introduced into the system. The authoritative restore restores the entire Active Directory structure and sets the update sequence number so that the other servers will rewrite their Active Directory data with the correct restored data.
2. NTBACKUP is not the only way to create an incremental backup. The Backup Wizard is just as effective, but the Backup Wizard cannot be called from a batch file.
3. Banks and financial institutions have to keep a picture of their accounts from day to day. They must be able to show every transaction performed. They must also be able to guarantee the validity of the transactions. WORM media provide that guarantee. WORM devices, once written, cannot be changed. Thus, the picture is both complete and unchangeable. Magnetic media can be changed from day to day, providing no guarantee of its validity.
4. Every organization should back up its data. By designating a backup operator, the organization ensures that no confusion exists regarding who should perform that work. Also, in the event of a failure, the designated employee can be held accountable. The designated person is usually a trusted employee who has a good record with the organization. Being designated as backup operator should be viewed as an honor.
5. Large-scale system crashes can have several causes. One possibility is a power surge or outage. Uninterruptible Power Supplies (UPSs) and generators can usually prevent those occurrences. Another cause is viruses. The prudent network administrator will have at least one up-to-date virus protection package running on every machine in the organization. Finally, hardware failures can cause system crashes. Hardware failures are difficult to prevent. One way to reduce the likelihood of a hardware failure is to purchase all equipment from manufacturers with a good track record.

ANSWERS TO KEY TERM QUIZ

1. non-authoritative
2. NTBACKUP
3. incremental
4. System State
5. append

MCSE
MICROSOFT CERTIFIED SYSTEMS ENGINEER

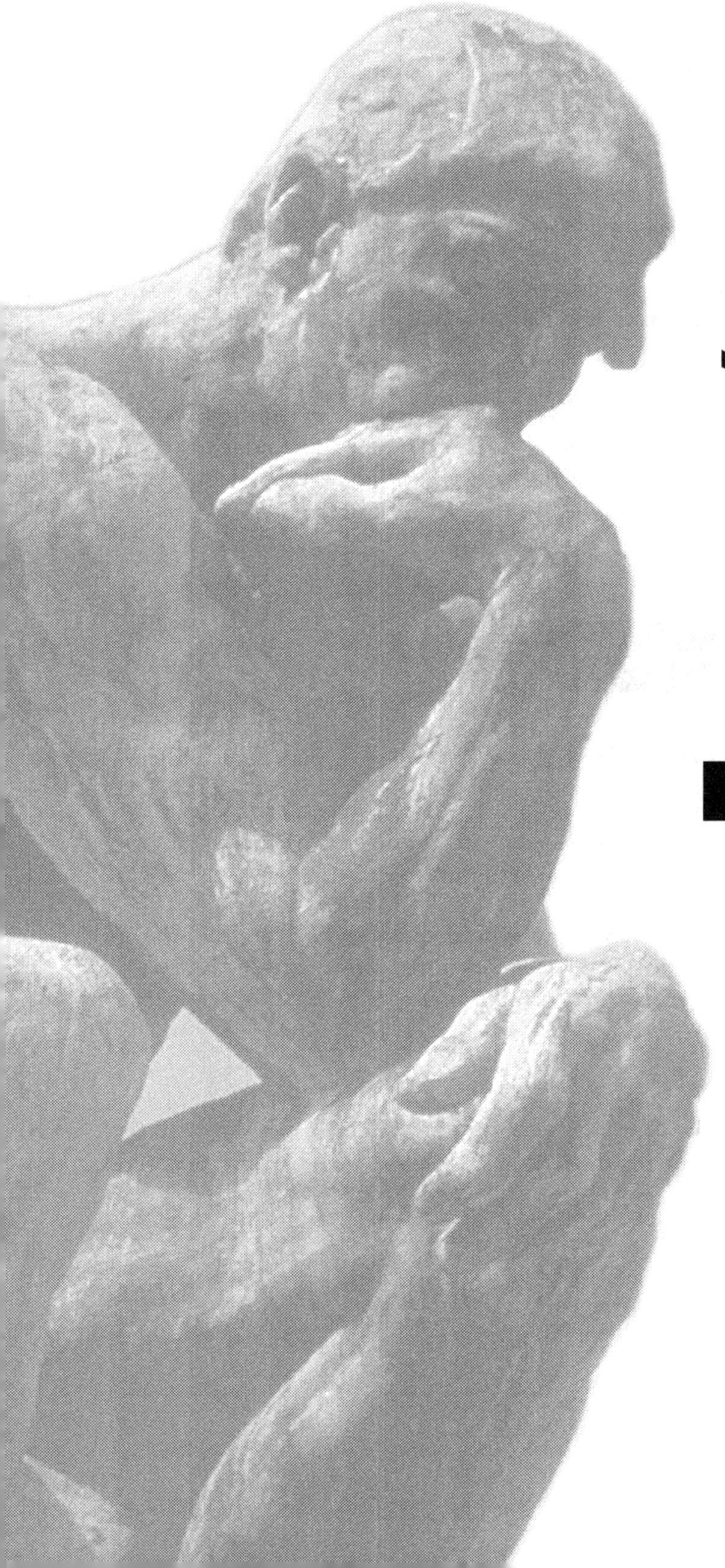

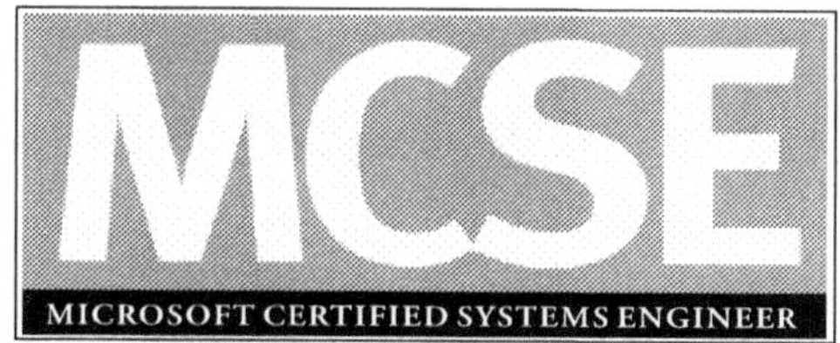

5

Integrating Domain Name Service with Active Directory

LAB EXERCISES

On one of your trips to the C&C Main site, Joanne asks you to speak with her for a while. She is concerned about the status of the DNS server. DNS entries often get added to a table, and then very quickly become outdated. If the table is not cleaned up, the DNS server can get bogged down. She asks how the DNS table might automatically be cleaned up.

You understand that obsolete entries can be a big issue. Active Directory can be incorporated into the DNS service. Active Directory zones, when coupled with Dynamic DNS, can automatically prune the DNS tree as nodes become obsolete. You tell Joanne that Active Directory will again solve the problem, and you get right to work.

LAB EXERCISE 5.01

Setting Up an Active Directory Zone

10 Minutes

Windows 2000 supports Dynamic DNS (DDNS), but only in an Active Directory integrated zone. Active Directory integrated zones do a better job of updating DNS tables. They are the first step in solving Joanne's problem.

More information on Active Directory integrated zones can be found in the* MCSE Windows 2000 Directory Services Administration Study Guide *in the Switching to Active Directory–Integrated Zones section of Chapter 5.

Learning Objectives

In this lab, you set up an Active Directory integrated zone in the DNS server. At the end of the lab, you'll be able to upgrade existing DNS zones to Active Directory integrated zones.

Lab Materials and Setup

To convert the zone, you need these materials:

- Administrative access to the server
- Microsoft DNS installed on the server

Getting Down to Business

Step 1. Start the DNS console from the Start button.

Step 2. In the left pane, select the forward lookup zone (or zones) to be converted.

Step 3. Go to the Properties dialog for the chosen zones.

Step 4. Change each of the chosen zones to Active Directory–Integrated.

LAB EXERCISE 5.02

20 Minutes

Setting Up and Configuring a Dynamic Domain Name Service

Converting the zone to Active Directory–Integrated solves a problem with updating multiple servers, but it doesn't solve Joanne's problem. She needs to ensure not only that the DNS tables are up to date, but also that dead links are removed. DDNS has features to age and remove (scavenge) dead links. DDNS prefers to work with the Active Directory zones that you created in Lab Exercise 5.01.

Learning Objectives

In this lab, you install and configure DDNS. At the end of the lab, you'll be able to:

- Install DDNS
- Set aging and scavenging properties on DDNS zones

Lab Materials and Setup

Again, you will be converting a zone. You need these materials:

- Administrative access to the server
- An Active Directory integrated zone

Getting Down to Business

Step 1. If DNS console is not already running, start it.

Step 2. Go to the Properties dialog for the zone.

Step 3. Switch on dynamic updates for the zone.

Step 4. Right-click the DNS server, and select Set Aging/Scavenging for All Zones.

Step 5. Set the refresh interval to 2 days.

Step 6. Manually enable "Scavenge stale resource records" for all non–Active Directory zones. (These will probably be the reverse lookup zones.)

LAB EXERCISE 5.03

15 Minutes

Adding a Record to the DNS Table

Joanne is happy that the servers will automatically update entries and remove old ones. However, she'd like to have the servers preloaded in the DNS table. She is unsure how to add the servers to the DNS table.

You tell her that new hosts are easy to add and that you'll take care of it immediately.

Learning Objectives

In this lab, you add a DNS entry for each server in C&C's network. At the end of the lab, you'll be able to add a new host to a zone.

Lab Materials and Setup

You will create several server entries in the DNS tables. You need these materials:

- A private IP address for each server
- Administrative access to the server
- DNS installed on the server

Getting Down to Business

Step 1. Start the DNS Snap-in from the Start button.

Step 2. Expand the forward lookup zone to see CandC.com.

Step 3. Add the new host to the forward lookup zone. Use these IP addresses for the servers:

Machine	IP Address
Main	192.168.1.1
South	192.168.1.128
North	192.168.1.192
Hill	192.168.1.224
Library	192.168.1.240

LAB EXERCISE 5.04

Building Baselines for Performance Console

10 Minutes

After you set up the DNS hosts, you ask Joanne how she plans to monitor network performance. She looks at you a little oddly and then says that when the network is slow she looks at the performance console to find the problem.

You immediately see a difficulty. If an administrator looks at the performance console for the first time when the network is slow, the problem won't be noticeable. The administrator needs to know what the performance console looks like at normal times as well as at peak usage times. You decide to show Joanne how to build baselines for her network.

lab hint

"Normal times" are when most of the users are logged in and working at their terminals. Times vary by the industry, but they tend to concentrate in the second hour of work and in the second hour after lunch. Peak times vary by industry and by season. In general, the beginning and end of a fiscal quarter are peak times. So is the time immediately after lunch, when employees return to their desks and start logging in. You should get a picture of the network during all of those times.

Learning Objectives

In this lab, you build a baseline for comparison with future performance statistics. At the end of the lab, you will be able to:

- Start the performance console
- Add tasks to watch
- Save the baseline

Lab Materials and Setup

You will create a baseline for a period of light demand on the network. You need administrative access to the server to complete the lab.

Getting Down to Business

Step 1. Choose Performance from the Start button.

Step 2. Add all counters.

Step 3. Wait for about 2 minutes to let performance console record the counter data.

Step 4. Record a picture of the screen as an HTML file.

Step 5. Open the HTML file in a browser, and print it for future reference.

See Table 5-1 in the textbook for descriptions of the DNS counters. Some useful counters to track include TCP Query Received, Total Query Received, and Total Response Sent/Sec.

LAB EXERCISE 5.05

10 Minutes

Using NSLOOKUP

Joanne is excited about the baseline for Performance Console. She understands the need to know what "normal" is for the network.

Joanne, having administered an NT network, remembers that occasionally a computer at a particular IP address would crash the network with a bad job. She always had a hard time identifying which computer was the culprit.

Joanne asks how a person can get a computer name from an IP address. You tell her that that trick is quite easy in Windows 2000. NSLOOKUP can provide the IP address of a machine on a network if reverse lookups are switched on.

You decide to demonstrate NSLOOKUP using the Internet.

Learning Objectives

In this lab, you use NSLOOKUP to trace machine names using IP addresses. At the end of the lab, you'll be able to:

- Start NSLOOKUP
- Find the machine name that corresponds to a given IP address

Lab Materials and Setup

You will test NSLOOKUP on some well-known Web sites. You need these materials:

- An account on the server
- Internet access

Getting Down to Business

Step 1. Connect to the Internet.

Step 2. Using Start | Run, start NSLOOKUP.

Step 3. At the prompt (>), enter these IP addresses: 206.79.171.55, 207.46.197.102, and 18.7.14.127.

lab hint

NSLOOKUP can find private IP addresses as well as public ones.

LAB ANALYSIS TEST

The following questions will help you to apply your knowledge in a business setting.

1. Start the performance console. Perform some routine tasks on your system and watch how the CPU time reacts. Perform simple tasks such as opening a file, moving the mouse, and minimizing and maximizing a window. What can the results tell you about the impact of using a network server as a workstation?

2. Besides being able to view a server's performance, what additional benefits can having baselines provide for the network administrator?

3. You set the refresh time for scavenging/aging to 2 days. That setting is shorter than the default of 7 days. What are the possible consequences of having shorter scavenging times?

4. A Windows 2000 box and a Linux box both control the DNS for your organization. You are having a hard time managing the Linux DNS from the Windows box. What is the problem?

5. You are using NSLOOKUP on the local LAN, and you're not getting names back from IP addresses. What could be the problem?

KEY TERM QUIZ

Use the following vocabulary terms to complete the sentences below. Not all of the terms will be used.

aging

BIND

cache

DDNS

DNS

IPCONFIG

NSLOOKUP

scavenging

TTL

zone

1. One example of a non-Microsoft DNS solution is abbreviated ____________________.
2. When DDNS is enabled on a zone, the ____________________ property removes old records and the ____________________ property sets the date for possible removal.
3. The command ____________________ will, among other things, provide the IP address and the Dynamic Host Configuration Protocol (DHCP) settings for a local Windows 2000 machine.
4. A query to a DNS zone has a ____________________ that represents the amount of time until the query is erased.
5. The command ____________________ can provide the name of a remote computer.

LAB WRAP-UP

Congratulations! You have successfully configured DNS for C&C. You have eased Joanne's worries about old DNS records clogging her server and met her need to ensure that the server is running at peak efficiency. In addition, you used NSLOOKUP to get information about a remote computer.

All of the users on the network will use DNS. The proper setup will make their Internet and local browsing much more efficient. In a real-world scenario, you will likely be asked to set up a DNS solution for a network.

LAB SOLUTIONS FOR CHAPTER 5

The sections that follow walk you through the steps to solve the lab exercises. You should avoid looking at these sections unless you are stuck on a particular exercise.

Lab Exercise 5.01

Select DNS from the Administrative Tools section of the Start button.

Expand the forward lookup zones in the left pane:

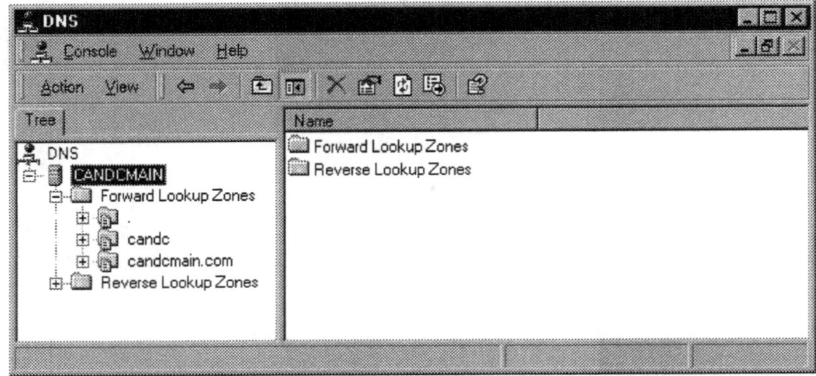

Select the first zone. Right-click the zone, and select Properties to open the Properties dialog for the zone (Figure 5-1).

Click the Change button to see the possibilities for changing the zone type.

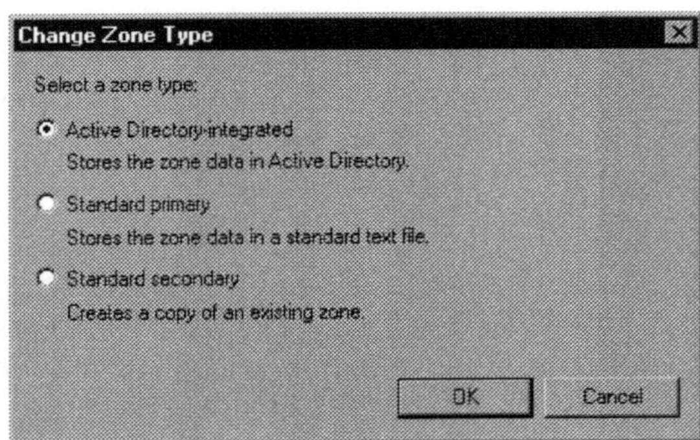

FIGURE 5-1

Integrating DNS zones with Active Directory

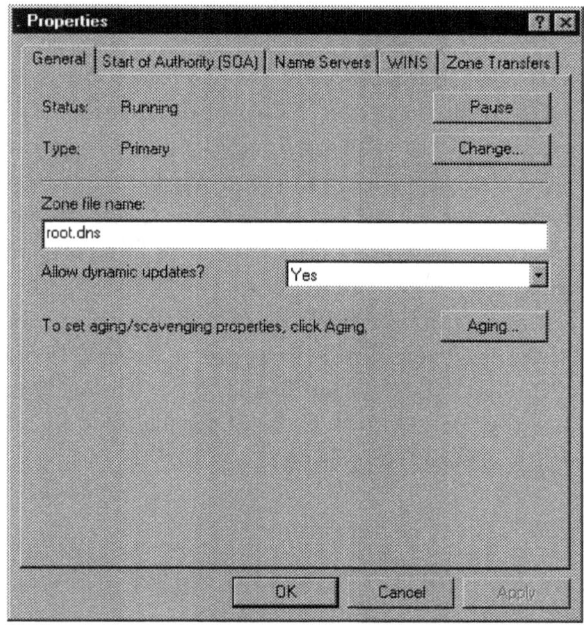

Select Active Directory as shown, and then click OK three times to return to the display of the forward lookup zones. Repeat the process for each forward lookup zone.

When you've finished, select Forward Lookup Zones in the left pane:

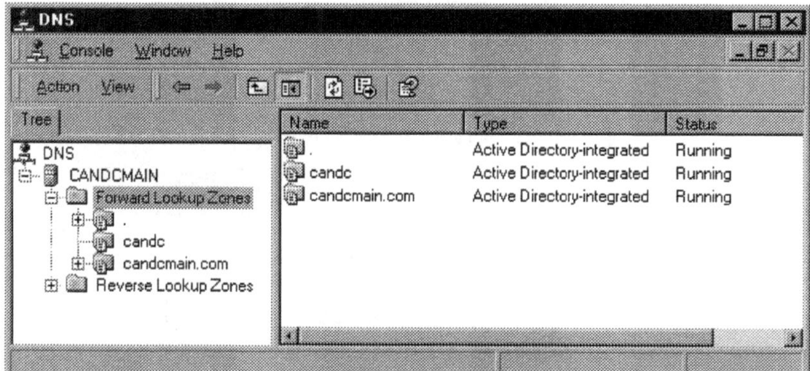

You can see that three Active Directory-integrated zones were created.

Lab Exercise 5.02

Start DNS as described for Lab Exercise 5.01.

Go to the Properties dialog for the first forward lookup zone. Click the Aging button to see the Zone Aging/Scavenging Properties dialog (Figure 5-2).

Set the properties as shown in Figure 5-2. Be extra careful to select the check box for Scavenge Stale Resource Records. Click OK to accept the changes.

Repeat the process for each Active Directory-integrated zone in Forward Lookup Zones.

You need to switch on DDNS for the reverse lookups as well. Go to the Properties dialog for the first zone in Reverse Lookups Zone (Figure 5-3).

Be sure that the drop-down box for Allow Dynamic Updates reads "yes." Again, click the Aging button and edit the dialog to match Figure 5-2. Click OK until you return to the DNS console.

FIGURE 5-2

Setting the aging properties of a zone

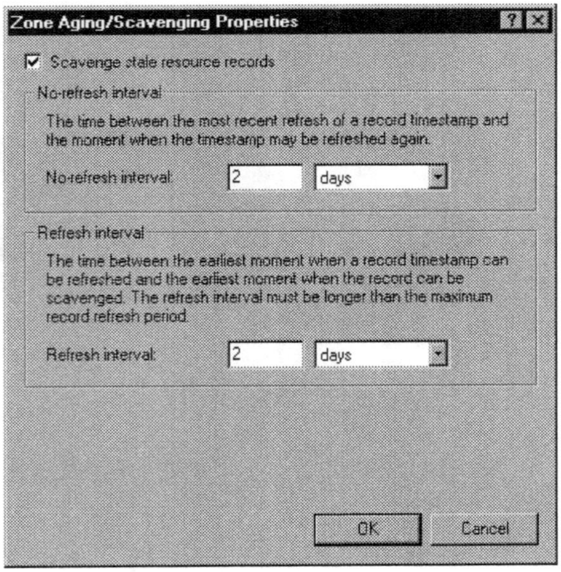

FIGURE 5-3

Viewing the general properties of a reverse lookup zone

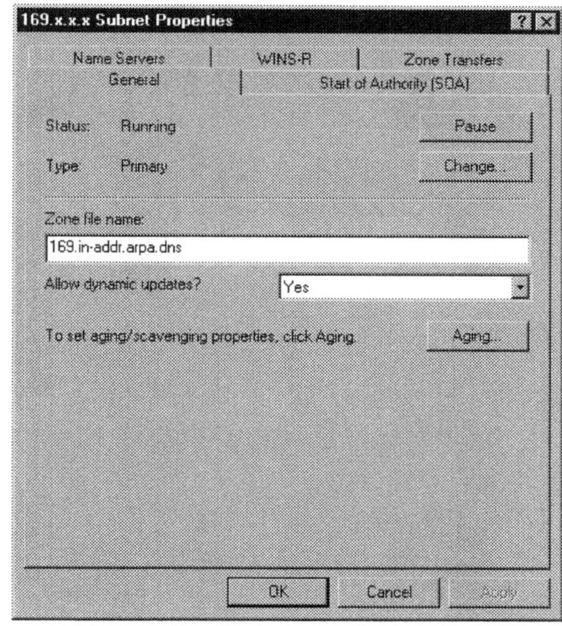

Lab Exercise 5.03

Start DNS. Expand to see the CandC.com zone. Right-click that zone, and select New Host. Configure the screen as shown here:

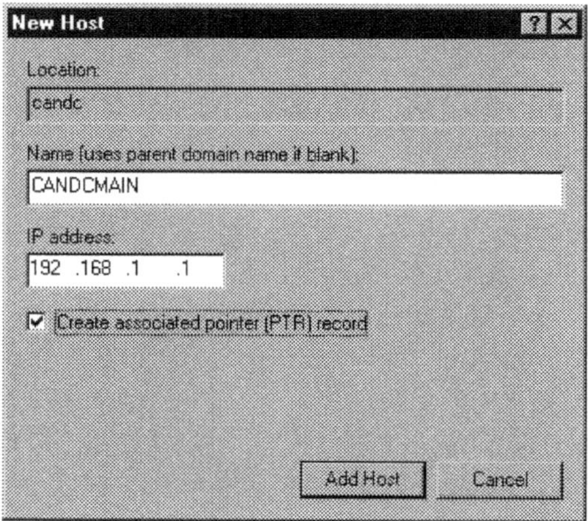

Click Add Host.

Add the remaining servers using these IP addresses:

Machine	IP Address
Main	192.168.1.1
South	192.168.1.128
North	192.168.1.192
Hill	192.168.1.224
Library	192.168.1.240

When you are done, the DNS screen should look like this:

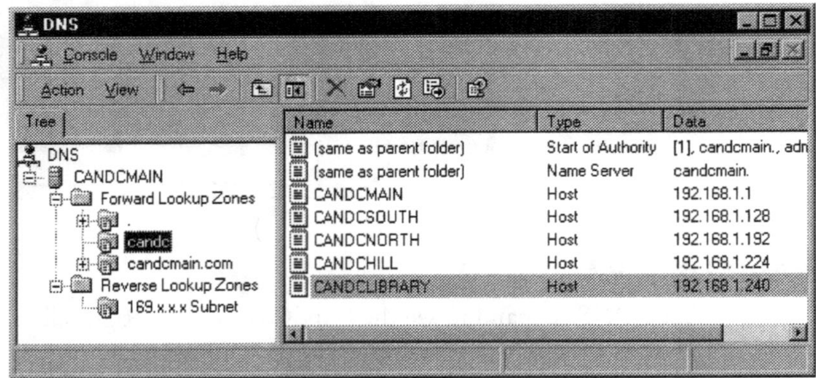

Lab Exercise 5.04

Select Start | Programs | Administrative Tools | Performance.

Right-click the right pane to see the menu shown in Figure 5-4.

Select Add Counters, and configure the Add Counters dialog as shown in Figure 5-5.

Click Add, and then Close to return to the performance console. Wait for about 2 minutes to allow the console to get a good picture of the network. Your screen will look something like Figure 5-6.

FIGURE 5-4

Preparing to add counters to the performance console

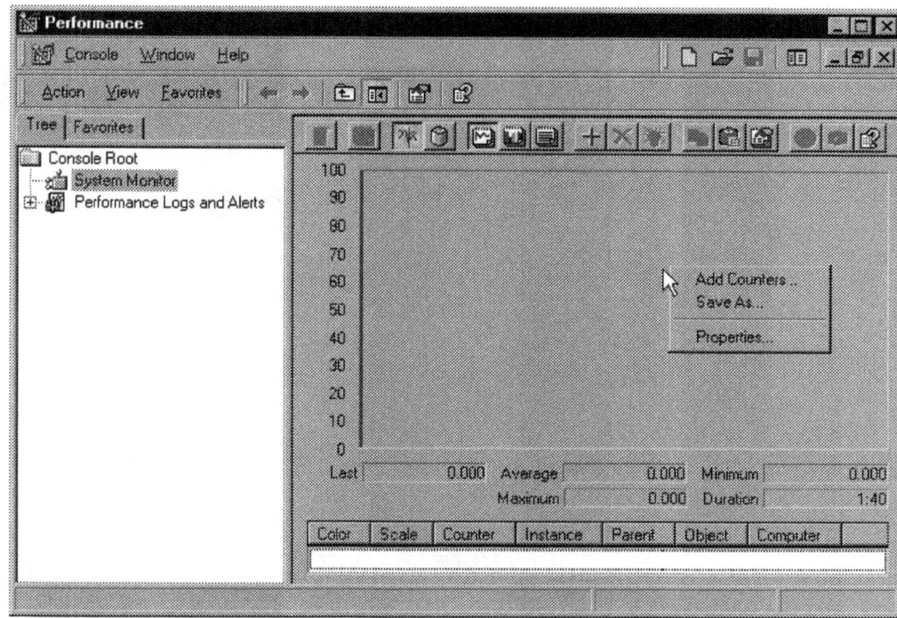

FIGURE 5-5

Choosing the counters to add

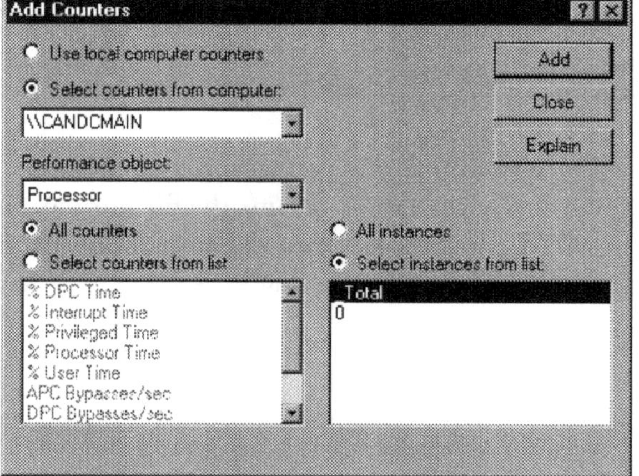

FIGURE 5-6 Viewing the typical performance console display

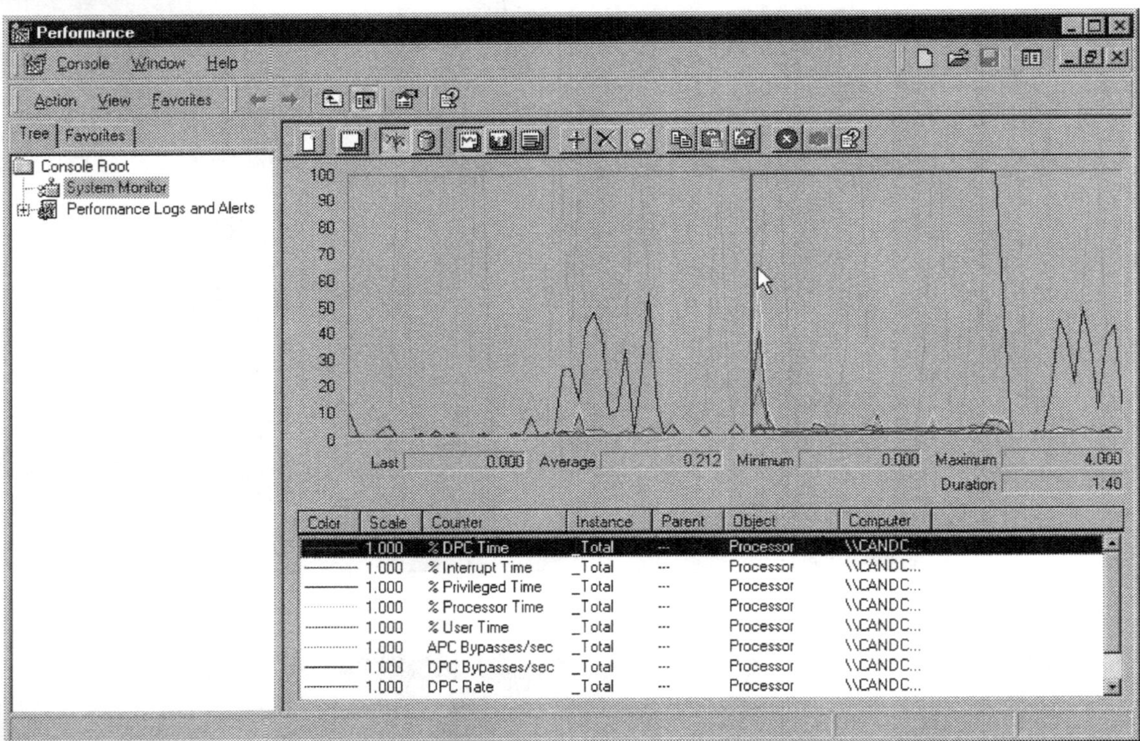

Once you think that you have a good picture of the network, right-click the graph and select Save As. Name the file **normal**, and make sure you are saving it as an HTML document. Open the normal.htm file in Internet Explorer or in Netscape to see the captured image (Figure 5-7).

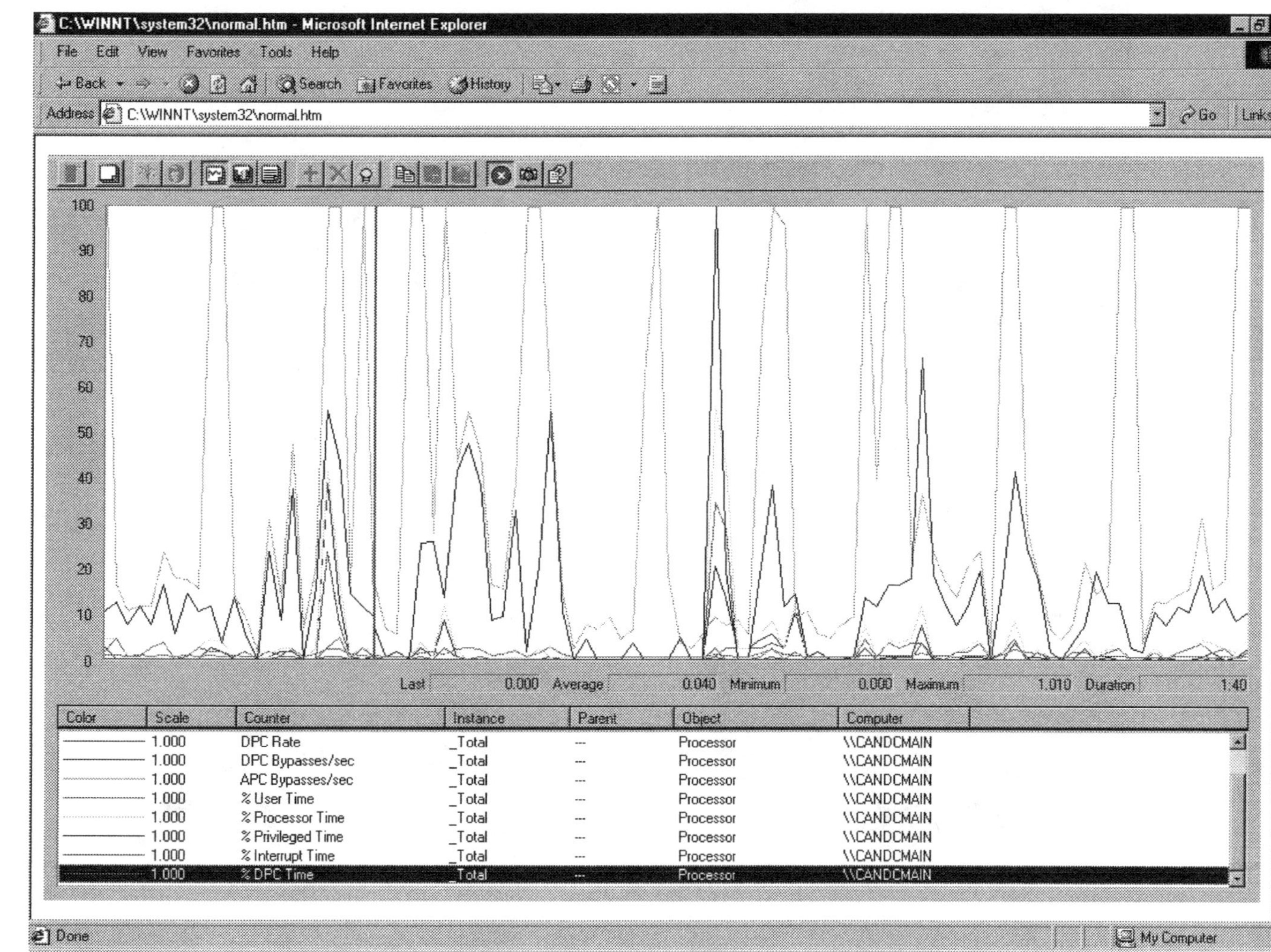

Figure 5-7 Viewing a saved performance console display in a browser

Lab Exercise 5.05

Connect to the Internet. Choose Start | Run, and start NSLOOKUP. A system window opens to show a command-line prompt:

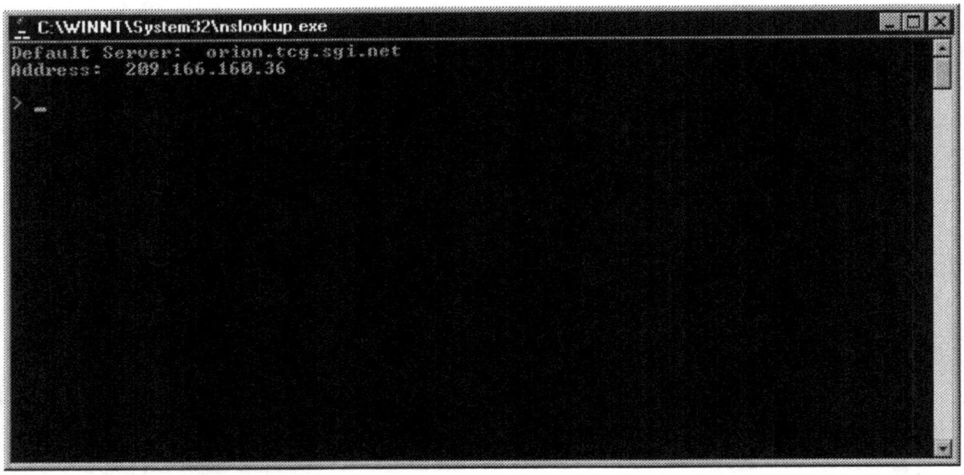

```
C:\WINNT\System32\nslookup.exe
Default Server:  orion.tcg.sgi.net
Address:  209.166.160.36

> _
```

At the prompt (>), enter an IP address. The response will be the DNS name. For example:

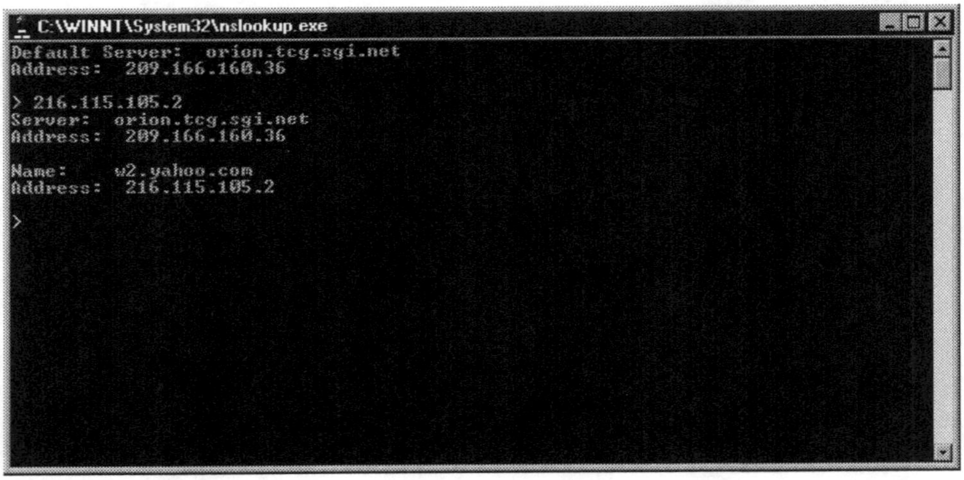

```
C:\WINNT\System32\nslookup.exe
Default Server:  orion.tcg.sgi.net
Address:  209.166.160.36

> 216.115.105.2
Server:  orion.tcg.sgi.net
Address:  209.166.160.36

Name:    w2.yahoo.com
Address:  216.115.105.2

>
```

The "Server" line represents the DNS server being queried. It is determined either by the host's TCP/IP settings for the preferred DNS server, or (as in this case) by the DNS server of the ISP. The name represents the name of the machine at the IP address. Try these IP numbers: **206.79.171.55**, **207.46.197.102**, **18.7.14.127**.

To obtain an IP address from a name, enter a URL. For example:

```
C:\WINNT\System32\nslookup.exe
Default Server:  orion.tcg.sgi.net
Address:  209.166.160.36

> www.pitt.edu
Server:  orion.tcg.sgi.net
Address:  209.166.160.36

Non-authoritative answer:
Name:    www.pitt.edu
Addresses:  136.142.42.14, 136.142.185.79, 136.142.185.69

> _
```

Press CTRL-C to exit NSLOOKUP.

ANSWERS TO LAB ANALYSIS TEST

1. Watching seemingly innocuous tasks—such as moving the mouse in a circle—can demonstrate very clearly that a server should be used as a workstation as little as possible. As user CPU time increases, the CPU time for networked applications drops considerably. The result is a certain amount of network congestion.

2. Two additional benefits can be derived from having baselines. The first is to protect your job status. Quite often, managers will make noise about the network "being slow." You, as the administrator, will be called on the carpet to explain why. If you have benchmarks for "normal" and the current performance console display is similar to those benchmarks, then the network is not slow and the problem is the manager's machine. A second benefit will arise if the network is truly slow. You then have justification that the money you request for network upgrades will be well spent to solve the "speed problem."

3. A shorter aging property on a DNS zone in a small-to-medium-sized organization typically has little impact on the quality of a DNS server. As the organization grows or becomes more mobile, a shorter aging property can accidentally remove needed DNS links from the table. For example, a server with a statically assigned IP address goes down for 3 days. With a 2-day aging cycle, that server is out of the DNS table and is hard to reach even after it comes back up.

4. The problem is that Windows 2000 DNS Console can control only other Windows 2000 DNS systems. BIND and other non-Microsoft solutions must use their own or third-party software to manage the DNS.

5. Several problems are possible. One is that the local machine is not properly connected to the network. A second might be a TCP/IP difficulty. Finally, NSLOOKUP cannot generate a name for a zone that does not have reverse lookup enabled.

ANSWERS TO KEY TERM QUIZ

1. BIND

2. scavenging, aging

3. IPCONFIG

4. TTL

5. NSLOOKUP

6

Implementing and Troubleshooting Group Policy

LAB EXERCISES

- 6.01 Creating a Group Policy
- 6.02 Applying Rules to Policies
- 6.03 Linking Policies to a Domain
- 6.04 Delegating Policy Authority
- 6.05 Exploring Policy Inheritance
- 6.06 Creating a Filter for Library Users
- 6.07 Importing an Administrative Template
- 6.08 Creating a User Script
- Lab Analysis Test
- Key Term Quiz
- Lab Wrap-Up
- Lab Solutions

One Monday morning as you are getting some coffee, Joanne confronts you with a problem. One of the Library computers was compromised over the weekend. An enterprising user set up an adult picture as the desktop wallpaper. Library staff were able to handle the fix, but they expressed concern about desktop control. Joanne would like to stop users from modifying local settings without having to resort to modifying the existing "acceptable use" policy.

You shake your head about the image and assure Joanne that the desktop can be controlled, within reason. You explain the concept of "group policy," and its effects on local computers. You further explain that no network security policy is completely secure; a very determined individual can bypass the security controls in Windows 2000. Despite the possible risk, Joanne seems excited and asks you to implement a group policy.

lab hint

Having a second computer on which to practice policies is helpful, but not required. By logging into a networked computer, you can see the effects of your changes while you remain logged on as administrator on the server.

The exercises that follow work only with Windows 2000 clients.

LAB EXERCISE 6.01

10 Minutes

Creating a Group Policy

Joanne asked you to create a group policy (GPO). First, you need to build the rules specific to a GPO. The policy itself you will apply in a later lab.

Learning Objectives

In this lab, you build a blank GPO. At the end of the lab, you'll be able to:

- Create a new policy
- Save the new policy

Lab Materials and Setup

To build a group policy you need these materials:

- Administrative access to the server
- Active Directory installed

Getting Down to Business

To build a GPO for C&C, you begin by creating a blank group policy.

Step 1. Start MMC, and add the Group Policy Snap-in.

Step 2. Select the Browse button.

Step 3. Right-click Browse for Group Policy, and select New Policy.

Step 4. Give the policy the name **Users**.

Step 5. Finish the add process, and return to MMC.

LAB EXERCISE 6.02

Applying Rules to Policies

20 Minutes

The Users policy is completely blank. You need to apply some rules to the policy. The rules will enforce a standard desktop "look and feel." In particular, you will set up a wallpaper for all computers in C&C's network.

Learning Objectives

In this lab, you prepare to force a standard desktop "look and feel" on the users. At the end of the lab, you will be able to:

- Browse policies
- Set policies

Lab Materials and Setup

To create rules in a GPO, you need to be logged in as administrator.

Getting Down to Business

To fix the desktop wallpaper problem, you need to add some rules to the blank Users policy:

Step 1. Expand the User Configuration tab to see Desktop, and then Active Desktop.

Step 2. Set the rules that will control the desktop. Disallow non-bitmapped backgrounds, pick the greenstone.bmp file for the background, and enable the Active Desktop.

Step 3. Expand the Control Panel to see Display.

Step 4. In Display, switch off the ability to change backgrounds.

Step 5. Save the policy as **Users**.

LAB EXERCISE 6.03

20 Minutes

Link Policies to a Domain

Now that the Users policy is built, you can apply it to users and to sites. But, before you continue, you need to create a test account. You will use the test account to verify the policy as you modify it.

It is usually a good idea to play with policies after hours when the business users have gone home. An accidental policy decision can affect the users' ability to work.

Learning Objectives

Policies are useless unless linked to users and sites. In this lab, you set up the necessary links. At the end of the lab, you'll be able to:

- Create a user
- Link a policy to a domain

Lab Materials and Setup

Linking policies to users and accounts is fairly simple, but you need administrative access to the server.

Getting Down to Business

You first create an account for testing the policy, and then you apply the policy to the entire domain. Here's how:

Step 1. Select Active Directory Users and Computers from the Start button.

Step 2. Create a new user called **testpolicy** in the Users folder. Provide a simple password; prevent the user from changing the password; and set the password never to expire.

Step 3. Go to the properties for the domain, and remove from the list any existing GPO objects.

Step 4. Browse and add the Users policy created in Lab Exercise 6.02.

Step 5. Apply the change.

Step 6. Log on as testpolicy, and verify that the policies have been correctly implemented. You may need to log on twice.

LAB EXERCISE 6.04

20 Minutes

Delegating Policy Authority

Joanne is happy with your policy work to date, but seems overwhelmed by the sheer number of rules that can be set within a GPO. She has enough tasks in her day and prefers to give the job to someone else.

You decide to create a user called "policy" that has rights to manage the policies for C&C. As you explain to Joanne, this approach gives a non-administrator special access to the server.

Learning Objectives

Delegating responsibility is the goal of many administrators. Simple tasks that can be given to typical users can relieve some of the administrative burden. In this lab, you set up a user to handle delegated policy duties. At the end of the lab, you'll be able to:

- Add a user to the security list of an object
- Add a user to a group
- Apply full control over an object

Lab Materials and Setup

To delegate authority, you need to be logged on as an administrator.

Getting Down to Business

To create the user called "policy" and to give that user control over the users policy for C&C, here are the steps you follow:

Step 1. Start Active Directory Users and Computers.

Step 2. Under the Users folder, create a user called **policy**. Apply a password different from that for the administrator account. Set the password never to expire.

Step 3. Add the User "policy" to the Group Policy Creator Owners group.

Step 4. Start MMC, and open users.msc.

Step 5. Go to the properties of the Users policy.

Step 6. Select the Security tab, and add the Group Policy Creator Owners group. In the Advanced Properties, set the group's permission to full access, and the application of the permission to "This object and all child objects."

Step 7. Exit out of all windows, saving as necessary.

LAB EXERCISE 6.05

Exploring Policy Inheritance

20 Minutes

Joanne is concerned about the scope of the Users policy. She wants to turn off several rules such as printer setups and other control panel functions. She would like the users to be able to perform the occasional control panel task, but she doesn't want to have to mess with the Users policy. Instead, she wants a series of policies that together build one large policy.

You understand Joanne's need. You explain to her how GPOs inherit settings from higher to lower position in a hierarchy. For example, Users currently sets the wallpaper for all computers. You suggest that a ControlPanel policy could be built to switch off all access to the Control Panel. You explain that, by having two policies, Joanne (or her delegate) can switch off the ControlPanel policy as needed, and switch it back on when machine configuration is complete.

Learning Objectives

In this lab, you see inheritance in action. Inheritance is an important concept in the application of Windows 2000 Active Directory. At the end of the lab, you'll be able to:

- Set up multiple policies
- Assign policy priorities
- Arrange for settings to be inherited from higher priority policies

Lab Materials and Setup

To set up a new policy, you need to be logged on as administrator.

Getting Down to Business

The new policy that you create in this lab will switch off access to the entire control panel.

Step 1. Start MMC, and add the Group Policy Snap-in.

Step 2. Create a new policy as you did in Lab Exercise 6.01. Give the policy the name **ControlPanel**.

Step 3. Disable the Control Panel and all subpanels.

Step 4. Link the new policy to the C&C domain.

Step 5. Give the new policy the highest precedence.

Step 6. To switch the new policy off, right-click it, and select Disabled.

LAB EXERCISE 6.06

Creating a Filter for Library Users

15 Minutes

Joanne is still concerned about the Library users. The library computers are public-access machines. She is concerned that a determined person could gain access to the policies and disable all security for the local machine.

You agree that Joanne's concern is valid, and you suggest a filter. The filter will specify a Library group. The Library group can then be assigned specific security settings that allow users in that group only to read and apply settings. In other words, users of Library computers will have C&C's policies applied to their accounts, but they will not be able to hack into the system and change system policies.

You again warn Joanne that this defense is not 100% effective, but it will ward off most attempts.

Learning Objectives

Applying a filter involves creating a list of users to be filtered, and applying that list to the GPO. In this lab, you'll practice that procedure. At the end of the lab, you will be able to:

- Create a security group
- Create a computer object
- Add members to the security group
- Apply limitations to the security group

Lab Materials and Setup

Creating users and groups requires an account with administrator privileges.

Getting Down to Business

You need to create a security group and to add users to it. Once the group is built, you will set the group permissions to ensure that no group member may change C&C's policies. Here's how:

Step 1. Start Active Directory Users and Computers.

Step 2. Select the Computers tab.

Step 3. Create two computers called **Lib1** and **Lib2**.

Step 4. Create a security group called **LibraryGroup**.

Step 5. Make Lib1 and Lib2 members of LibraryGroup.

Step 6. Call up the properties for the Users policy.

Step 7. Add LibraryGroup to the security list.

Step 8. Set the permissions for LibraryGroup to "read" and to "apply."

LAB EXERCISE 6.07

5 Minutes

Importing an Administrative Template

Joanne has a problem with Internet usage at C&C. By default, Windows Media Player accesses the Web to download the CODEC when a user plays a CD. The CODEC itself is small, but having many users downloading the CODEC wastes bandwidth that could be used for more important tasks. She wants to know if policies can put a stop to the problem.

You know that wmp.adm is present on the Windows 2000 server. That template allows the administrator to control how Media Player works. One of the settings controls the automatic downloading of the CODEC.

Learning Objectives

In this lab, you'll see how to use an administrative template to solve Joanne's problem. At the end of the lab, you'll be able to:

- Import an existing administrative template
- Modify the wmp.adm settings in the policy editor

Lab Materials and Setup

To import a template, you need administrative access to the server.

Getting Down to Business

Your plan to import the wmp.adm template into the group policy and to set a policy requires you to complete these steps:

Step 1. Start MMC, and open the users.msc file.

Step 2. Find the administrative templates under Users. Add the wmp.adm template.

Step 3. Expand the new tab in the Policy dialog to see "Prevent automatic CODEC download." Enable that policy.

Step 4. Save your changes.

LAB EXERCISE 6.08

15 Minutes

Creating a User Script

You corner Joanne in a hallway to discuss one additional problem with the wallpaper policy that is now in place. Users can still modify the wallpaper file locally. Thus, even though the policy forces the use of the greenstone.bmp file as the background, a local user can still save a different image under that name on the local computer.

You suggest copying the file greenstone.bmp to the local computer every time someone logs on. A user can change the image for the duration of a session, but at the next logon, the original image returns.

Learning Objectives

In this lab, you create a logon script—a task similar to creating an old-style DOS batch file. All that you need to do is to list commands in the order you need them to be executed. In this case, you'll be asking for a copy command to be executed at each logon. At the end of the lab, you'll be able to write a logon script.

Lab Materials and Setup

A script is a list of commands that runs every time someone logs onto a computer. To complete your proposed script, you need these materials:

- Administrative access to the server
- A copy of the greenstone.bmp file
- A shared netlogon folder (default Windows 2000 setup) or another shared folder

Getting Down to Business

You plan to copy the greenstone.bmp file to the netlogon share and to write a script that automatically copies the file to the remote computer.

Step 1. Copy C:\winnt\greenstone.bmp to C:\winnt\sysvol\sysvol\www.candc.com\scripts, where C: is the drive containing Windows 2000 and www.candc.com is the domain.

Step 2. Start Notepad or another text editor.

Step 3. In the editor, type a DOS command that copies the greenstone.bmp file to C:\winnt.

Step 4. Save the file as **logon.bat** in C:\winnt\sysvol\sysvol\www.candc.com\scripts.

Step 5. Start MMC, and open user.msc.

Step 6. Add the logon script as a logon script to the Users policies.

lab hint

The procedure described here can also be used to copy customized default wallpaper to remote stations.

LAB ANALYSIS TEST

The following questions will help you to apply your knowledge in a business setting.

1. What is the difference between a filter and inheritance?

2. Why is it helpful to delegate control of policies to another user?

3. Suppose that you need to control the speed of a mouse click. That option is not controlled in the policies. How can you make the control change?

4. What is the difference between "block policy inheritance" and "no override"?

5. Describe at least two uses for a logon script other than copying a file to the local system.

KEY TERM QUIZ

Use the following vocabulary terms to complete the sentences below. Not all of the terms will be used.

disabled
enabled
inherit
link
logon script
netlogon
policy
registry
remote
share
template

1. A policy that is switched off can be said to be ____________________.
2. The ____________________ folder is shared by default.
3. Before a policy can be implemented by a remote computer, the administrator must ____________________ it to the domain.
4. A domain with several policies will ____________________ rules from each policy.
5. A ____________________ is a program that runs at logon or logoff.

LAB WRAP-UP

Congratulations! You have successfully set up group policies for C&C. Group policies are one way of controlling and protecting an organization's network. You solved several security problems, including unauthorized display changes and policy changes. You reduced the company's frivolous Internet usage and wrote a script that discourages users from changing their local copies of the standard wallpaper.

The next chapter continues in the same vein. You will practice ensuring that local machines remain consistent by using the group policy to deploy software.

LAB SOLUTIONS FOR CHAPTER 6

The sections that follow walk you through the steps to solve the lab exercises. You should avoid looking at these sections unless you are stuck on a particular exercise.

Lab Exercise 6.01

Select the Run option from the Start button, and run MMC.

Add the Group Policy Snap-in (Figure 6-1) by selecting it and clicking Add.

When the wizard opens (Figure 6-2), click the Browse button to see the Browse for Group Policy window.

Right-click the white area, and select New. Give the name **Users** to the new policy. Your screen should look like this:

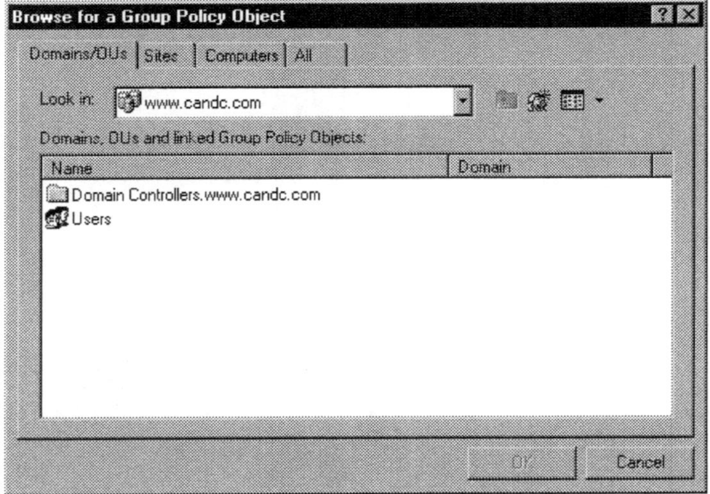

Select Users, and click OK. You are returned to the wizard (Figure 6-2), except that now, Users is the selected group policy.

Click Finish, and then Close, and then OK until you reach the Group Policy editor screen (Figure 6-3).

Save the screen contents as **users.msc**.

FIGURE 6-1

Adding the Group Policy Snap-in

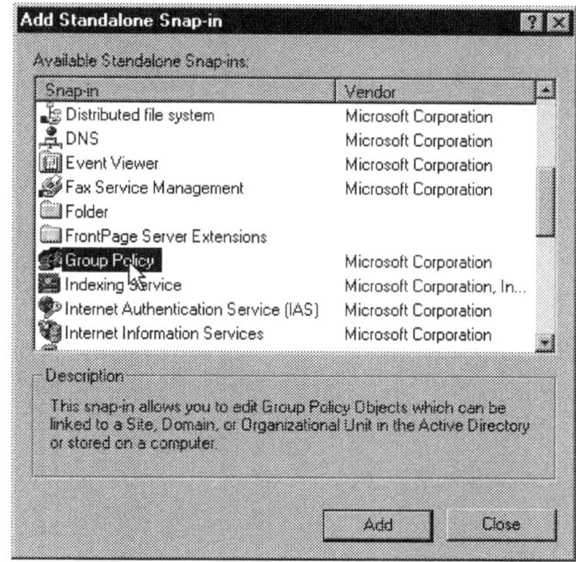

FIGURE 6-2

Preparing to create a new Group Policy Object

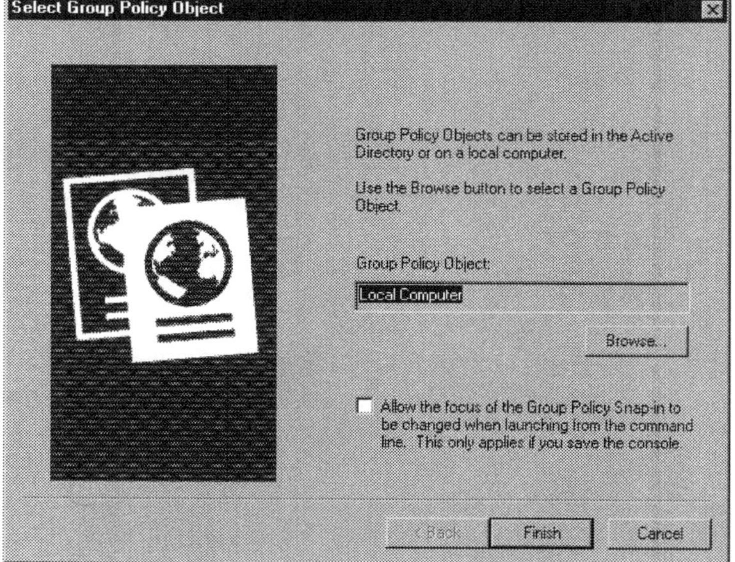

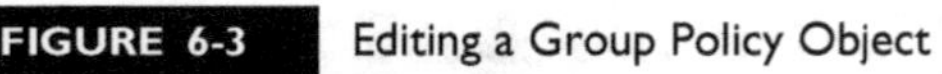

FIGURE 6-3 Editing a Group Policy Object

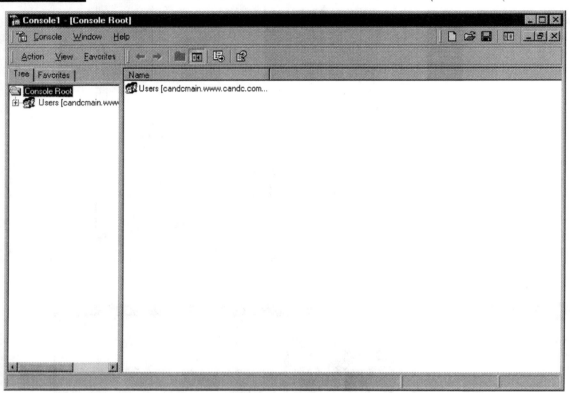

Lab Exercise 6.02

After Lab Exercise 6.01, you should still be in users.msc. If not, open the users.msc file in MMC.

Expand the folders to see the Active Desktop and its policies (Figure 6-4).

Start by enabling the Active Desktop as shown in Figure 6-5.

Next, force the wallpaper under the Active Desktop Wallpaper policy. Make the dialog look like Figure 6-6.

Enable "Allow only bitmapped wallpaper." Your screen should look like Figure 6-7.

Now, expand the Control Panel tab. Enable the rule to disable changes in the wallpaper. Save the screen as **users.msc**. Close MMC.

FIGURE 6-4

Viewing current Active Desktop policies

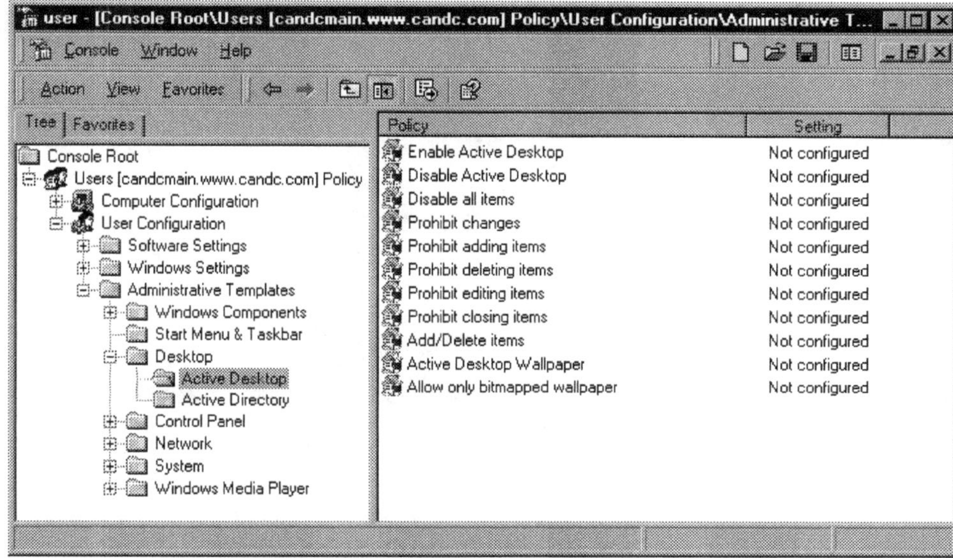

FIGURE 6-5

Enabling the Active Desktop

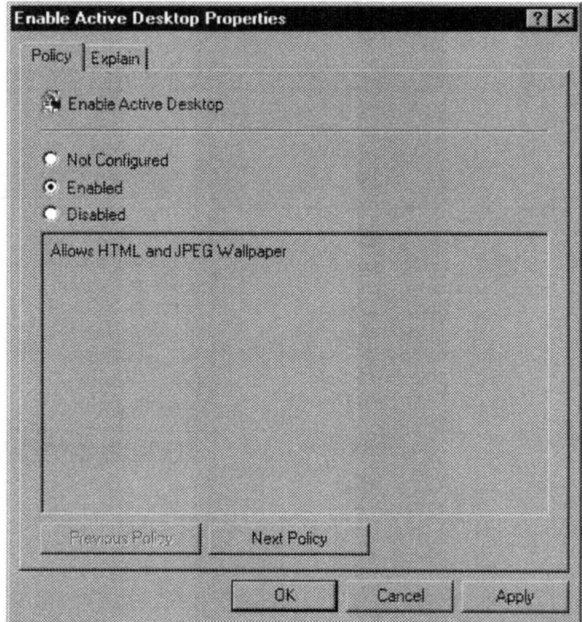

FIGURE 6-6

Setting the Wallpaper policy rules

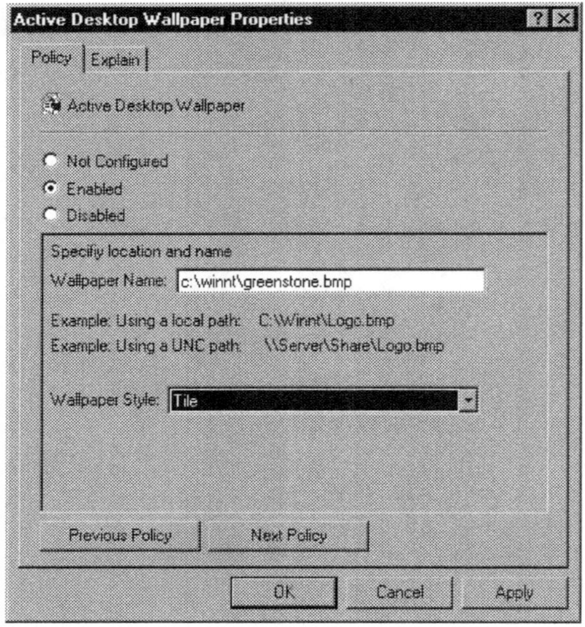

FIGURE 6-7

Enabling the "Allow only bitmapped wallpaper" rule

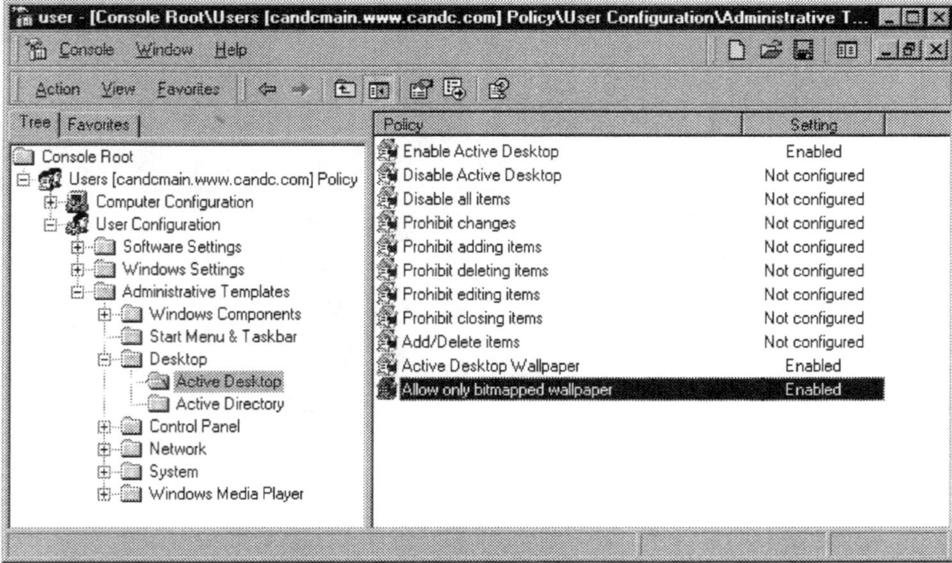

Lab Exercise 6.03

From the Start button, choose Active Directory Users and Computers.

Right-click the domain name at the top of the left pane, and select Properties.

Click the Group Policy tab (Figure 6-8). (Your version of this dialog may be slightly different.)

Remove the policies currently on the list (if any), except for the Default Domain Policy. Be sure only to remove them from the list, as shown:

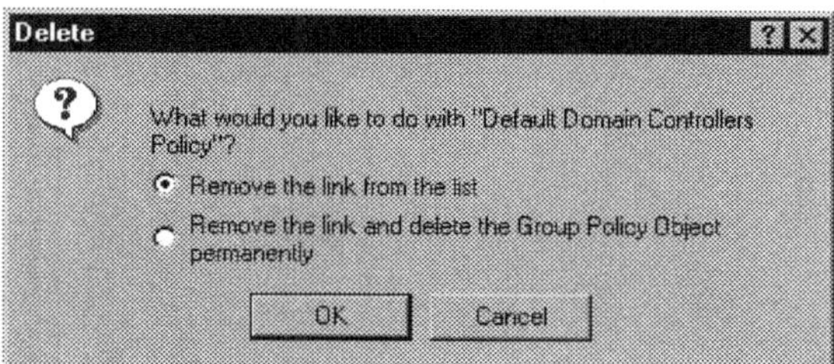

Click the Add button to begin the process of selecting the Group Policy. Click the All tab to see the list of Group Policy Objects (Figure 6-9).

FIGURE 6-8

Reviewing the Group Policy tab for the C&C domain

FIGURE 6-9

Reviewing the list of available Policy Objects

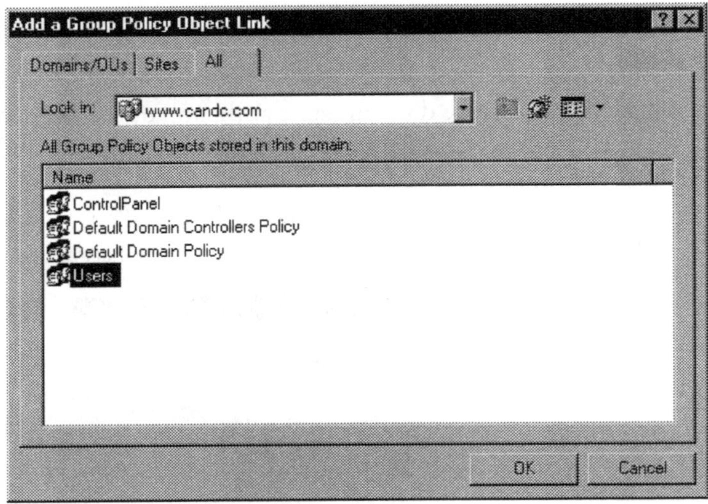

Select Users, and click OK. You are returned to the Group Policy tab for the domain (Figure 6-10).

Click Apply, and then OK.

FIGURE 6-10

Adding the Users Policy Object to the domain

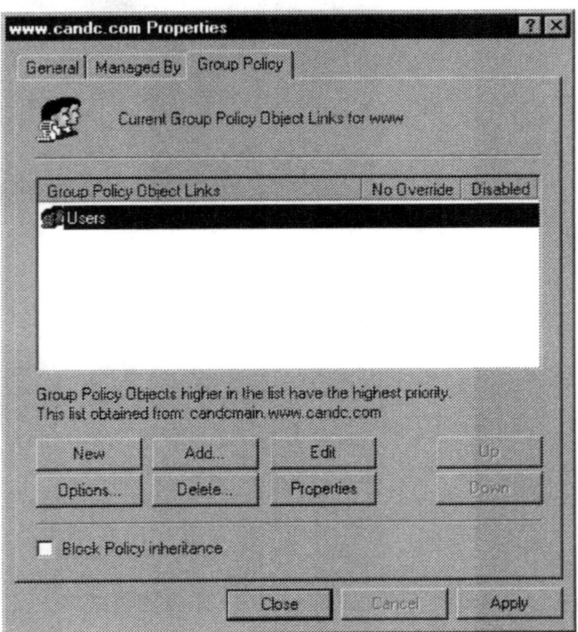

To create the user, right-click the Users tab. Select New | User. Complete the form so that it looks like this:

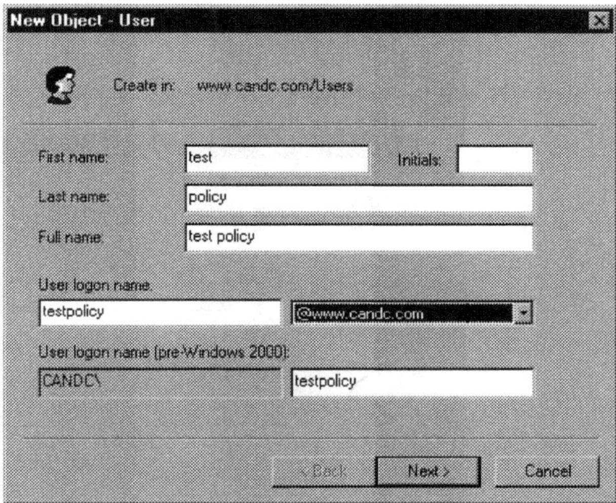

Select Next. Then set a password and options as shown here:

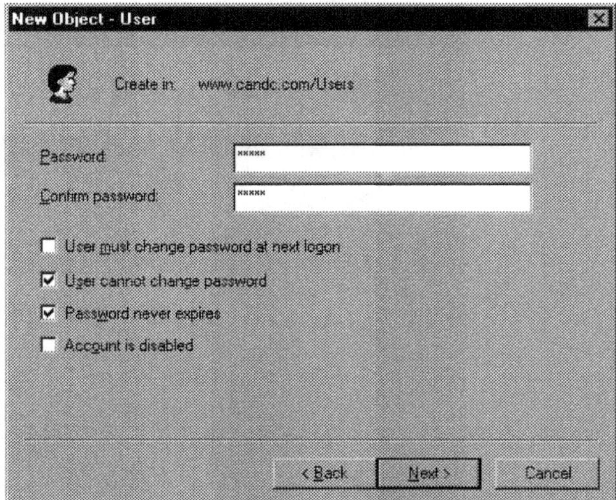

Select Next, and then Finish. The system then creates the user. You should see your test user in the folder.

Log onto a workstation under the test username to test your policies.

Lab Exercise 6.04

Start Active Directory Users and Computers from the Start button.

Expand to view the Users tab.

Right-click Users, and, remembering the procedure from Lab Exercise 6.03, create the new user with the information shown here:

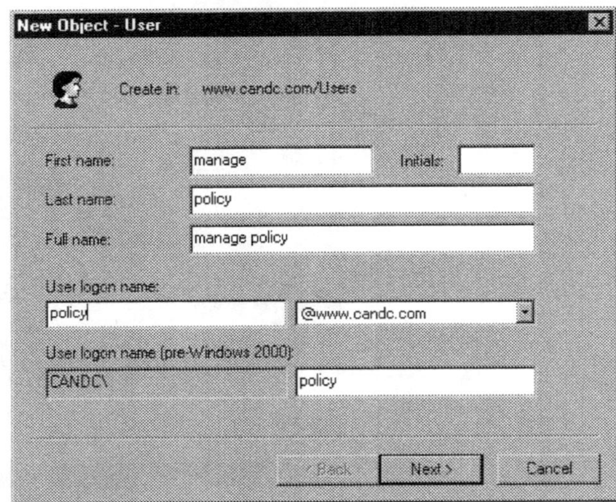

Select Next, and then set these password rules:

New Object - User
Create in: www.candc.com/Users
Password: ********
Confirm password: ********
User must change password at next logon
User cannot change password
Password never expires
Account is disabled
< Back
Next >
Cancel

Select Next, and then Finish.

You should be able to see the new user in Users list.

Find the Group Policy Creator Owners group under the Users tab and double-click it.

In the dialog that opens, click the Members tab (Figure 6-11).

Click the Add button. Add the "manage policy" user to the lower list in the dialog (Figure 6-12). Click OK.

The "manage policy" user should now be listed at the resulting screen.

Close Active Directory Users and Computers, and open MMC.

In MMC, open the file user.msc. Right-click Users, and select Properties. Click the Security tab (Figure 6-13).

Click Add, and, when the Add dialog opens, pick Group Policy Creator Owners (Figure 6-14), and click OK.

At the Security page, give full control to the Group Policy Creator Owners. Then, select the Advanced button to review the advanced security settings (Figure 6-15).

Select the Group Policy Creator Owners, and click View/Edit.

Change the "Apply onto" list box to read "This object and all child objects," as shown in Figure 6-16.

FIGURE 6-11

Reviewing the members of the Group Policy Creator Owners

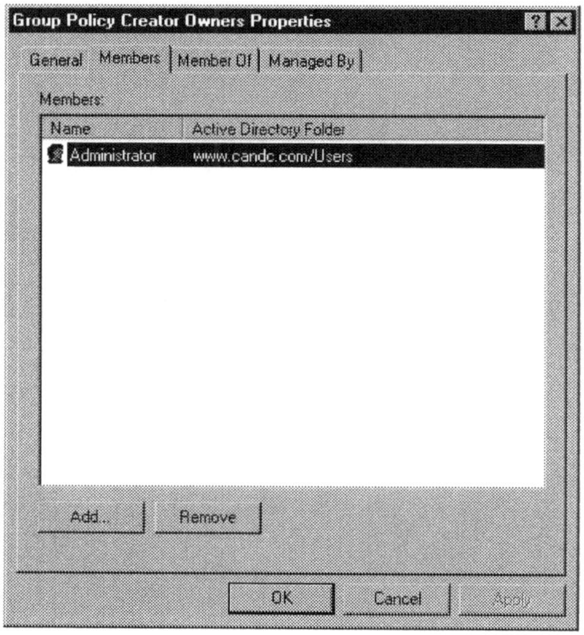

FIGURE 6-12

Adding a selected user to the Group Policy Creator Owners

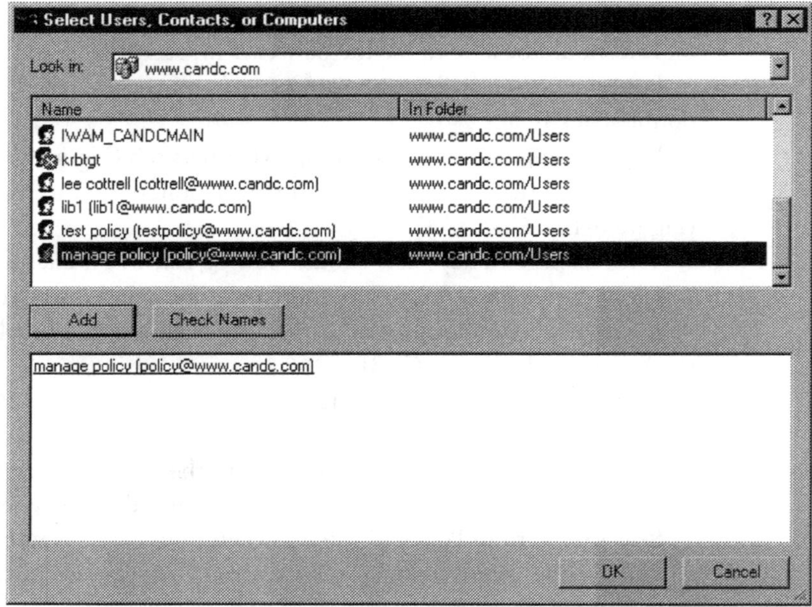

FIGURE 6-13

Choosing the Group Policy security settings

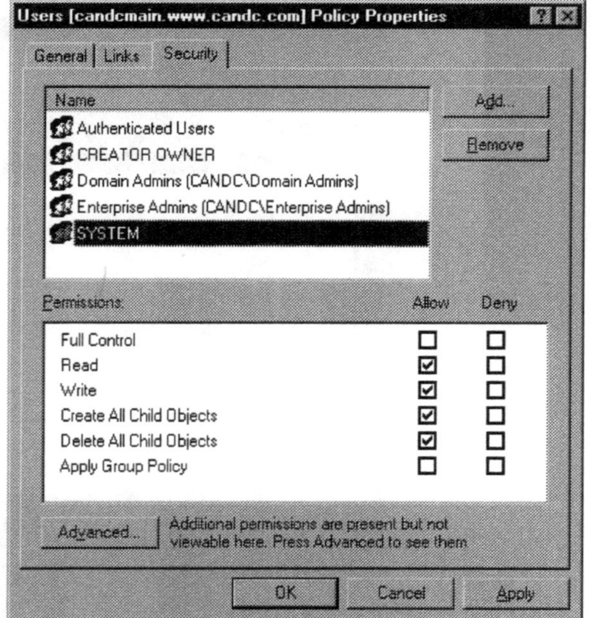

FIGURE 6-14

Choosing the group to whom to apply the policy

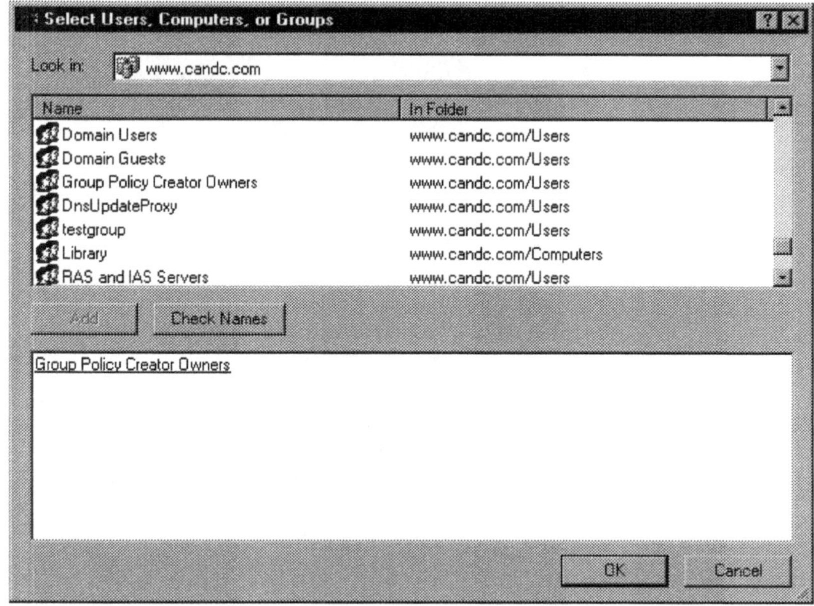

FIGURE 6-15

Working with the advanced security settings

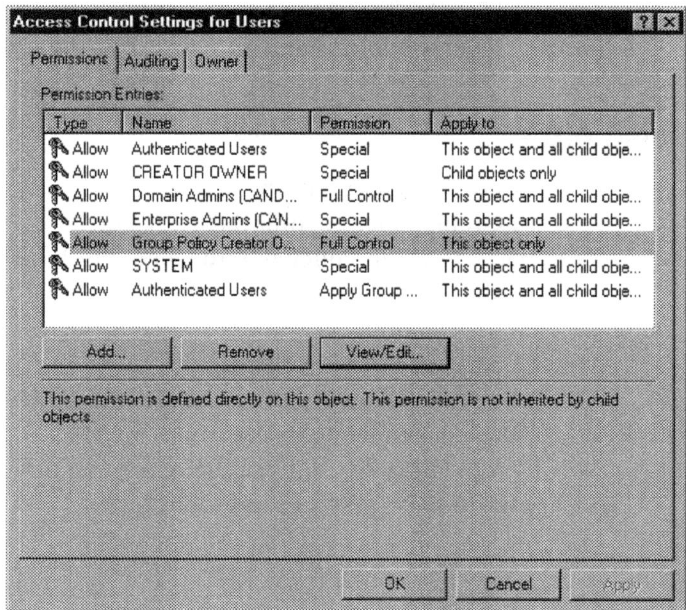

FIGURE 6-16

Setting the permissions entry for a selected user

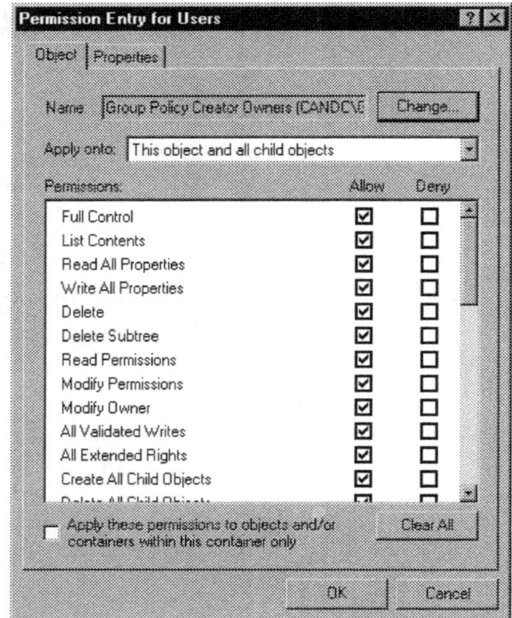

Click Apply, and then OK until you return to the Active Directory Users screen. Close the MMC window, saving the content as **user.msc**.

Lab Exercise 6.05

Select Run from the Start button, and enter MMC.

Add the Group Policy Snap-in (Figure 6-1).

At the Select Group Policy wizard (Figure 6-2), select the Browse button to open the group policy window for browsing. Right-click the white area, and select New.

Call the new policy **ControlPanel**.

Close out of all dialogs until you return to the console screen, which you should then expand as shown in Figure 6-17.

Switch on the Disable Control Panel policy. Set other rules as desired. (See Figures 6-18 through 6-20 for suggestions.)

FIGURE 6-17 Expanding the Control Panel to see the policy folder

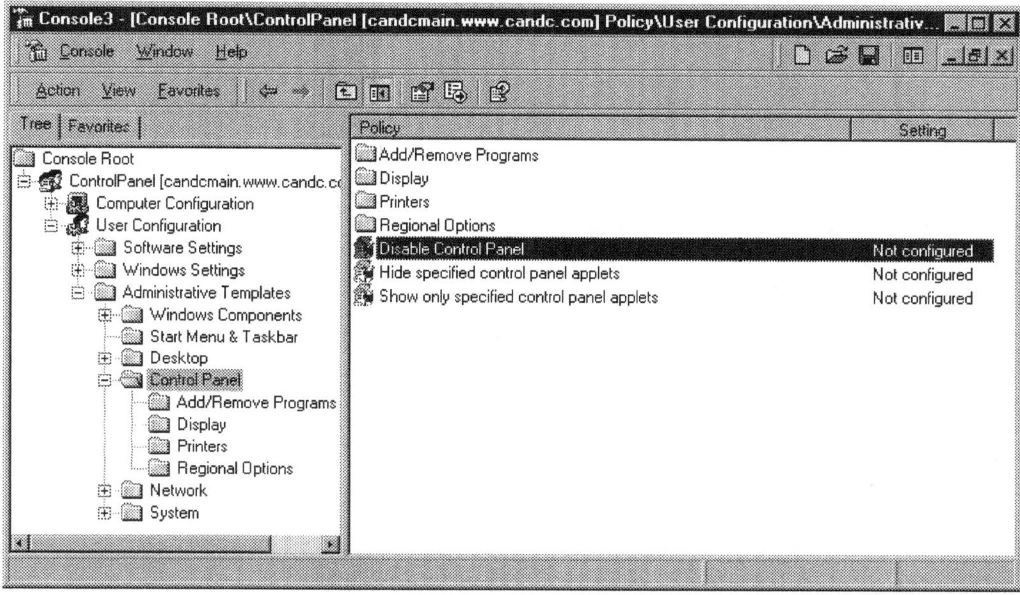

FIGURE 6-18 Choosing policies for adding and removing programs

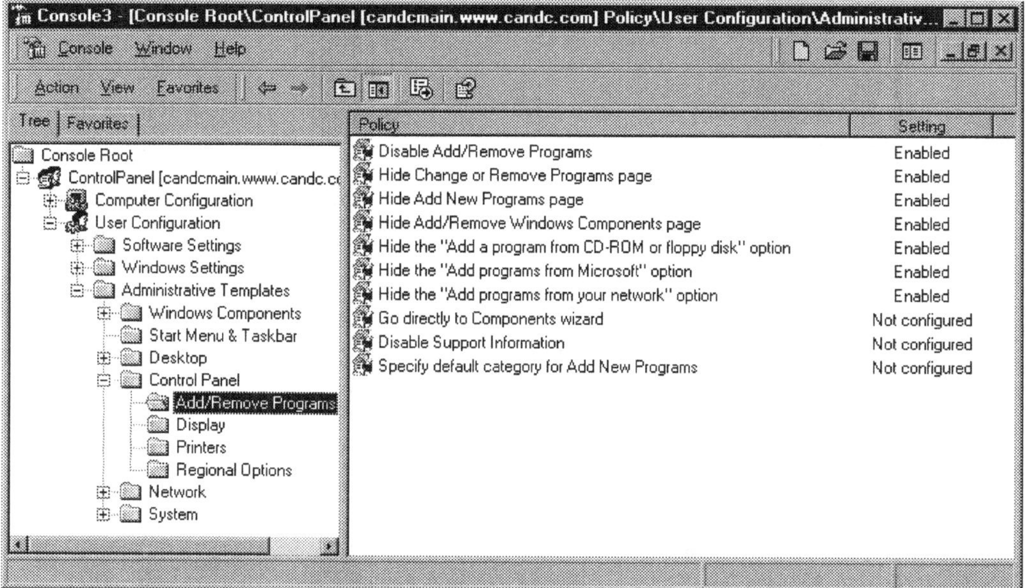

FIGURE 6-19 Choosing policies for the computer display

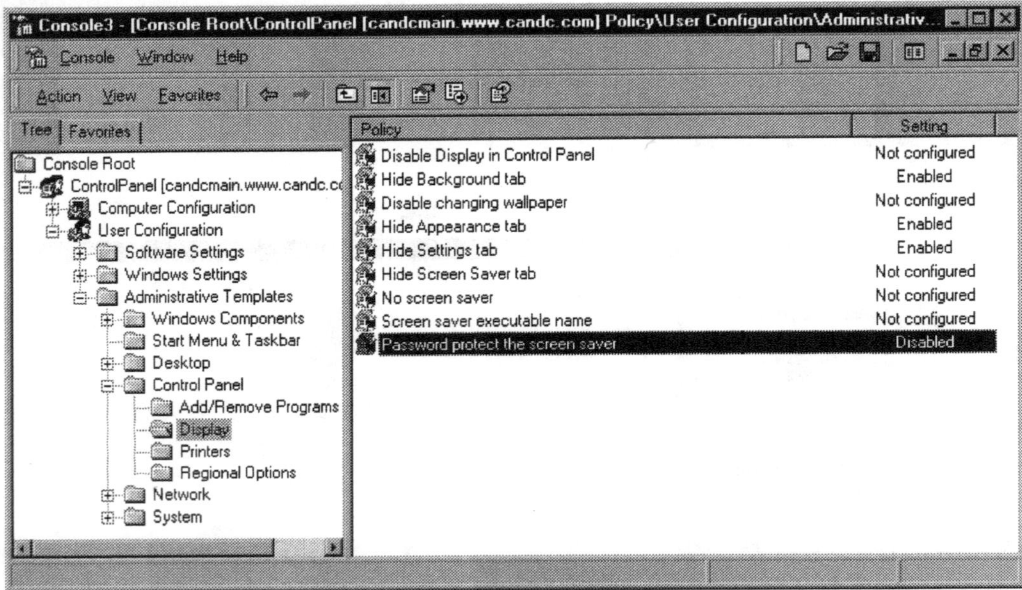

FIGURE 6-20 Choosing policies for printer use

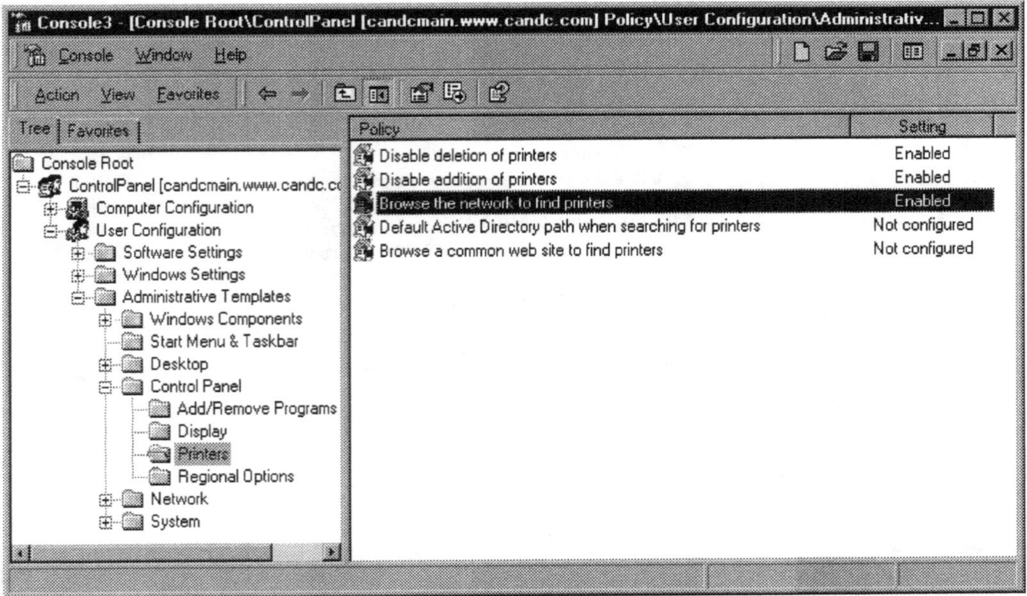

Lab Exercise 6.06

Start Active Directory Users and Computers from the Start button.

Click the computer folder. Right-click the right-hand pane, and select New | Group.

Define the **Library** group as shown here:

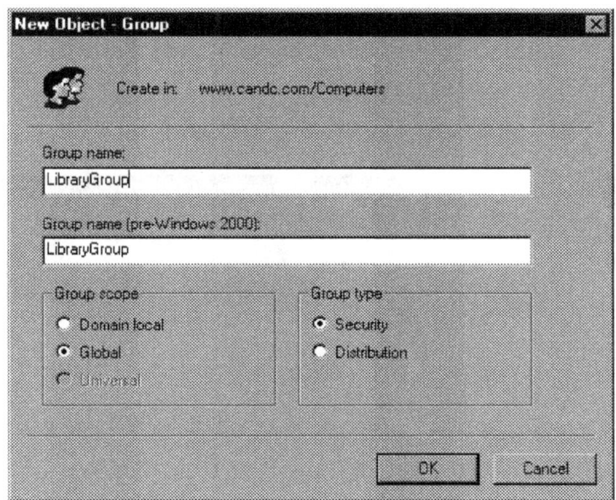

Click OK to create the Library group.

Right-click the right-hand pane again, and select New | Computer.

Define the computer **Lib1** as shown here:

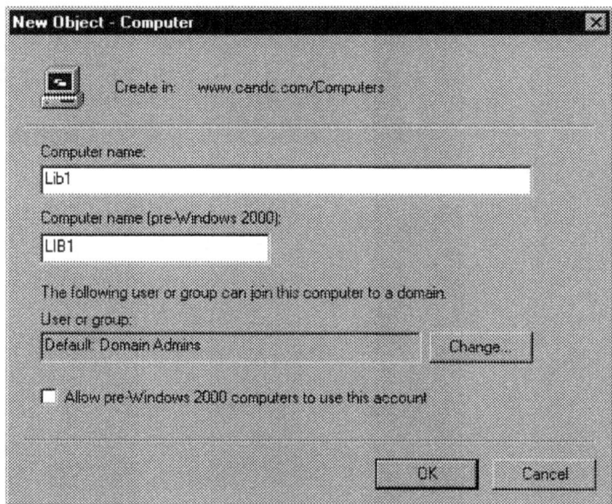

Click OK to create the Lib1 computer. Repeat the process to create **Lib2.**

Double-click the LibraryGroup icon to open the group properties dialog, and click the Members tab (Figure 6-21).

Select Add, and make Lib1 and Lib2 members of the group (Figure 6-22).

Right-click the domain name in the left pane, and select Properties. Click the Group Policy tab (Figure 6-23).

Right-click the Users icon, and select Properties. Click the Security tab (Figure 6-24).

FIGURE 6-21

Viewing the empty members list of a new policy group

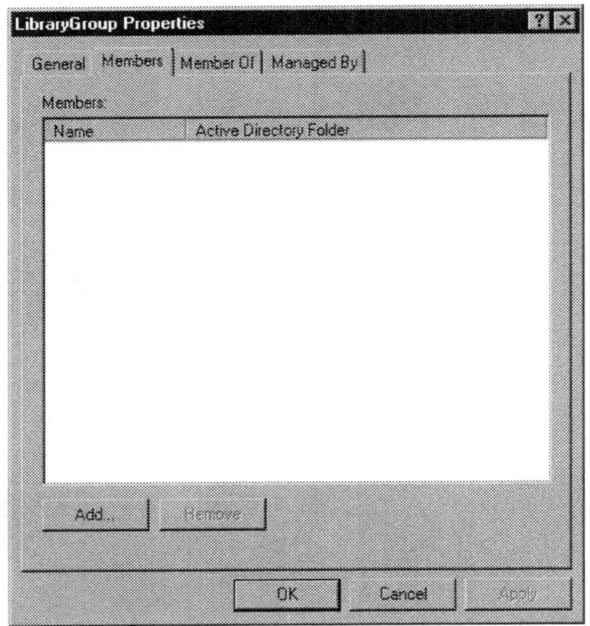

FIGURE 6-22

Adding members to a policy group

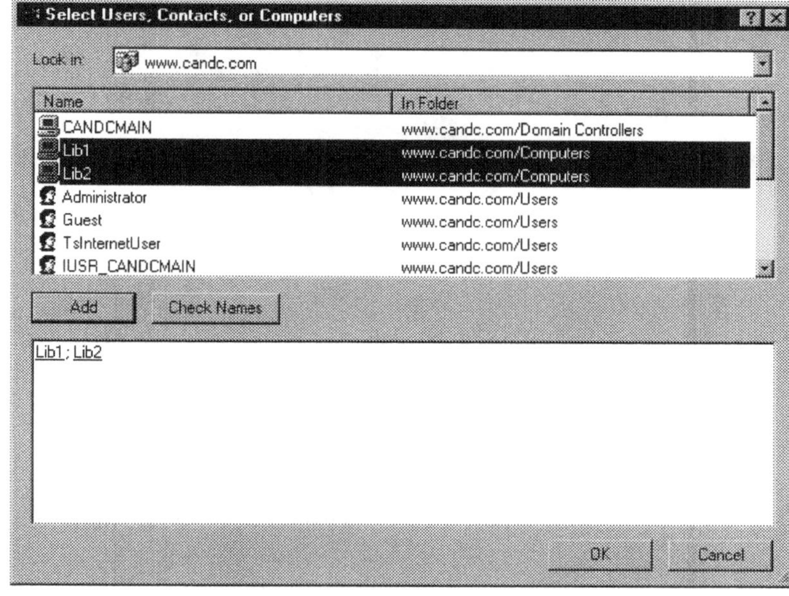

FIGURE 6-23

Viewing the group policies assigned to a policy group

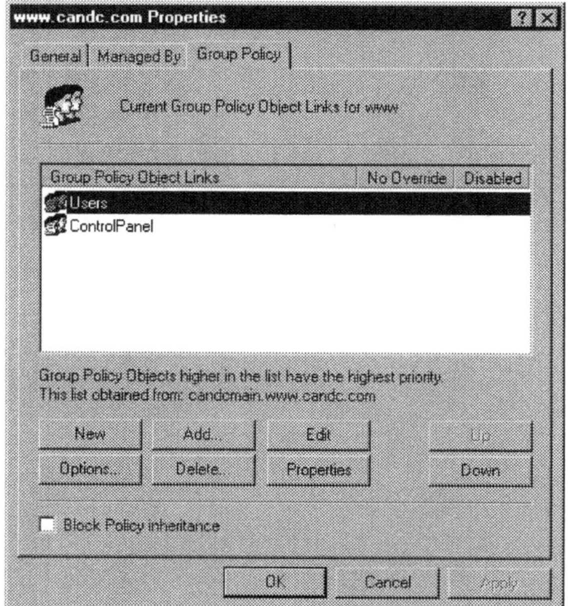

FIGURE 6-24

Viewing the security properties of the users in a policy group

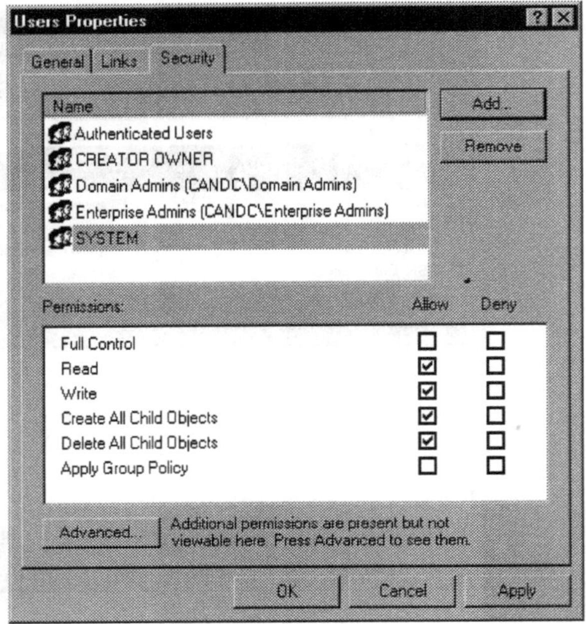

Select Add, and add the LibraryGroup as shown:

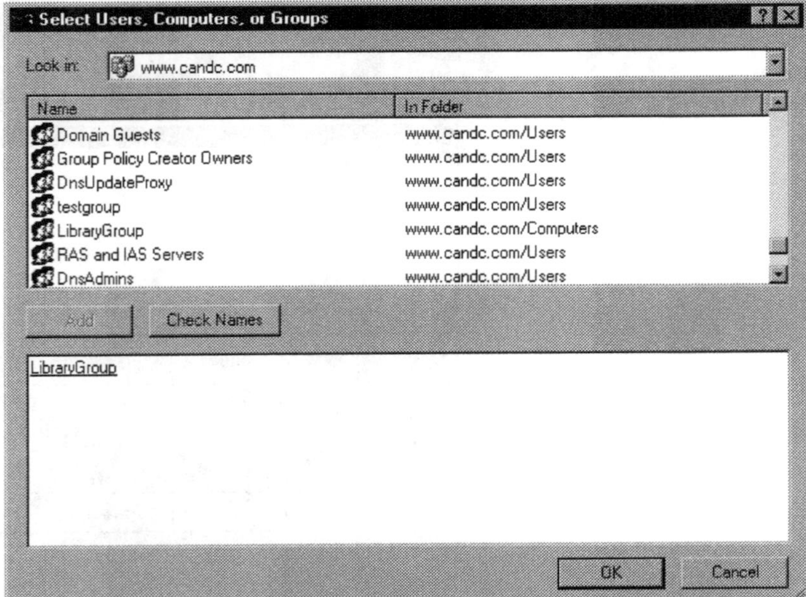

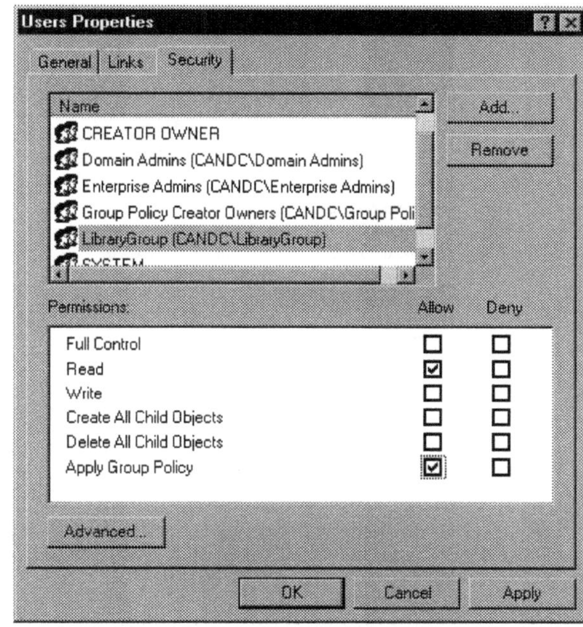

FIGURE 6-25

Giving "full control" permissions to the LibraryGroup

Give full control to the Group Policy Creator Owners as shown in Figure 6-25. Repeat the process for the Control Panel policy.

Lab Exercise 6.07

Select Run from the Start button, and enter MMC.

Open the user.msc file.

Expand the tree to see the administrative templates (Figure 6-26).

Right-click Administrative Templates, and select Add/Remove Template to open the template list, which shows any templates that are currently installed:

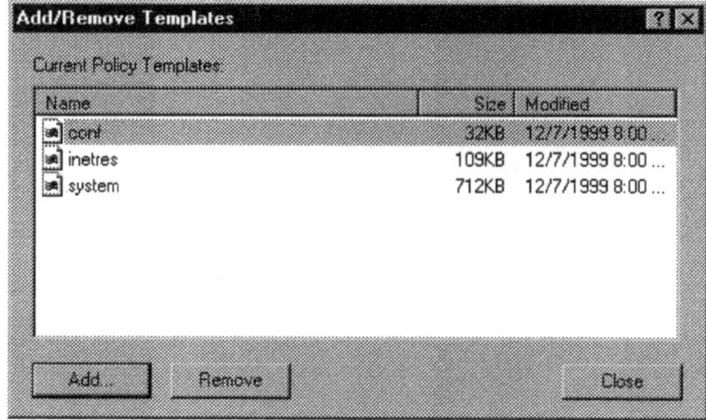

FIGURE 6-26

Expanding the view of the Administrative Templates

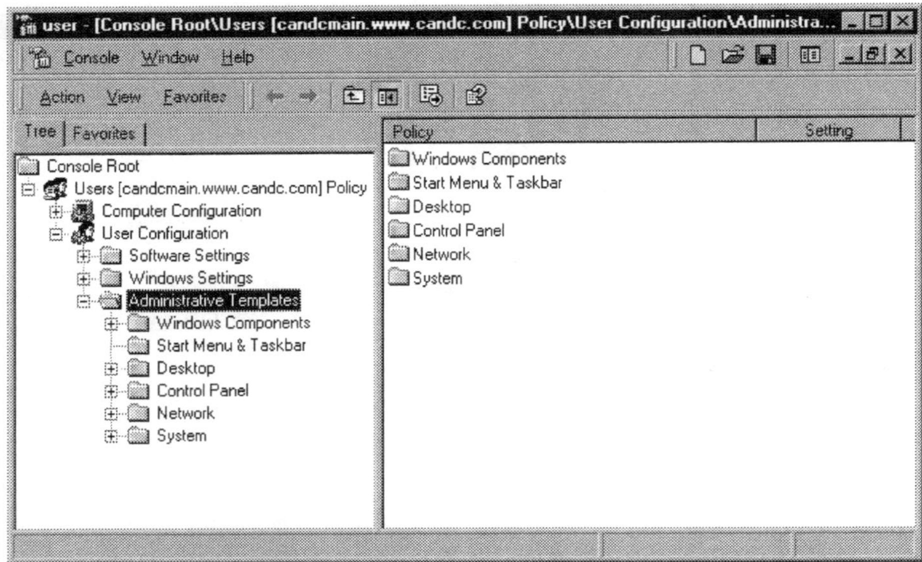

Click Add and choose wmp.adm (Figure 6-27).

Click Open, and then click Close to return to the policy screen. Windows Media Player should be added under Administrative Templates.

Set the rules for Windows Media Player as shown in Figure 6-28.

FIGURE 6-27

Choosing the Windows Media Player Policy Template

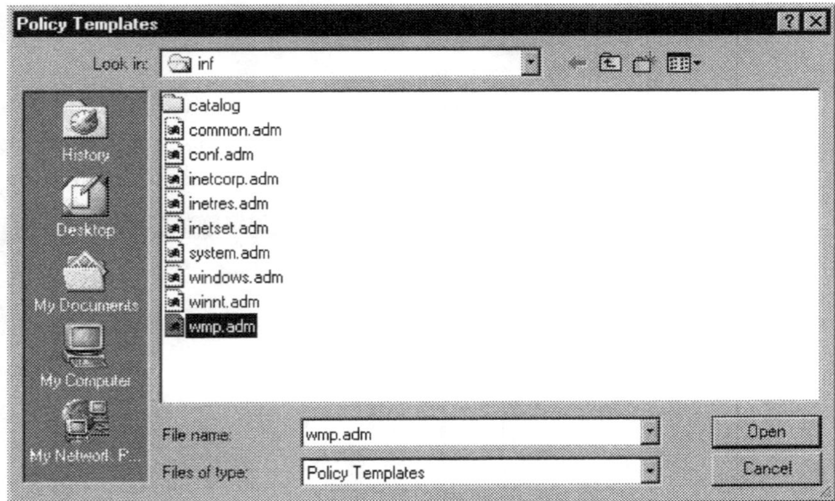

FIGURE 6-28

Setting the policies for Windows Media Player

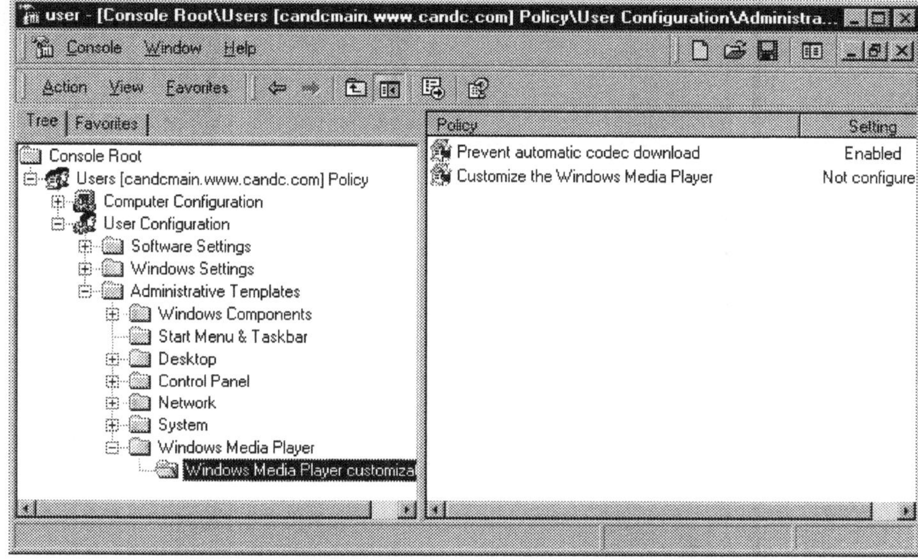

Lab Exercise 6.08

Open My Computer. Browse to C:\winnt, or to wherever your Windows folder is stored. Show the files in that folder.

Find the greenstone.bmp file and copy it.

Open the folder C:\winnt\sysvol\sysvol\www.candc.com\scripts, where C: is the drive containing Windows 2000 and www.candc.com is the domain. Paste the greenstone.bmp file into the folder.

Start Notepad or another text editor. Enter this code into Notepad *on a single line*:

```
xcopy \\candcmain\netlogon\greenstone.bmp c:\winnt\greenstone.bmp /y
```

Save this command as **logon.bat** in the C:\winnt\sysvol\sysvol\www.candc.com\scripts folder.

Start MMC, and open user.msc.

Expand the tree to see the Logon and Logoff Scripts (Figure 6-29).

In the right-hand pane, right-click the Logon icon, and select Properties. Click Add, and then again Add, and then Browse. Browse to the C:\winnt\sysvol\sysvol\www.candc.com\scripts folder and add logon.bat.

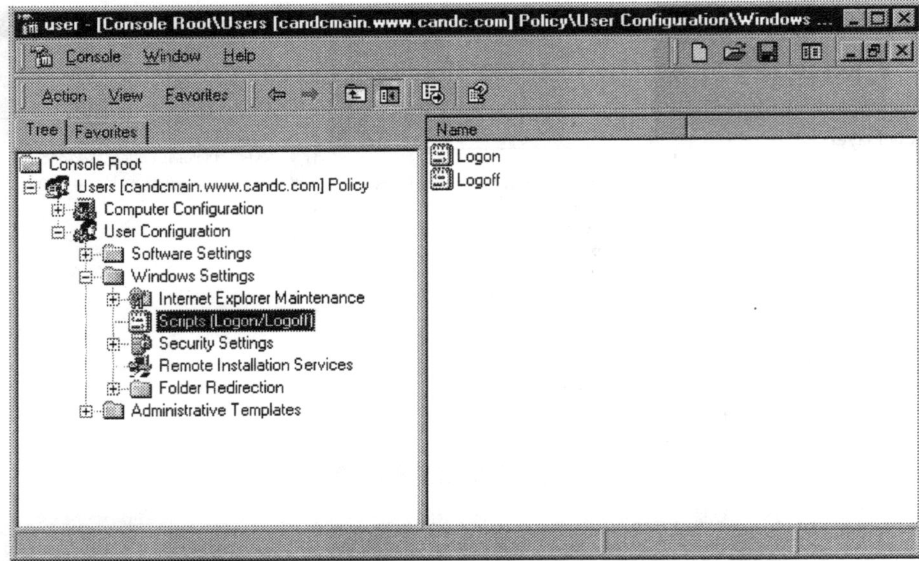

FIGURE 6-29 Viewing the Logon and Logoff Scripts

ANSWERS TO LAB ANALYSIS TEST

1. As used in the exercises in this chapter, a filter is applied to security, and inheritance is applied to multiple policies. Filters ensure that the only rights applied are the ones that you specify. Inheritance allows you to write modular policies for application to user accounts.
2. A typical network administrator has several duties throughout the day. System policies, while relatively easy to create, are complex and demanding to maintain. Delegating the job of maintaining the policies to one person does two things: it gets a demanding responsibility off the administrator's hands, and it allows the delegate to specialize in the application of group policies.
3. Anything held in the client's registry can be controlled by policies. In this instance, you first create a template that contains the policies to be implemented. Once you have created the template, you add it to the group policy and administer it as needed. Creating templates is a difficult task, well beyond the scope of this lab.
4. The Block policy option prevents lower level group policy objects from inheriting the settings of higher level group policy objects. A Block policy is set at the level of the lower policy object, where the block is to take effect. The No Override option allows an administrator to force lower level policy objects to inherit settings from a higher level object. You cannot block group policy settings from higher level objects if those settings have been defined with a No Override option. In other words, the No Override option takes precedence over the Block option.
5. Logon scripts have many uses. For consistency, administrators use the Net Use command to map a network drive. Port settings for legacy print devices can be set up in a script. Removal of unwanted files (games, for example) can be handled in a logon script. Anything that needs done to many computers—either every time the machine is used, or periodically—can be handled with a logon script.

ANSWERS TO KEY TERM QUIZ

1. disabled
2. netlogon
3. link
4. inherit
5. logon script

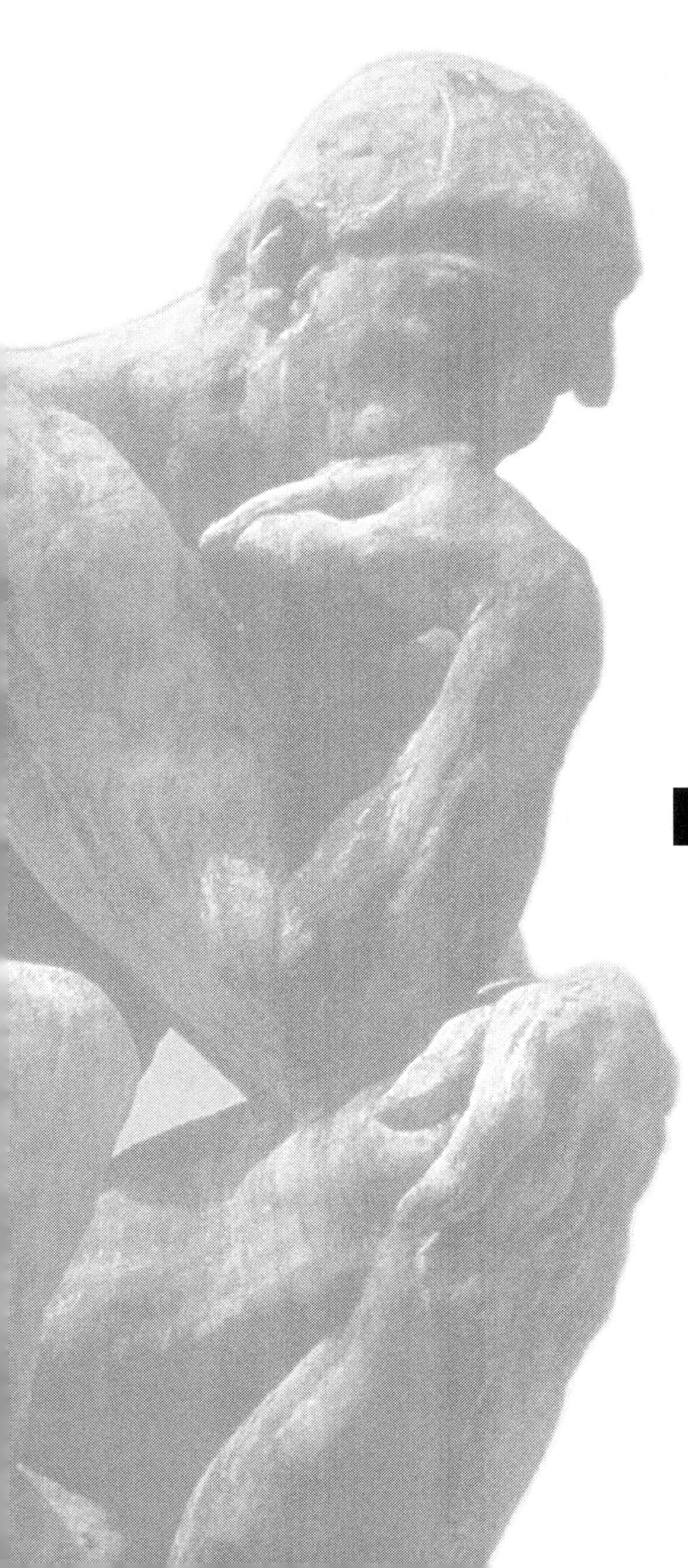

7

Managing Software and Network Configuration Using Group Policy

LAB EXERCISES

- 7.01 Installing WinINSTALL
- 7.02 Creating a Microsoft Installer Package
- 7.03 Deploying Software to a Computer
- 7.04 Applying a Filter for the Server Computers
- 7.05 Redeploying Updated Software
- 7.06 Troubleshooting a Publish Software Problem
- 7.07 Configuring Internet Explorer
- 7.08 Troubleshooting Using Event Viewer
- Lab Analysis Test
- Key Term Quiz
- Lab Wrap-Up
- Lab Solutions

Joanne is excited about the prospect of managing user settings remotely. She sees a potential for fewer user configuration problems. What she would like to do is to maintain the software for her servers and client computers. Installing service packs and patches is a tedious task in a large organization. She asks if Group Policies can be used to install and maintain software remotely.

You know that Group Policies can install and maintain software remotely. You discuss the concept of a Microsoft Installer Package (MSI) and published software. Joanne asks you to implement that solution immediately in preparation for the MS Office upgrade due in the near future.

The labs in this chapter talk about installing a payroll software program. "Payroll" could be any software that you need to install across your organization. Check out www.tucows.com for some small but useful shareware programs that you can use to practice building MSI software.

LAB EXERCISE 7.01

Installing WinINSTALL

15 Minutes

Joanne has a new payroll program that simplifies the task of entering employee hours and pay information into the computer. She would like the payroll program to be installed on every server in the organization. She asks you to create an MSI.

You know that the first item of business is to install the WinINSTALL software. WinINSTALL is included on the Windows 2000 server CD.

Learning Objectives

In this lab, you install the WinINSTALL program in a process similar to most program installations. At the end of the lab, you will be able to install a program on the server.

Lab Materials and Setup

To install a program from the Windows 2000 CD, you need these materials:

- Windows 2000 CD
- Administrator account

Getting Down to Business

You install WinINSTALL on the CANDCMAIN server using these steps:

Step 1. Insert the Windows 2000 CD into the drive. Hold down the SHIFT key to stop the CD auto run procedure.

Step 2. Explore the CD to \valueadd\3rdparty\mgmt\winstle\swiadmle.msi.

Step 3. Follow the on-screen prompts, accepting the default choices if you are unsure.

Step 4. Using the default settings, share the folder created by the install. Make sure that users can read the folder and that administrators can write to the folder.

LAB EXERCISE 7.02

Creating a Microsoft Installer Package

15 Minutes

Using the WinINSTALL program that you just installed on the server, you can take a snapshot of settings and files created or modified during an install. Next, you will install a simple payroll program and use WinINSTALL to create an MSI for it.

Learning Objectives

In this lab, you create an MSI for a simple application. At the end of the lab, you will be able to:

- Install a program on the server
- Create a snapshot of the install

Lab Materials and Setup

Installing a program and creating a snapshot of the install is the foundation of using WinINSTALL. You need these materials for the job:

- Install file for the application
- WinINSTALL installed on the server
- Administrator account

Getting Down to Business

Joanne would like the payroll program installed on all C&C servers. Here's how to proceed:

Step 1. Create a "before" picture by running discoz.exe from the Winstall folder.

Step 2. Install the payroll program, accepting all default suggestions.

Step 3. Create an "after" picture by running discoz.exe from the Winstall folder.

LAB EXERCISE 7.03

20 Minutes

Deploying Software to a Computer

Now that you have an MSI for the payroll program, you would like to automatically install it on other servers. You decide to deploy the package to computers rather than to users. That method ensures that the software is installed only once per computer. Deploying to users installs the software once for every different user on the computer.

Learning Objectives

In this lab, you deploy software to a computer—a common network task. Many administrators have found that deploying to computers is easier on network usage than is deploying to users. At the end of the lab, you will be able to set up for deploying software to a computer.

Lab Materials and Setup

Deploying software is part of the Active Directory Group Policy. You need these materials:

- Active Directory installed
- Group Policies installed
- Administrator account

Getting Down to Business

To finish solving Joanne's problem, you create a group policy (GPO) that installs the payroll program to a computer. Here's how:

Step 1. Run Microsoft Management Console (MMC), and add the Group Policy MMC.

Step 2. Create a new policy called **installpayroll**.

Step 3. Add the payroll.msi file created in Lab Exercise 7.02 to the Software Install policy of the Computer Software Settings.

Step 4. Link the GPO to the domain.

LAB EXERCISE 7.04

Applying a Filter for the Server Computers

20 Minutes

Joanne notices that the solution you've just finished creating has a slight problem. Right now, any computer that logs on receives the payroll program. She wants the payroll program limited to the servers.

From Chapter 6, you recall that the properties of a particular organizational unit (OU) can be set to read a policy.

Learning Objectives

In this lab, you apply the filtering trick and make an OU that contains only servers read the software policy. Administrators and the Group Policy Creator Owners still retain full control. At the end of the lab, you'll be able to apply and remove permissions for the payroll GPO.

Lab Materials and Setup

You will set the permissions for the server OU. You need these materials for the task:

- Active Directory installed
- Payroll GPO created
- Administrative access to the server

Getting Down to Business

To create an security group for servers and to apply permissions for the group to read the payroll GPO, use these steps:

Step 1. Start Active Directory Users and Computers.

Step 2. Create a computer for each server.

Step 3. Create a security group called Servers.

Step 4. Make each server a member of Servers.

Step 5. Go to the properties of the Payroll GPO.

Step 6. Add the server group with "read" and "apply" permissions. Switch off the Authorized Users group "read" and "apply" permissions.

LAB EXERCISE 7.05

5 Minutes

Redeploying Updated Software

lab hint ***Use the same software package as in the previous lab exercises.***

A couple of days after you deploy the payroll program, Joanne tells you that the software was updated. The servers need the new version to be installed and the old version to be removed. She wants to know if the changeover is possible. She has already built the new MSI file, using the same payroll name as before.

You tell Joanne that redeploying the changed software is very easy. Several settings in the software install policy allow the change. In particular, forcing the install and a redeploy will put the new version of the software on the servers.

Learning Objectives

In this lab, you redeploy the payroll package. Because Joanne built the package for you, and nicely left the name the same, you can reuse the original package. At the end of the lab, you will be able to redeploy software installations.

Lab Materials and Setup

To redploy the payroll package, you need these materials:

- Install file for the application
- WinINSTALL installed on the server
- Administrator account

Getting Down to Business

Redeploying involves telling Windows 2000 to reinstall the package.

Step 1. Start MMC, and open the payroll.msc file.

Step 2. Right-click the Payroll object and redeploy.

LAB EXERCISE 7.06

5 Minutes

Troubleshooting a Publish Software Problem

It's late on a Friday, and you're about to head home for a long weekend. Joanne rushes into your office obviously frustrated. She explains that she has created a perfectly valid software package. She set the properties to publish the package for users. The problem is that the users can't see the control panel to run Add/Remove Software.

You think for a moment. You believe that you know what the problem is. One of the rules installed in the Users policy disables the control panel and the Add/Remove Software option. You will have to switch these items on before the users can install the package, however, the rest of the control panel still needs to be disabled.

Learning Objectives

In this lab, you troubleshoot a problem with a GPO. At the end of the lab, you'll be able to:

- Change policies
- Fix problems with the Publish option of the GPO

Lab Materials and Setup

To modify settings in the GPO, you need these materials:

- Users policy
- Administrator account

Getting Down to Business

Fixing the problem requires you to open the Users file and change the settings for control panel.

Use the Search option on the Start button to find the path for Control Panel (*.cpl) objects.

Step 1. Start MMC, and open the users.msc file.

Step 2. Expand the Control Panel under the User settings.

Step 3. Enable Control Panel and the Add/Remove Programs option.

Step 4. Ensure that only the control panel for the Application Wizard is visible.

LAB EXERCISE 7.07

Configuring Internet Explorer

15 Minutes

One of the C&C directors saw something on a colleague's computer that he wants implemented at C&C. The Internet Explorer task bar included the name of the company. In addition, every computer in the company had the same home page and list of favorites. Finally, the local computers seemed to block offensive pages. Naturally, the director asked Joanne to make it happen, and she is delegating the task to you.

You know that one of the GPO options is to manipulate Internet Explorer (IE) settings. Each of the required settings is included with Windows 2000. In addition to IE, MS Office resource kits include policy templates that an administrator can use with GPO editors to manage Office products.

Learning Objectives

In this lab, you modify the policy settings for IE. At the end of the lab, you'll be able to:

- Modify an existing policy
- Use policy settings for an application

Lab Materials and Setup

Modifying the settings in the GPO requires you to have these items:

- Users policy file
- Administrator account

Getting Down to Business

Using these steps, you make the necessary changes to the Users policy:

Step 1. Start MMC, and open the users.msc file.

Step 2. Expand to the Users Software Setting Administrative templates.

Step 3. Apply the desired policies to IE.

LAB EXERCISE 7.08

15 Minutes

Troubleshooting Using Event Viewer

A little after 11:00 P.M. one evening, just as you are about to leave after a long day, the administrator from South Side calls. He thinks that the payroll software did not install correctly on his server. He asks you to verify that the settings are correct.

You are fairly sure that you set all of the policies correctly. You know that the event viewer is the best way to quickly determine if the payroll install ran.

Learning Objectives

In this lab, you run the event viewer to prove that the software installed. At the end of the lab, you'll be able to:

- Use the event viewer
- Verify system events

Lab Materials and Setup

To run event viewer, all you need is an administrator account.

Getting Down to Business

You check the event viewer logs for today to see if any errors occurred.

Step 1. Start Event Viewer, and open the application log.

Step 2. Sort the list by type.

Step 3. Verify that the installer ran.

LAB ANALYSIS TEST

The following questions will help you to apply your knowledge in a business setting.

1. In Lab Exercise 7.07, you modified the Users policy to control IE's policy. Could you have done it in a different way?

2. Why should the "after" snapshot be taken immediately after the software is installed? What can happen if you wait for a time before taking it?

3. When should you *publish* an application as opposed to *assign* one?

4. MSI is a nice management tool for installing software packages. What scenarios with this tool would cause network lag and downtime?

5. What is the difference between assigning a package to a user and assigning a package to a computer?

KEY TERMS QUIZ

Use the following vocabulary terms to complete the sentences below. Not all of the terms will be used.

- assign
- category
- deploy
- discoz
- IntelliMirror
- MSI
- package
- publish
- snapshot
- transforms

1. A(n) ____________________ is used to change the typical software install.
2. Administrators can create a(n) ____________________ to store different but related applications.
3. The ____________________ program is run to build the package.
4. To automatically install software, the administrator is said to ____________________ the software.
5. When building an MSI, administrators take a(n) ____________________ both before and after an install.

LAB WRAP-UP

Congratulations! You have successfully mastered remote installation and maintenance of software. As a network administrator, you should always strive to keep the organization's computers consistent. By making use of software installation policies, you can be sure that the software is installed exactly as you want it to be installed.

A policy of consistency can cause some friction with users—especially the computer-savvy ones. Those users often resent the organization's desire to control "their" computer. Be sure to remind those users that the equipment is not theirs; it belongs to the company.

In the next chapter, you take the remote software install to a new level by installing an entire computer from a server. That procedure avoids the need for you to manually build new computers or to rebuild broken ones.

LAB SOLUTIONS FOR CHAPTER 7

The sections that follow walk you through the steps to solve the lab exercises. You should avoid looking at these sections unless you are stuck on a particular exercise.

Lab Exercise 7.01

Insert the Windows 2000 CD, holding SHIFT to stop auto run. If auto run starts anyway, close the Windows dialog.

Open My Computer and browse to D:\valueadd\3rdparty\mgmt\winstle\, where D: is the CD drive.

Double-click the file swiadmle.msi to start the installation. A progress display remains open during the install:

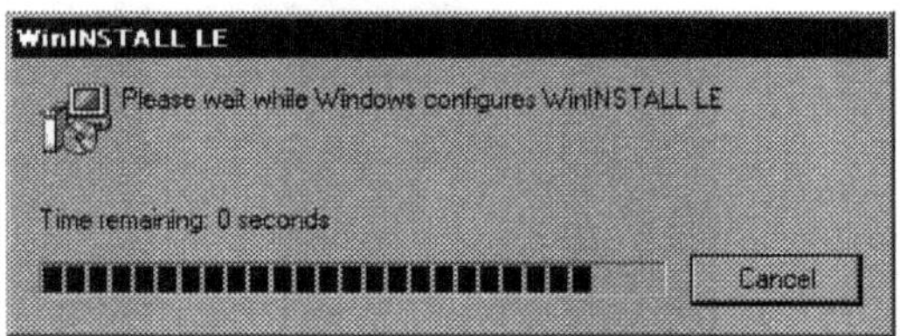

Once the software is installed, you need to share the WinINSTALL folder. Browse to C:\program files\VERITAS Software\Winstall.

Right-click the folder, and select Sharing to open the Winstall Properties dialog. Set the option buttons as shown in Figure 7-1.

Click Permissions.

Change the access for Everyone to "read only." Add the administrator group, giving them full control (Figure 7-2).

Click OK. Exit all of the dialogs.

Lab Exercise 7.02

Browse to C:\program files\VERITAS Software\Winstall.

Run the file **discoz.exe** to start the WinINSTALL Discover wizard (Figure 7-3).

Select Next to start the process.

FIGURE 7-1

Setting the sharing options for the WinINSTALL folder

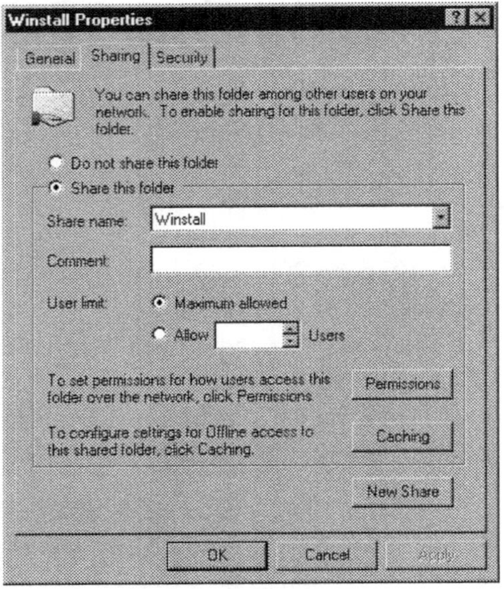

FIGURE 7-2

Setting permissions for the administrator group

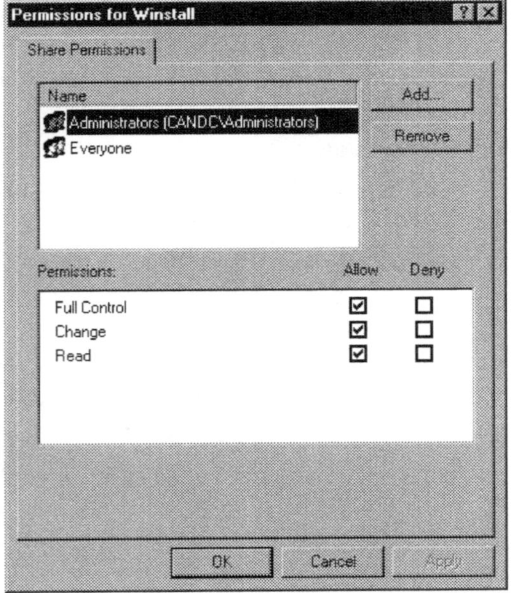

FIGURE 7-3

Launching the WinINSTALL Discover wizard

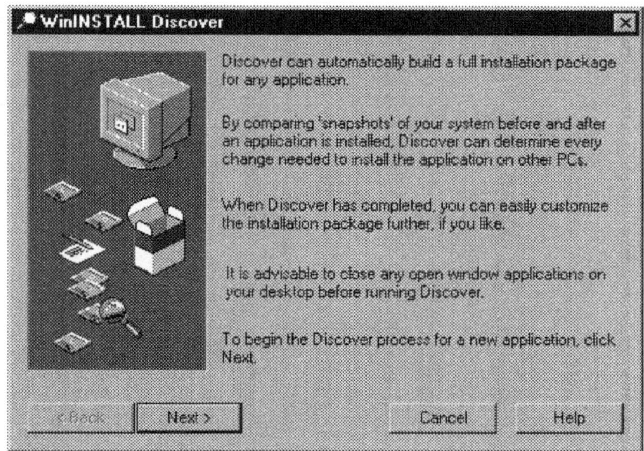

Enter the name of the software to be installed, and the uniform naming convention (UNC) path to its location on the server (Figure 7-4).

Click Next.

On the subsequent screen (Figure 7-5), you set the temporary storage location for install files.

Accept the default location by clicking Next.

The next screen (Figure 7-6) is where you select the drives to scan.

Select only the drives that will change during the installation. Click Next after you've made your choices.

At the next screen (Figure 7-7), you can select folders to ignore during the scan.

Add folders unlikely to be affected by the install. Good candidates are My Documents and third-party folders. Click Next to begin taking the snapshot.

FIGURE 7-4

Setting the install path and the name of the software program

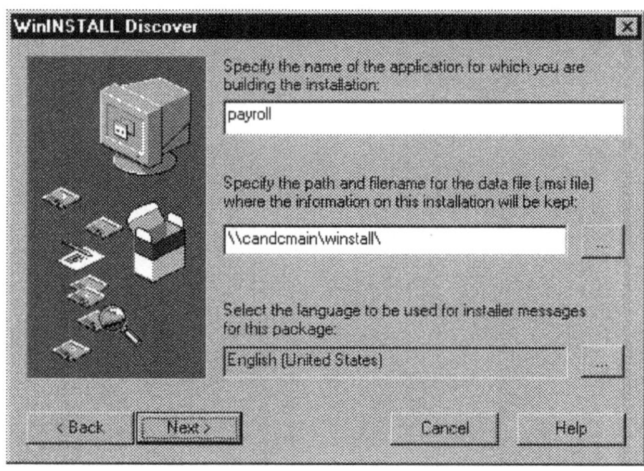

FIGURE 7-5

Choosing a temporary file location

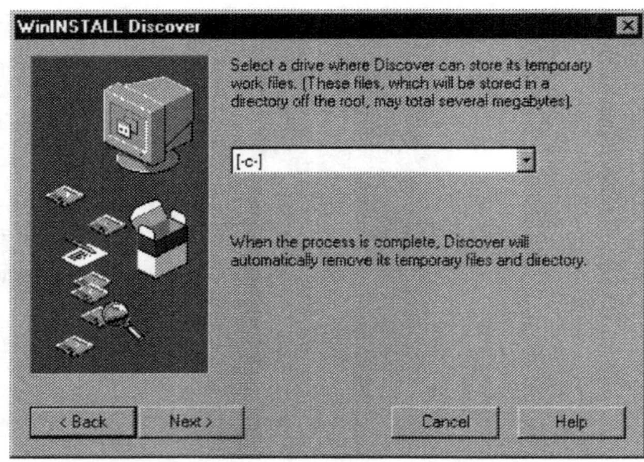

FIGURE 7-6

Selecting the drives to scan for changes after the install

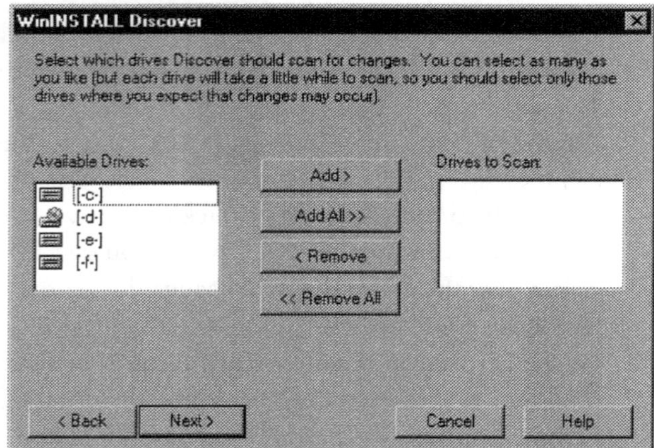

FIGURE 7-7

Selecting folders to exclude from the scan

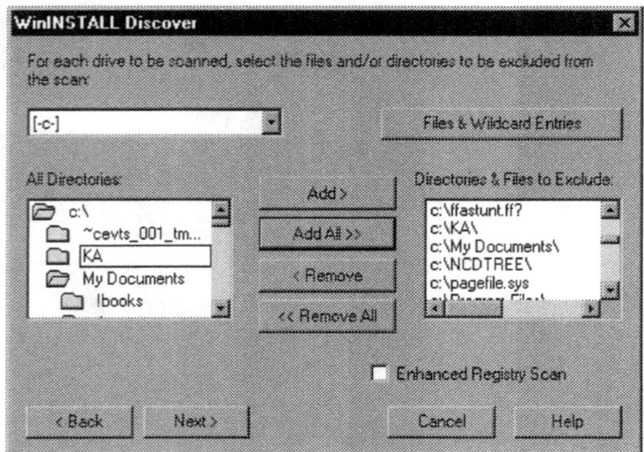

As discoz runs, you see this progress display:

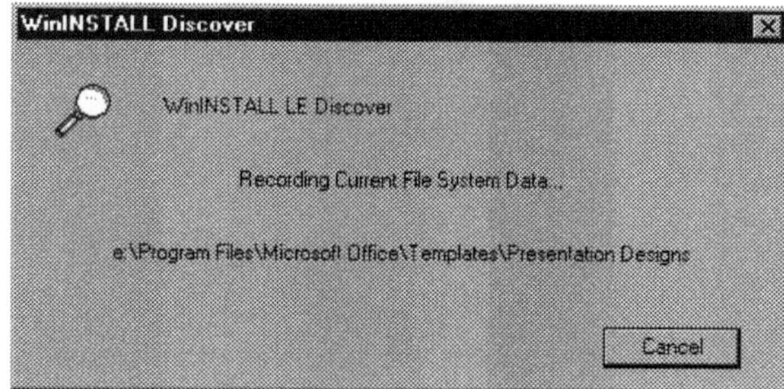

When the "before" snapshot is complete, you see this message:

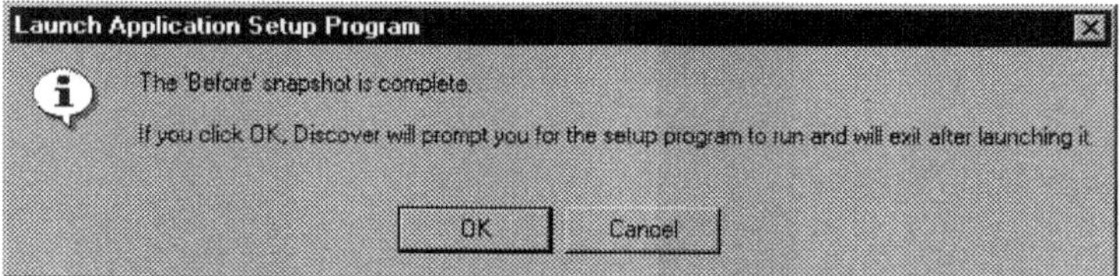

Click OK to install the software package.

Browse to the location of the install routine. Double-click the setup program. Follow the install steps, accepting all the default choices.

Once the install is complete, you need to take the "after" picture.

Again browse to C:\program files\VERITAS Software\Winstall, and run discoz.exe. The opening screen (Figure 7-8) verifies that you want to build an "after" snapshot. It also permits you back out of a botched install.

A message informs you when the snapshot is finished:

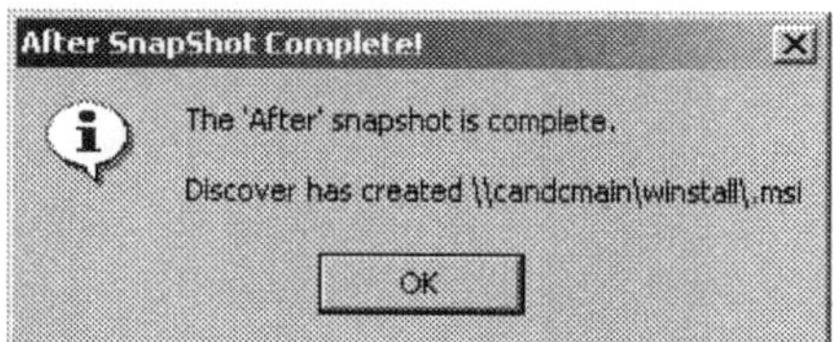

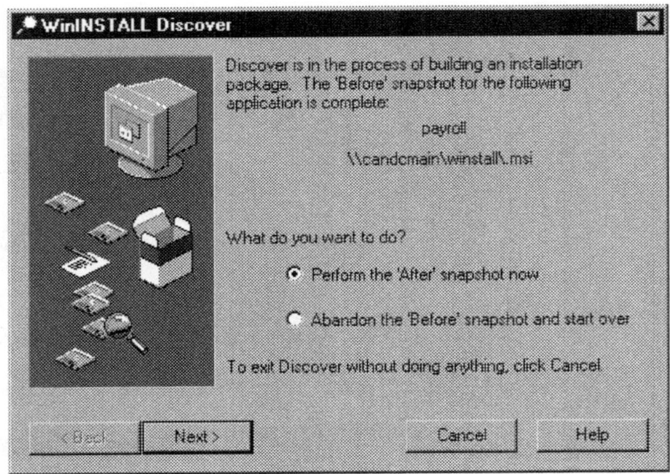

FIGURE 7-8 Starting an "after" snapshot

Lab Exercise 7.03

Select Run from the Start button, and run MMC.

Add the Group Policy snap-in, and create a new policy called **Payroll**, using the procedure that you learned in Chapter 6.

Expand the Computer Settings to see Software Installation. Right-click Software Installation, and "Add a new package."

Browse to \\candcmain\winstall and select payroll.msi. Click Open to see the Deploy Software dialog:

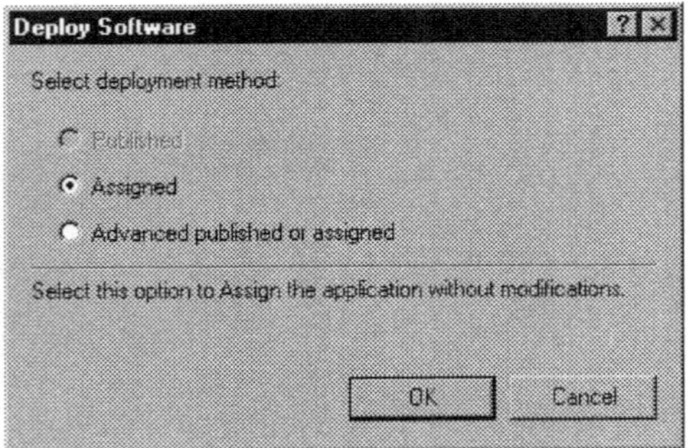

Select the default option (Assigned), and click OK. When the assign operation finishes, you see Payroll in the right-hand pane, as shown here:

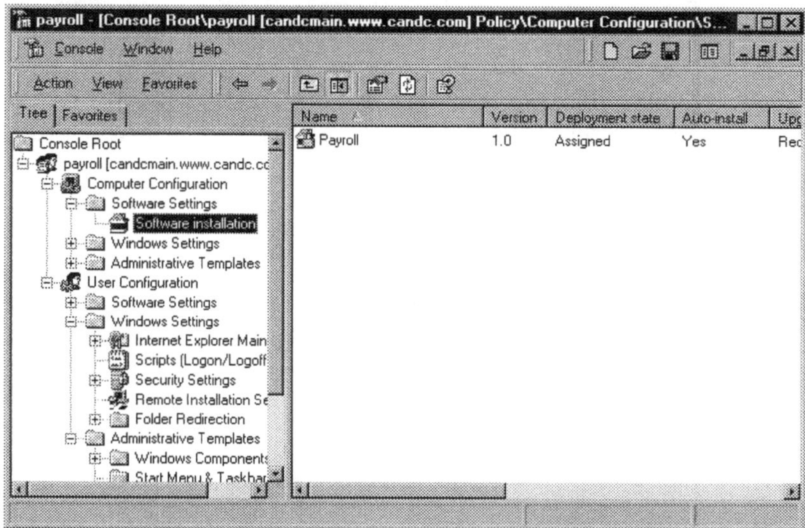

Now you need to assign the policy to the users. You learned the steps in Chapter 6.

Save the current screen as C:\winnt\system32\payroll.msc. Open Active Directory Users and Computers from the Start button. Right-click the domain object, and select Properties. Click the Group Policy tab. Add payroll.msc to the list of policies. Click Apply to finish linking the policy.

Lab Exercise 7.04

Start Active Directory Users and Computers.

Create a Security group called Servers.

Create a server object for each server in the organization. The names are **CandCHill**, **CandCLibrary**, **CandCMain**, **CandCSouth**, and **CandCNorth**. When you are finished, the screen should look like the one in Figure 7-9.

Go to the properties of the server group, and select the Members tab. Add each server to the list (Figure 7-10). Exit all of the dialogs.

Now you need to set the permissions of the payroll GPO so that only the server objects can read it.

Start Active Directory Users and Computers. Right click the domain object and select properties. Select the group policy tab and select the payroll object. Go to the properties of the payroll object and then select the security tab. Give the "read" and "apply group policy" permissions to the server group as shown in Figure 7-11.

FIGURE 7-9 Creating server objects

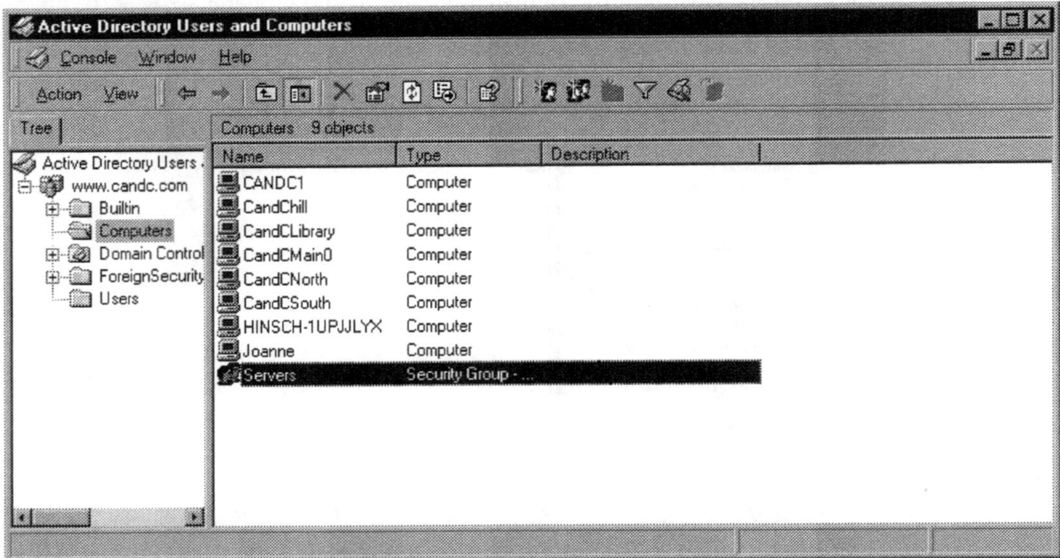

FIGURE 7-10

Adding servers to a server group

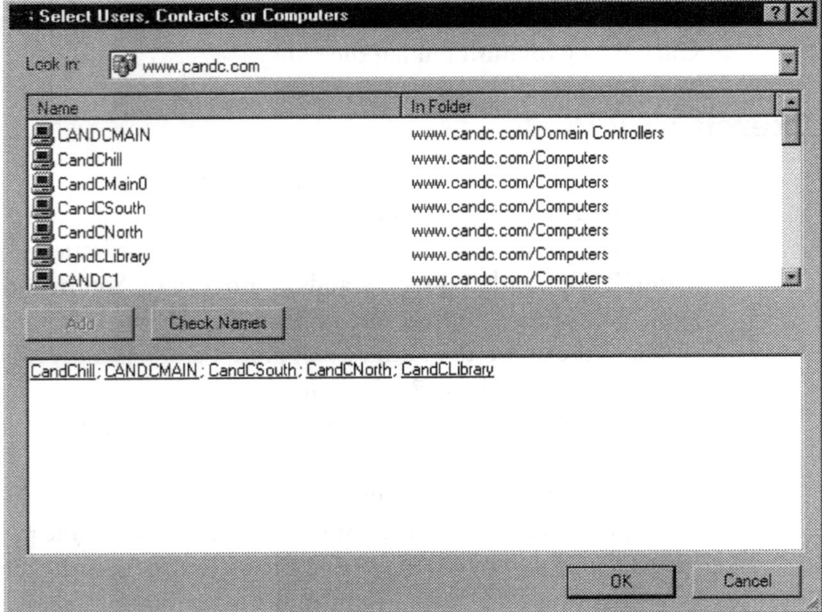

FIGURE 7-11

Assigning permissions to servers

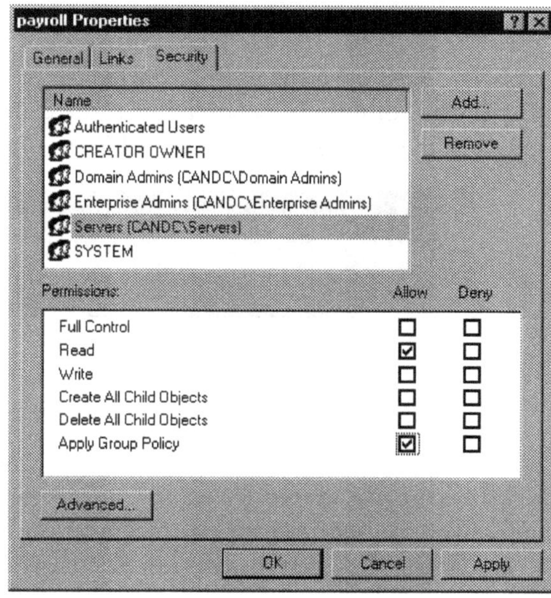

Now clear the "read" permission for authenticated users, as shown in Figure 7-12.

Add administrators with full control. Click OK to close the dialog box and save your changes.

FIGURE 7-12

Removing permissions from authenticated users

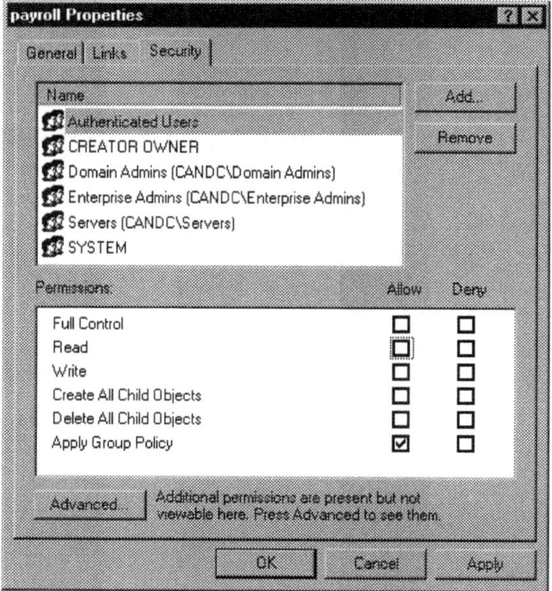

Lab Exercise 7.05

Start MMC, and open the payroll.msc file.

Expand to Software Installation under the Computer Configuration folder. Right-click the payroll object. Select All Tasks | Redeploy. You see this message:

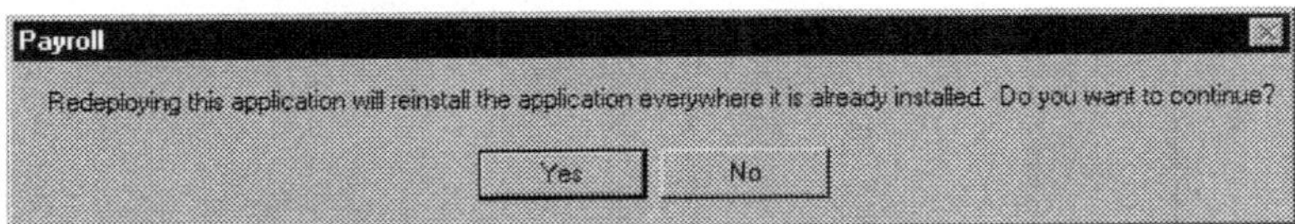

Click Yes.

Lab Exercise 7.06

The reason that the users can't see the control panel is the policies that are in place. You disabled control panel access in Chapter 6 when you built the user profile.

Start MMC, and open the user.msc file. Expand as shown:

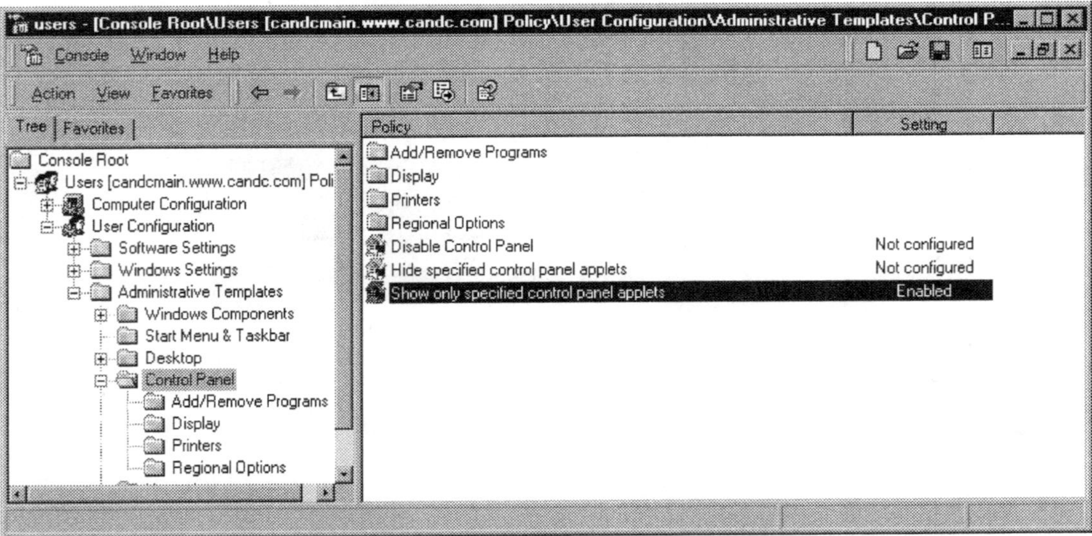

Disable the "disable control panel" policy, and enable the "Show only specified control panel applets." In the properties for the specified control panel applets, add appwiz.cpl to the list:

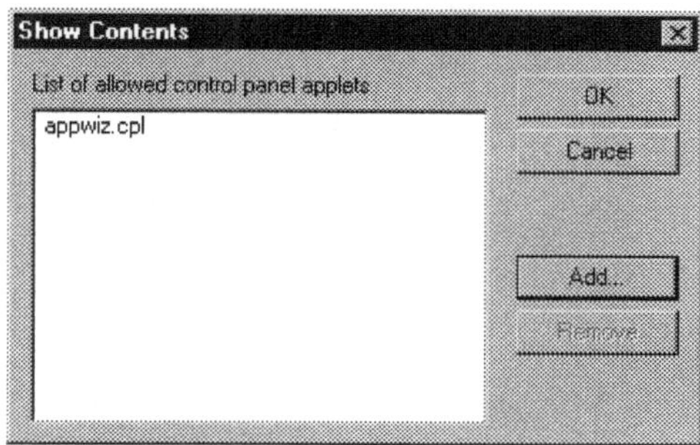

lab hint *To see the list of control panel applets, select Start | Search, and enter *.cpl.*

Lab Exercise 7.07

Open users.msc in MMC, and browse to Internet Explorer Maintenance as shown in Figure 7-13.

FIGURE 7-13 Reviewing the Internet Explorer maintenance policies

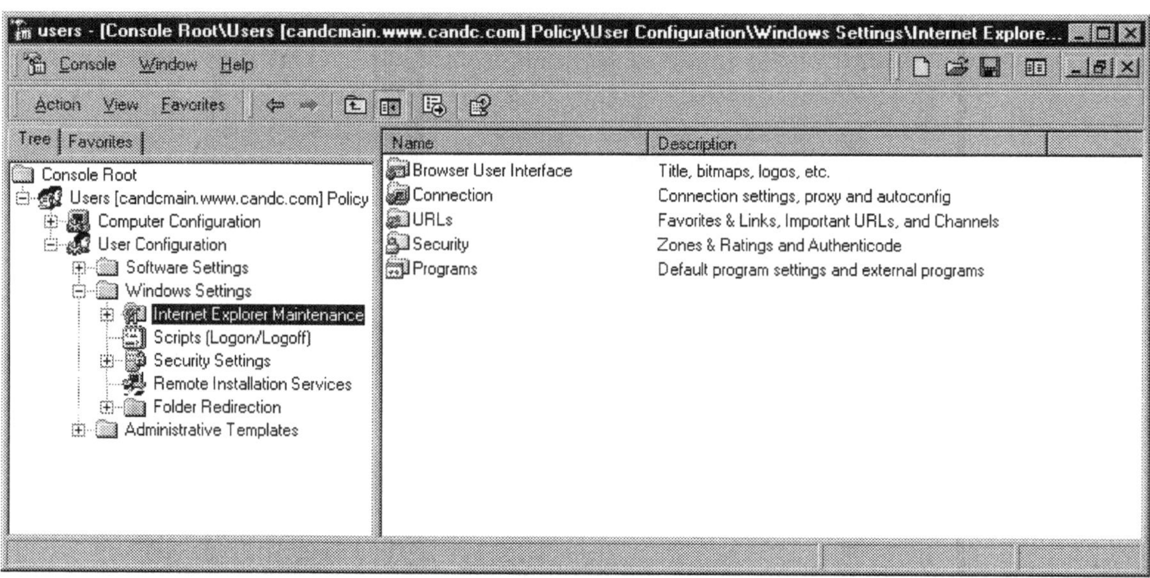

To set the title bar options, expand Browser User Interface, and double-click Browser Title. Make the browser title look like this:

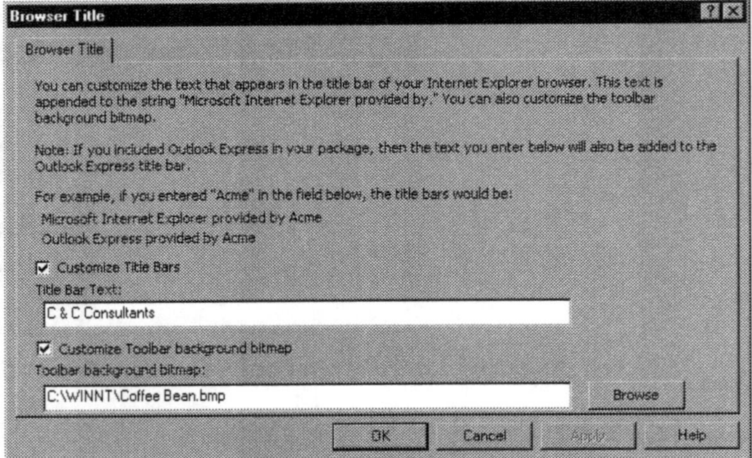

To set the content ratings, double-click Security, and import the content ratings. Click Modify Settings to open the Content Advisor dialog (Figure 7-14).

Set the nudity and sex rating to level 0 and the language and violence rating to level 1. (Many news pages are given a content rating of 1 for violence.)

When you click OK, you'll be asked to enter a password. Pick something long and hard to guess.

To set the home-page options, expand URLS, then double-click Important URLS. Set the home page as shown here:

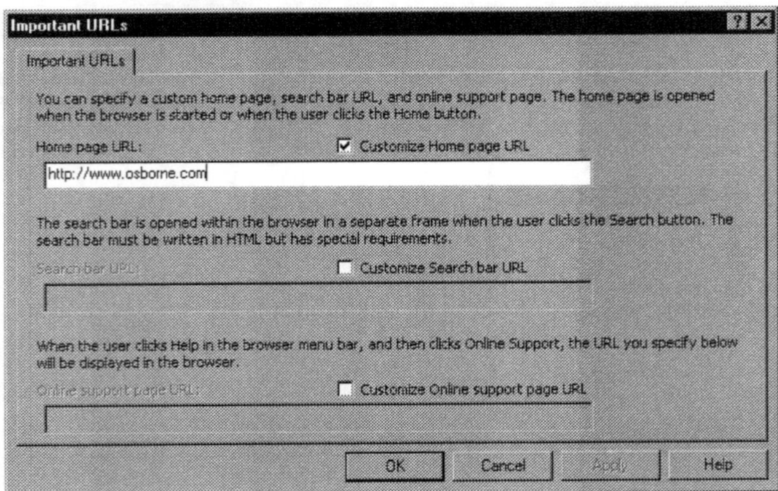

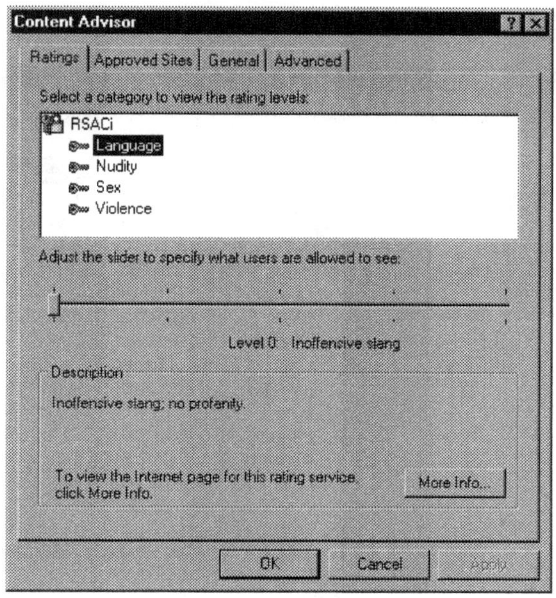

FIGURE 7-14 Setting levels for Internet content ratings

lab hint ***Many other IE options are available. Explore them at this policy and at the Internet Explorer policies under User Configuration.***

Lab Exercise 7.08

Choose Start | Administrative Tools | Event Viewer. Click the Application Log icon to see the current log content (Figure 7-15).

To sort the log by event type, click the heading bar labeled Source. Scroll until you see the group of MSI Installer events. Look for an error icon among the events for today's date.

As shown in the sample log (Figure 7-16), the MSI Installer ran at 10:04 and 10:07 on 9/28/2001. No errors were detected at that time. That information leads you to believe that the service ran as expected, and that the local user made an error.

lab hint ***The two errors were caused by a permissions mistake.***

FIGURE 7-15 Checking the Event Viewer log

Event Viewer

Action View

Tree

Event Viewer (Local)
- Application Log
- Security Log
- System Log
- Directory Service
- DNS Server
- File Replication Service

Application Log 861 event(s)

Type	Date	Time	Source	Cat
Information	11/25/2001	6:55:31 PM	MsiInstaller	Nor
Error	11/25/2001	6:54:14 PM	Userenv	Nor
Warning	11/25/2001	6:54:14 PM	SceCli	Nor
Error	11/25/2001	6:49:05 PM	Userenv	Nor
Warning	11/25/2001	6:49:05 PM	SceCli	Nor
Error	11/25/2001	6:43:57 PM	Userenv	Nor
Warning	11/25/2001	6:43:57 PM	SceCli	Nor
Error	11/25/2001	6:38:49 PM	Userenv	Nor
Warning	11/25/2001	6:38:49 PM	SceCli	Nor
Error	11/25/2001	6:33:41 PM	Userenv	Nor
Warning	11/25/2001	6:33:41 PM	SceCli	Nor
Information	11/25/2001	6:31:14 PM	MsiInstaller	Nor
Error	11/25/2001	6:28:32 PM	Userenv	Nor
Warning	11/25/2001	6:28:32 PM	SceCli	Nor
Error	11/25/2001	6:23:23 PM	Userenv	Nor
Warning	11/25/2001	6:23:23 PM	SceCli	Nor
Error	11/25/2001	6:18:15 PM	Userenv	Nor
Warning	11/25/2001	6:18:15 PM	SceCli	Nor
Information	11/25/2001	6:14:26 PM	ESENT	Log

FIGURE 7-16 Searching for MSI installer events

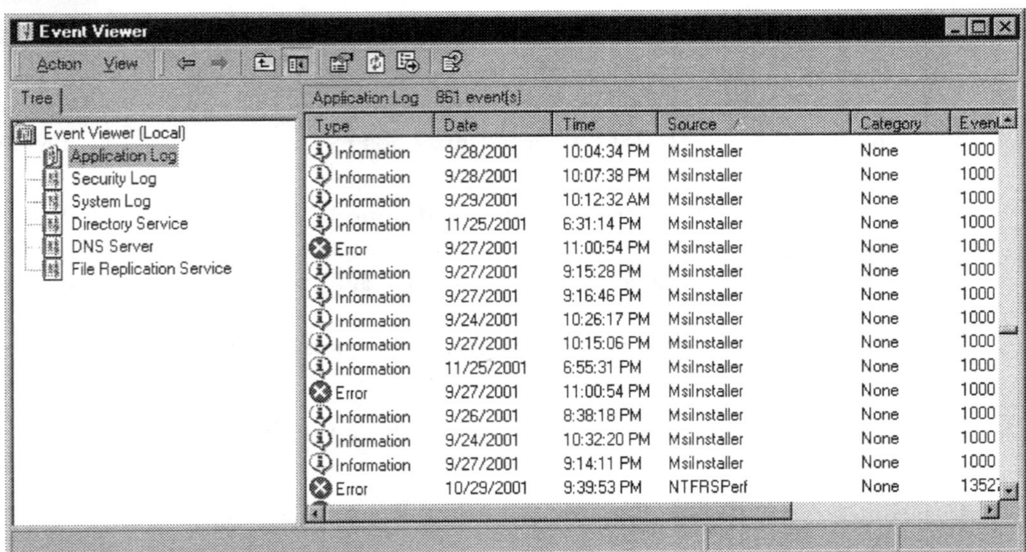

ANSWERS TO LAB ANALYSIS TEST

1. Another method would be to create a separate policy and let inheritance handle the IE tasks. The advantage of that approach lies in its modularity. Multiple policies make it easier to enable or disable specific policies as needed.
2. The snapshots capture the changes to a system after a program is installed. If the snapshot is not taken immediately, and if another user changes the system, then the snapshot may include files not needed for the installation.
3. An application that is published is installed at the user's discretion. If users feel that the application is important to them, then they install it. For example, everyone in the organization does not need MS Access. Only those who need Access will install it. An application that is assigned must be installed on every computer. The user is not given a choice. When that user logs on, the application is installed. Thus, if an application *must* be installed on the local computer, it should be assigned. If an application is optional, then it should be published.
4. The MSI service provided by Microsoft is a nice tool. It works well for small programs that need to be installed across the network. But using it to install a large software package—MS Visual Studio, for example—should be avoided. The install time over the network will be excessively long, and the traffic between the server and the client will bog down the entire network. If multiple users are installing the application, the network will be slowed even more.
5. The difference between assigning a package to a user and assigning it to a computer has to do with the number of times that the software will be installed. For a user-assigned package, the software will be installed every time the user logs onto a computer (unless the package is already installed). However, assigning to users allows the administrator to pick and choose the people who get the assignment, potentially increasing security. Computer-assigned software is installed one time. When the computer logs on, the software is installed. The administrator has a difficult time restricting the application to a given set of users.

ANSWERS TO KEY TERM QUIZ

1. transform
2. categories
3. discoz
4. deploy
5. snapshot

8

Installing and Configuring the Remote Installation Service

LAB EXERCISES

- 8.01 Installing and Configuring Dynamic Host Configuration Protocol
- 8.02 Installing the Remote Installation Service
- 8.03 Building a CD-Based Image
- 8.04 Configuring the Remote Installation Service
- 8.05 Building a Remote Boot Disk
- 8.06 Creating an Install User
- 8.07 Modifying an Answer File
- 8.08 Troubleshooting the Remote Installation Service
- Lab Analysis Test
- Key Term Quiz
- Lab Wrap-Up
- Lab Solutions

Joanne and the directors at C&C love the Microsoft Installer Package (MSI) process. It frees administrators and technicians from performing routine installations on client computers. However, a larger issue remains. Occasionally, client computers break and need to be rebuilt. Part of the rebuild involves reinstalling Windows 2000. That task ties up an administrator with a routine install for approximately 1 hour. Joanne asks if the MSI process can be used to install Windows 2000.

You know that MSI will not correctly install Windows 2000, but that Microsoft also provides the Remote Installation Service (RIS). With RIS, a client computer with no operating system can connect to the server and automatically install Windows 2000 Professional. The install process can be automated using an answer file and several images. You tell Joanne that you will set up RIS on the C&C server.

LAB EXERCISE 8.01

25 Minutes

Installing and Configuring Dynamic Host Configuration Protocol

You want to jump right in and install the RIS, but you know that it depends on the Dynamic Host Configuration Protocol (DHCP). C&C's servers are not currently using DHCP.

Installing a DHCP server in a network that already has a DHCP server can cause problems. Do not perform this lab exercise if your organization is already running DHCP. If you are unsure, consult your administrator.

Learning Objectives

In this lab, you install DHCP on C&C's main server. At the end of the lab, you'll be able to:

- Install DHCP
- Set a scope
- Set an exclusion range

Lab Materials and Setup

Installing DHCP is not much different than installing other Windows 2000 services. You need these materials:

- Windows 2000 Server CD
- Administrator account
- Static IP address for the server

Getting Down to Business

To install DHCP and configure the scope for C&C, here's what you do:

Step 1. Ensure that the server has a statically assigned IP address of 192.168.1.1.

Step 2. Go to the control panel, and select the Add/Remove Programs icon.

If your control panel is disabled by a group policy, add the Administrators group to the policy permissions, and switch off the "apply" permission.

Step 3. Select the DHCP check box under the Networking Services tab.

Step 4. Start the DHCP snap-in from the Start button.

Step 5. Create a new scope using the private IP range 192.168.1.2 to 192.168.1.255. Set the appropriate subnet mask. Exclude from the range any addresses that are statically assigned to machines in the network.

Step 6. Accept the default lease duration, but avoid configuring any other options.

Step 7. Select Manage Authorized Servers.

Step 8. Authorize the server with the IP address 192.168.1.1.

LAB EXERCISE 8.02

5 Minutes

Installing the Remote Installation Service

Now that DHCP is installed, you can install RIS. With RIS installed, client users can reinstall Windows 2000 as necessary. The maximum administrator involvement might be to provide a boot disk and directions.

Learning Objectives

Installing RIS is similar to installing any other Windows 2000 service. At the end of the lab, you'll be able to install RIS.

Lab Materials and Setup

To install RIS, you need these materials:

- Administrator account
- Windows 2000 Server CD

Getting Down to Business

To add RIS to the list of installed Windows programs, use these steps:

Step 1. Start the control panel.

Step 2. Using the Add/Remove applet, add the Windows component Remote Installation Service.

LAB EXERCISE 8.03

Building a CD-Based Image

30 Minutes

Joanne is pleased that RIS is installed, and she is anxious to see a user remotely reinstall the operating system. You tell her to slow down—you have no images built yet!

The RIS server must have an image to serve up. You start by building the simplest image—the CD-based image. That image is just a copy of the i386 folder from the Windows 2000 Professional CD. That image can run a basic Windows 2000 install onto a client machine.

Learning Objectives

The CD-based install is a typical image placed on RIS servers. At the end of the lab, you will be able to:

- Run RISetup
- Create a CD-based image

Lab Materials and Setup

To build the Windows 2000 Professional image, you need these materials:

- Administrator account
- RIS installed on the server
- Copy of the Windows 2000 Professional CD
- A 2GB or larger non-system drive formatted with NTFS

Getting Down to Business

You will run RISetup to build the CD image. Here's how:

Step 1. Run RISetup from Run on the Start button.

Step 2. Select the image location, but avoid responding to the request for clients.

Step 3. Specify the path to the Windows 2000 Professional CD, and name the folder and image.

Step 4. Confirm your choices and go to lunch. The process takes about 20 minutes, depending on the speed of your system.

LAB EXERCISE 8.04

10 Minutes

Configuring the Remote Installation Service

Joanne knows that each computer needs a unique name. She asks how Active Directory manages that trick. You know that, to answer her question, RIS needs to be configured. You proceed to configure RIS so that computer accounts are named automatically, including placement in an organizational unit (OU).

You decide to use the naming scheme CANDC#, where # is the next number in sequence. Each new computer will be placed in the Computer container.

Learning Objectives

In this lab, you set up the RIS server to properly place new computer accounts. At the end of the lab, you'll be able to:

- Change the properties of the RIS server
- Set up a computer-naming scheme.
- Force placement in an organizational unit

Lab Materials and Setup

Configuring the RIS server requires that you set the computer name and OU status. You will need these materials:

- Administrator account
- RIS installed on the server

Getting Down to Business

This exercise leads you in setting the rules for computer names and for the containers in which they reside.

Step 1. Start Active Directory Users and Computers.

Step 2. Call up the properties of the RIS server.

Step 3. Customize the name and container settings. Use the name **CANDC%#**. Give the container the name **Computers**.

LAB EXERCISE 8.05

Building a Remote Boot Disk

5 Minutes

Joanne asks how the remote computers will connect to the RIS server if they have no operating system. You tell her about the network boot option present in most new computers. Such computers, when configured to boot from the network, will automatically find the RIS server and start the image.

Joanne then asks about older computers that do not support network booting. You reply that you will create a Remote boot disk to start the install.

Learning Objectives

To build a boot disk, Windows 2000 RIS provides a tool called the Remote Boot Floppy Generator (RBFG). At the end of the lab, you'll be able to run RBFG.exe to build a boot disk.

Lab Materials and Setup

To run RBFG, you need these materials:

- RIS installed on the server
- A blank 1.44MB floppy disk and label

Getting Down to Business

Here's the procedure for running RBFG:

Step 1. From the Start button, run **D:\remoteinstall\admin\i386\rbfg.exe** where D: is the drive on which RIS is installed.

Step 2. Click Create Disk.

LAB EXERCISE 8.06

10 Minutes

Creating an Install User

Joanne is concerned that users will start reinstalling operating systems whenever a small problem occurs. She would like some control over the process.

You decide to create a user called Image. That user will have the rights to install an image and to create a computer account in the OU. By creating one user with the authority to install images, you can enable that user as needed. Thus, only when you switch on the Image user can an image be processed.

Learning Objectives

In this lab, you delegate to the Image account the right to reinstall from an image. At the end of the lab, you'll be able to:

- Create a new user
- Delegate authority to the user

Lab Materials and Setup

To delegate authority, you need these materials:

- Administrator account
- RIS installed and configured
- Active Directory installed

Getting Down to Business

By completing the steps that follow, you will create a new user and give that user the power to restore from the image and to join the computer to the domain.

Step 1. Start Active Directory Users and Computers.

Step 2. Create a new user called **Image**. Apply logical first and last names. Pick a password that's easy to remember.

Step 3. Go to the properties of the domain and delegate control.

Step 4. Following the steps in the wizard, apply the necessary rights to Image.

Step 5. Disable the Image user.

LAB EXERCISE 8.07

Modifying an Answer File

30 Minutes

Joanne presented your solution to the board, and all directors are pleased, except Vince. Vince believes that games are wastes of time and resources, and he would like them removed from the installation process. Joanne asks if that can be done.

You believe that the answer file includes choices for software packages to install. By removing the games package from the answer file, new installs won't include games.

Learning Objectives

In this lab, you modify the default answer file for the remote install. At the end of the lab, you'll be able to:

- Edit an answer file to disable games
- Associate an answer file

Lab Materials and Setup

To modify the answer file, you need these materials:

- Windows 2000 Server CD
- RIS installed
- A CAB Viewer or WinZip

Getting Down to Business

To disallow installation of games on client computers, use these steps:

Step 1. Open the file unattend.doc in the \support\Tools\Deploy.cab file. Read how to configure the disabling of games.

Step 2. Open ristndrd.sif in the image's folder.

Step 3. Add a [Components] section after the [Display] section.

Step 4. Turn off the Solitaire, FreeCell, Minesweeper, and Pinball options. Save the altered file as **nogame.sif**.

Step 5. Go to the properties of the RIS server in Active Directory Users and Computers.

Step 6. Add a new image and associate a new answer file to the existing image.

Step 7. Remove the original installation choice.

Step 8. Allow users to read nogames.sif.

LAB EXERCISE 8.08

5 Minutes

Troubleshooting the Remote Installation Service

Joanne is happy with the RIS server, but she wants some guidance regarding troubleshooting. In particular, when a user is having problems using RIS, Joanne wants to know how to verify that the server is okay, and that any mistakes can be attributed to the user.

You know how RIS appears in the event logs and what steps you can take to verify that RIS is working.

Learning Objectives

Troubleshooting any network service is tedious at best; but, at the end of the lab, you will be able to:

- Verify that the RIS server is valid
- Verify that DHCP is running
- Verify that no errors are present

Lab Materials and Setup

To troubleshoot the RIS server, you need these materials:

- RIS installed
- DHCP installed
- A working client computer

Getting Down to Business

Finding and checking the server properties, and reviewing the event log is a simple process.

Step 1. Select Verify Server in the properties of the RIS server.

Step 2. Verify that DHCP is running and that the scope is active.

Step 3. Verify that no BINSVL, TFTP (trivial file transfer protocol), DHCP, or DNS (domain name service) errors are present in the event log.

LAB ANALYSIS TEST

The following questions will help you to apply your knowledge in a business setting.

1. Why does RIS require a DHCP server?

2. When would you want to prestage a computer?

3. The naming scheme allows you to include media access control (MAC) access. How could MAC be used to troubleshoot bad machines or users?

4. What is required for RIS to be installed and configured?

5. Which is better, having one user with the permissions to reinstall images, or applying those permissions to individual users as necessary?

KEY TERMS QUIZ

Use the following vocabulary terms to complete the sentences below. Not all of the terms will be used.

answer file

delegation

DHCP

DNS

GUID (group user ID)

image

prestaging

PXE (preboot execution environment)

RIPrep

RISetup

1. The ____________________ service automatically assigns IP addresses to client computers.
2. A remote client computer ____________________ can be prepared using ____________________.
3. To prestage a computer, the administrator needs to have a(n) ____________________ for each computer.
4. The ____________________ selects the settings for the automated install.
5. Network cards must be ____________________-compliant to handle RIS.

LAB WRAP-UP

Congratulations, you have successfully set up RIS! Using RIS, you can create and distribute images that are used to build remote client machines. The service is designed to automate the rebuilding of client computers. When RIS is correctly set up, a user needs to know nothing more than the correct logon name and password to use.

The current chapter covered setting up and configuring the RIS server. In Chapter 9, you actually install software on a remote computer.

LAB SOLUTIONS FOR CHAPTER 8

The sections that follow walk you through the steps to solve the lab exercises. You should avoid looking at these sections unless you are stuck on a particular exercise.

Lab Exercise 8.01

On the desktop, right-click My Network Places. Select Properties to see the available Network and Dial-up Connections (Figure 8-1).

Right-click Local Area Connection, and select Properties. When the properties dialog (Figure 8-2) opens, go to the properties for TCP/IP.

Set the static IP address as shown in Figure 8-3.

Select OK until you are back at the desktop.

Go to the control panel. Start Add/Remove Programs. Click the Add/Remove Windows Components option.

Find Networking Services (Figure 8-4), and click Details.

Select DHCP as shown in Figure 8-5.

Click OK to return to Networking Services (Figure 8-4), and then click Next to continue the installation.

FIGURE 8-1 Viewing the properties of My Network Places

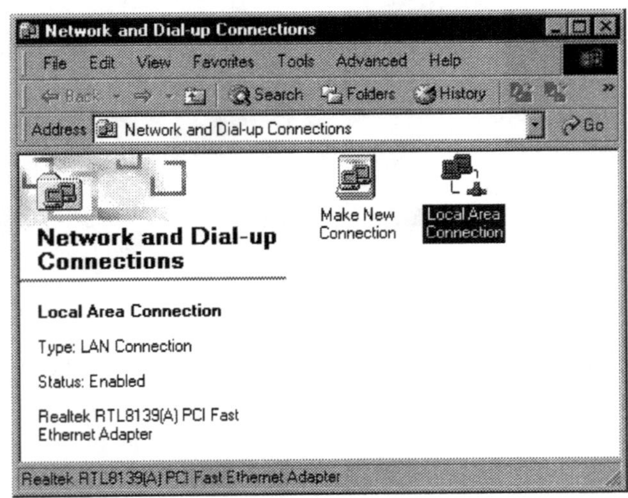

FIGURE 8-2

Viewing the properties of the Local Area Connection

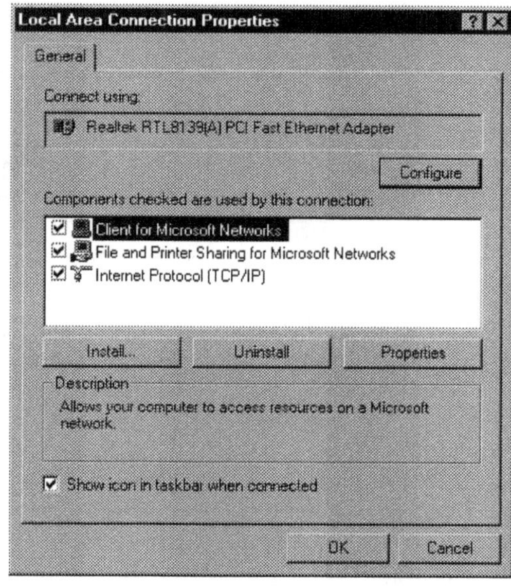

FIGURE 8-3

Setting the static IP address

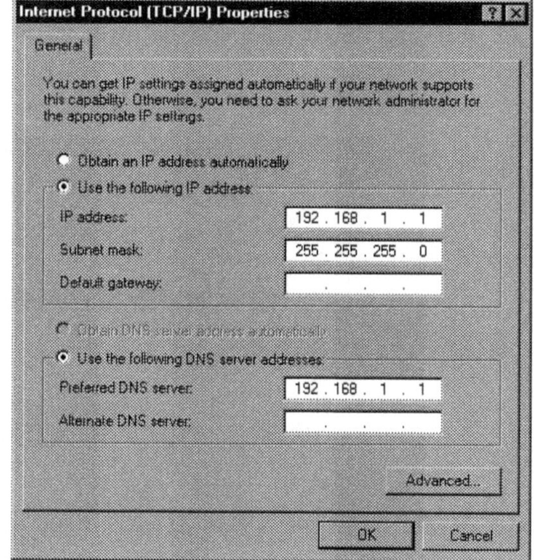

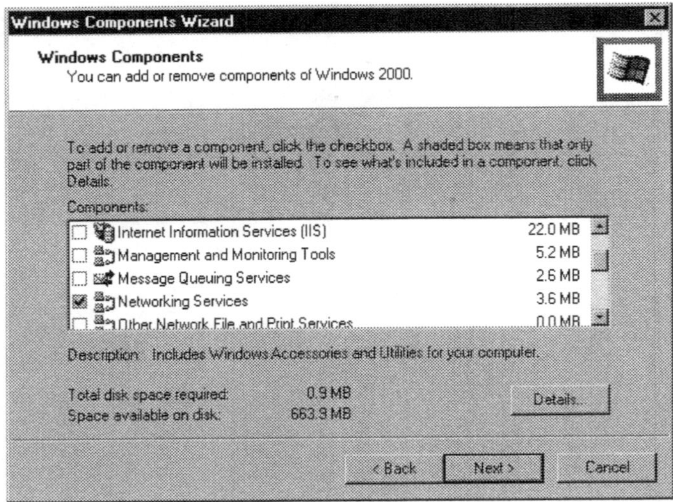

FIGURE 8-4 Finding the networking services

You can watch while the Windows Component Wizard runs. When the Wizard is done, click Finish.

Select Start | Programs | Administrative Tools | DHCP to see the DCHP folder (Figure 8-6).

To create a scope, first expand the server, next, right-click the server, and select New Scope.

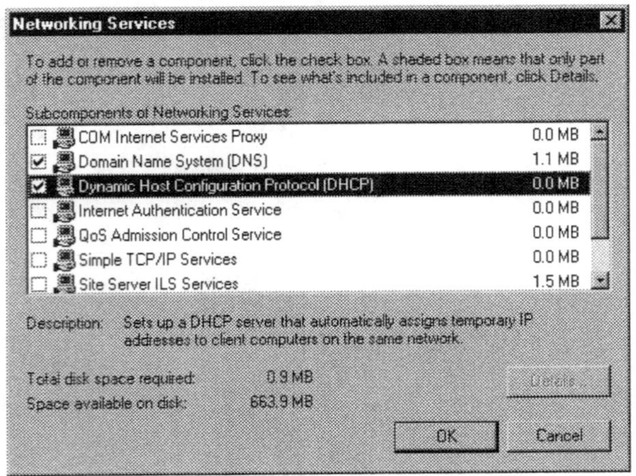

FIGURE 8-5 Selecting the Dynamic Host Configuration Protocol (DHCP)

FIGURE 8-6 Opening the DHCP folder

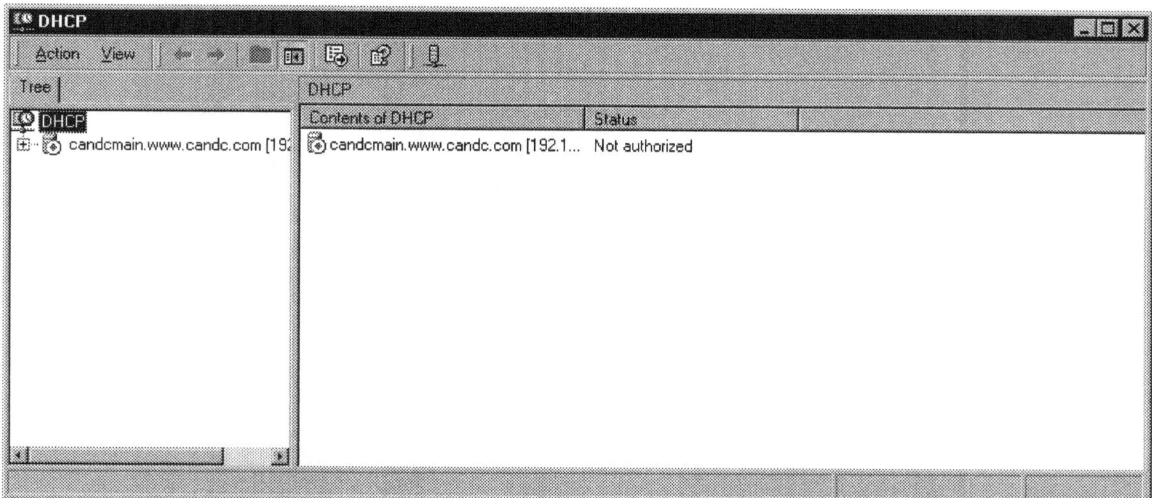

At the opening screen, click Next. Give the scope the name and description shown here:

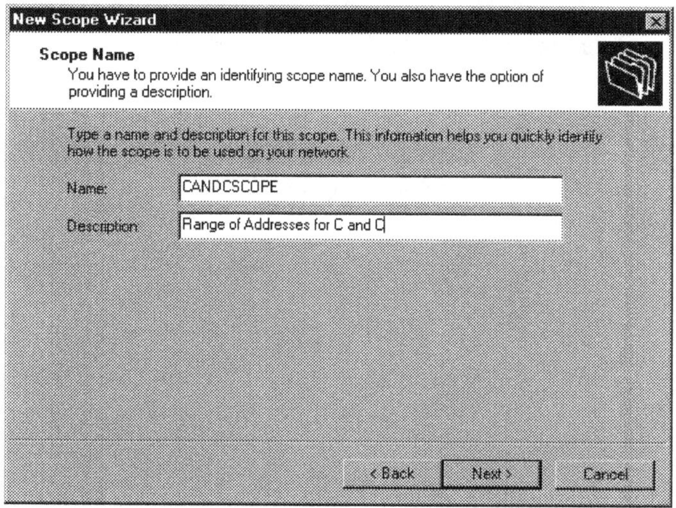

Click Next.

Configure the IP address range as shown:

New Scope Wizard

IP Address Range
You define the scope address range by identifying a set of consecutive IP addresses.

Enter the range of addresses that the scope distributes.

Start IP address: 192 . 168 . 1 . 2
End IP address: 192 . 168 . 1 . 254

A subnet mask defines how many bits of an IP address to use for the network/subnet IDs and how many bits to use for the host ID. You can specify the subnet mask by length or as an IP address.

Length: 24
Subnet mask: 255 . 255 . 255 . 0

< Back | Next > | Cancel

Click Next. Do not exclude addresses at this time. Leave the lease duration at 8 days. Click Next again.

Do not configure any additional options for now (Figure 8-7).

When you return to the DHCP folder, right-click the DHCP icon and select Manage Authorized Servers. When the list of authorized servers opens (Figure 8-8), select Authorize.

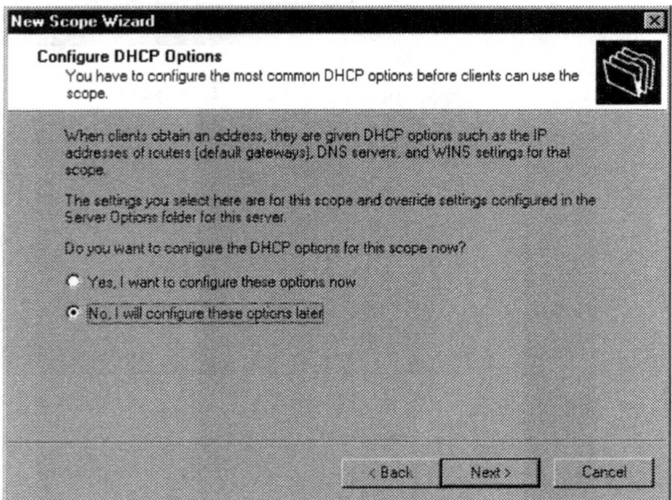

FIGURE 8-7 Skipping the configuration of other DHCP options

FIGURE 8-8

Viewing the (empty) list of DHCP-authorized servers

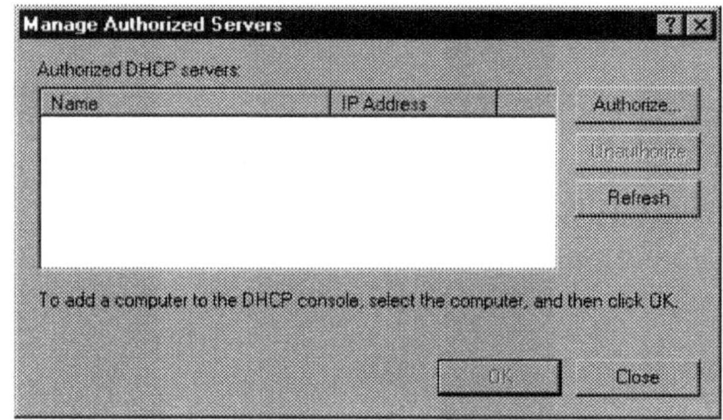

Configure the server for DHCP as shown:

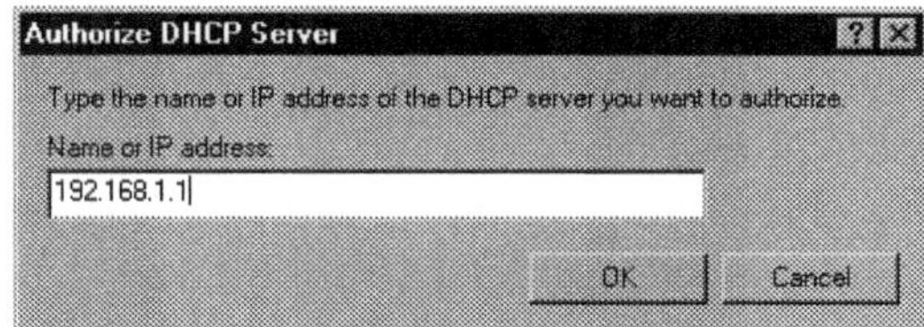

Confirm the authorization. After you confirm, you'll be returned to the main DHCP screen.

Select Action | Authorize. If errors occur, click OK, and then close and reopen DHCP. When DHCP opens, you see the new scope in the content of the server:

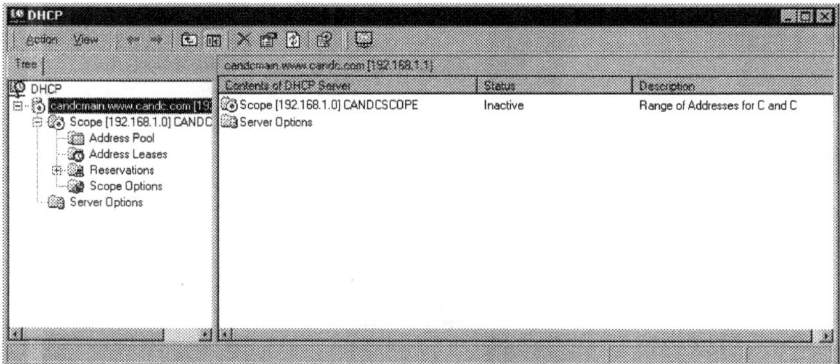

Right-click the scope, and select Activate. The scope is now active.

Close the DHCP window.

Lab Exercise 8.02

Go to the control panel. Start Add/Remove Programs, and click the Add/Remove Windows Components option.

Select Remote Installation Service, as shown in Figure 8-9.

Insert the Windows 2000 CD when prompted. When prompted, reboot your computer.

Lab Exercise 8.03

From the Start button, select the Run option. Into the Run box, type **RISetup**, and press ENTER. The opening screen of the RISetup Wizard (Figure 8-10) appears.

Click Next to choose the folder location for the RIS (Figure 8-11). Make sure that your choice reflects a non-system drive formatted with NTFS and having at least 2GB available space.

Click Next.

Avoid responding to the request for clients. (Accept the default choice. You'll respond later when an image is ready.)

Insert the Windows 2000 Professional CD, holding down the SHIFT key to stop the auto run feature. Enter the path to the CD as shown in Figure 8-12.

FIGURE 8-9 Choosing to install the Remote Installation Service

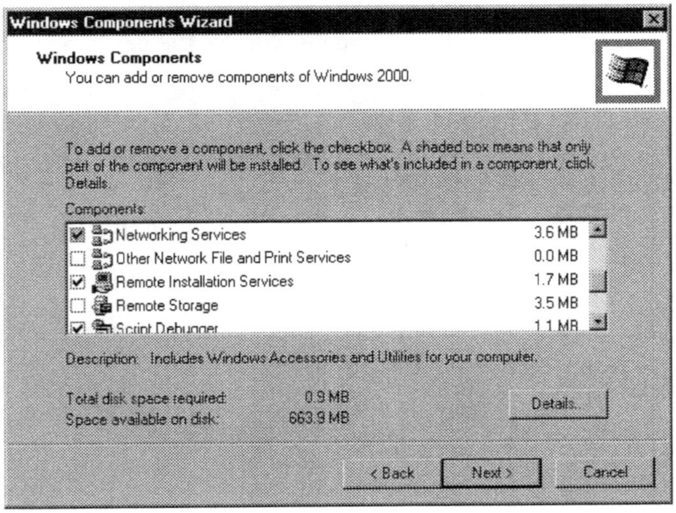

FIGURE 8-10

Starting the RISetup wizard

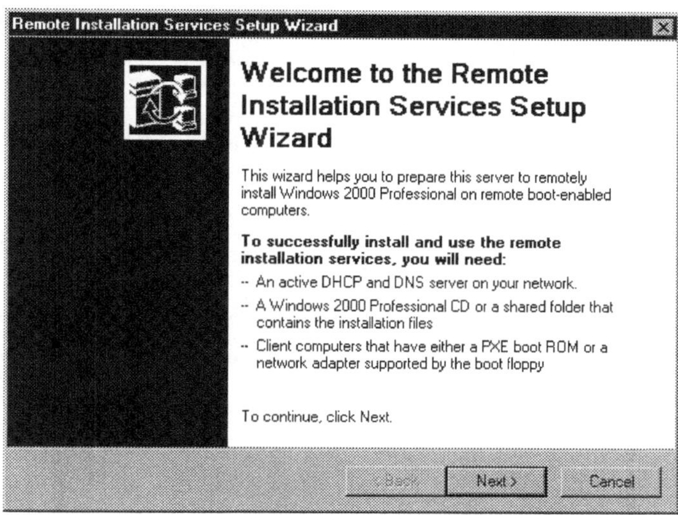

Accept the default entries on the next two screens. Verify the image as shown in Figure 8-13.

While the image is being copied, you see the progress tracking screen (Figure 8-14).

On an AMD Athlon 1.2 with 256MB RAM and a 32× CD drive, the copy operation took 5 minutes.

FIGURE 8-11

Selecting the RIS image location

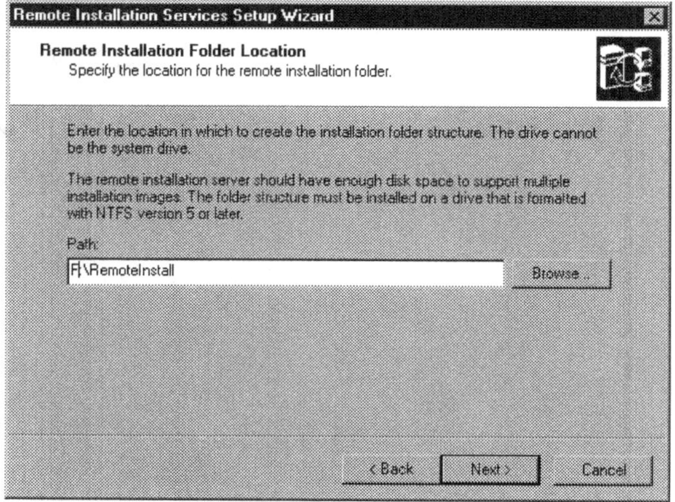

FIGURE 8-12

Specifying the path to the install files

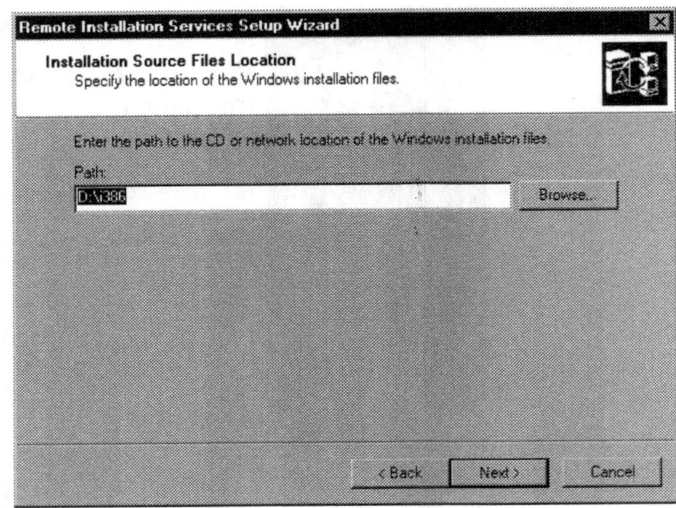

Lab Exercise 8.04

From the Start button, select Programs | Administrative Tools | Active Directory Users and Computers.

Expand the Domain Controller folder, and then call up the properties of CANDCMAIN.

Click the Remote Install tab. On that tab sheet (Figure 8-15), select Respond to clients requesting service, and then click Advanced Settings.

FIGURE 8-13

Verifying the image details

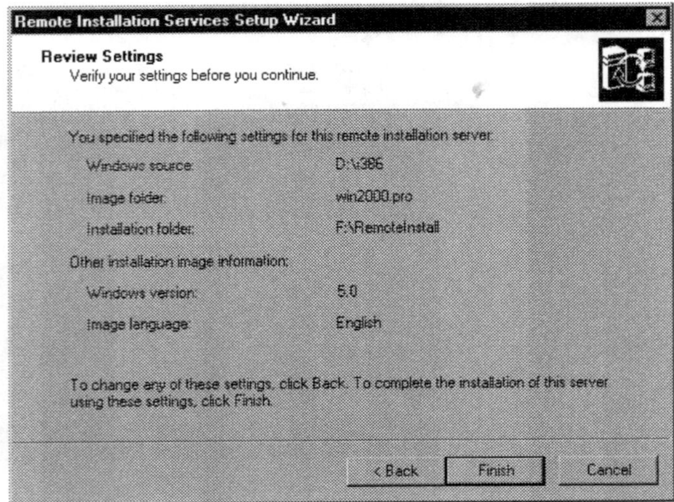

FIGURE 8-14

Tracking image creation on the progress screen

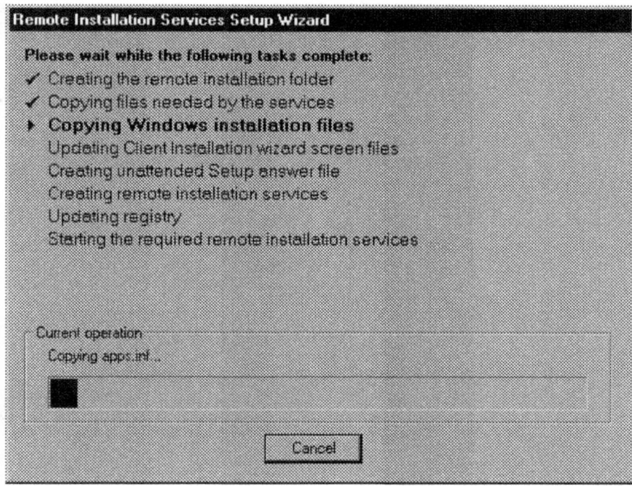

Click Customize, and enter the naming scheme shown in Figure 8-16. Now, set the Active Directory location as shown in Figure 8-17. Click Apply and then OK to return to the Active Directory screen.

FIGURE 8-15

Setting the Remote Install Properties

CANDCMAIN Properties
General | Operating System | Member Of
Location | Managed By | Remote Install
You can manage this remote installation server and control the way it interacts with existing and potential client computers.
Client support
☑ Respond to client computers requesting service
☐ Do not respond to unknown client computers
Check server
If this remote installation server is exhibiting problems, select the "Verify Server" option to perform an integrity check. If problems are encountered they will be fixed.
This option is only available from the server console.
Verify Server
Show Clients... | Advanced Settings...
OK | Cancel | Apply

FIGURE 8-16

Defining a custom naming scheme

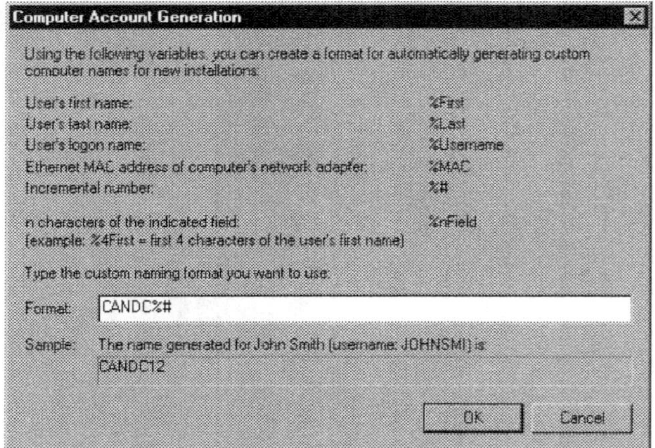

FIGURE 8-17

Accepting the default Active Directory location

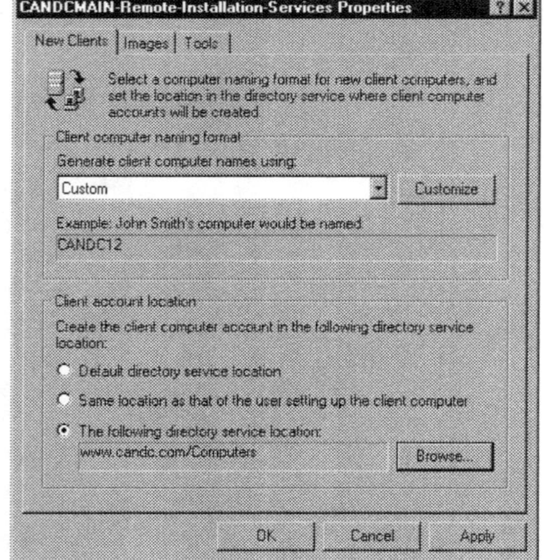

Lab Exercise 8.05

Choose Run from the Start button.

Enter **D:\remoteinstall\admin\i386\rbfg.exe** (where D: is the drive on which RIS is installed). The RBDG opens, as shown here:

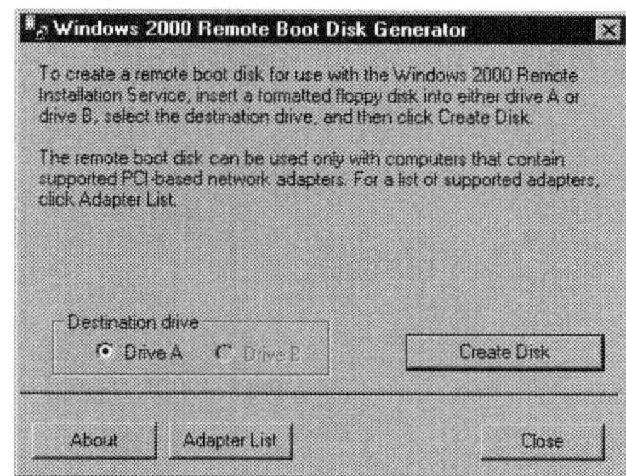

To build a remote boot disk, select Create Disk.

When the operation is complete, click No to stop creating boot disks. Afterward, click Close.

Lab Exercise 8.06

Start Active Directory Users and Computers. Expand the Users folder.

Right-click the right-hand pane, and select New | User. Complete the dialog box as shown:

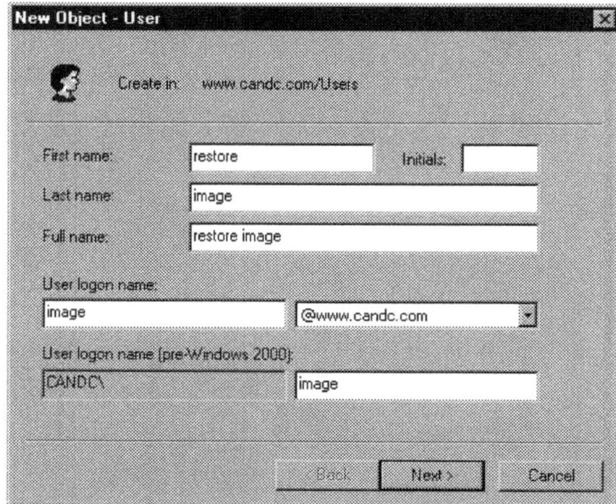

Click Next.

Now, set these password properties:

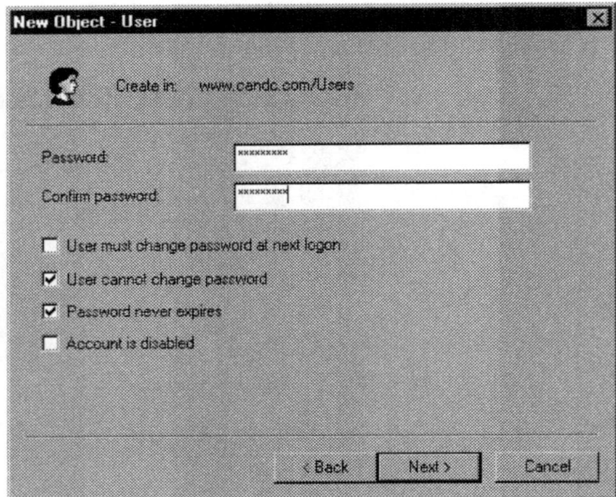

Click Next.

Right-click Users, and select Delegate Control to open the Delegate Control Wizard. Click Next.

Add the image as shown in Figure 8-18. Afterward, click Next.

Set the delegation properties as shown in Figure 8-19, and the permissions as shown in Figure 8-20, clicking Next to move on each time when you are done.

FIGURE 8-18

Adding a user image

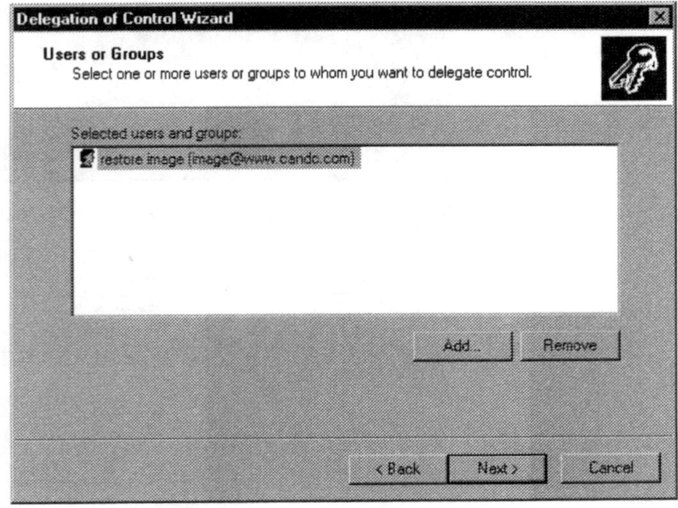

FIGURE 8-19

Specifying Computer Objects as the scope of the delegation

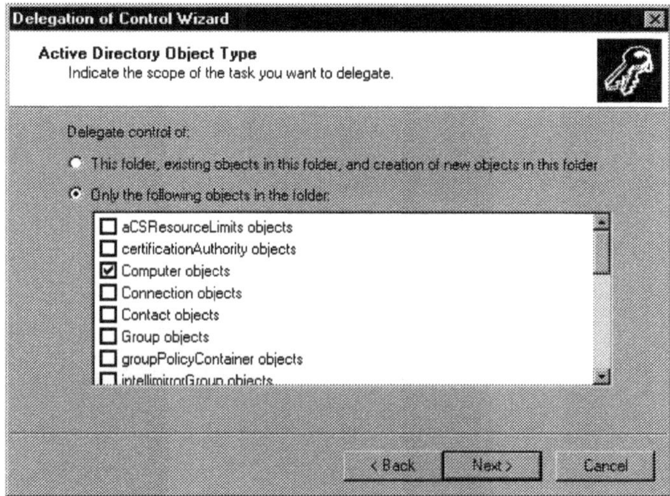

Click Finish to complete the delegation.

Right-click the domain name, and select Delegate Authority.

When the Tasks to Delegate dialog (Figure 8-21) opens, select "Join a computer to the domain." Click Next, and then Finish.

FIGURE 8-20

Specifying the permissions being delegated for specified objects

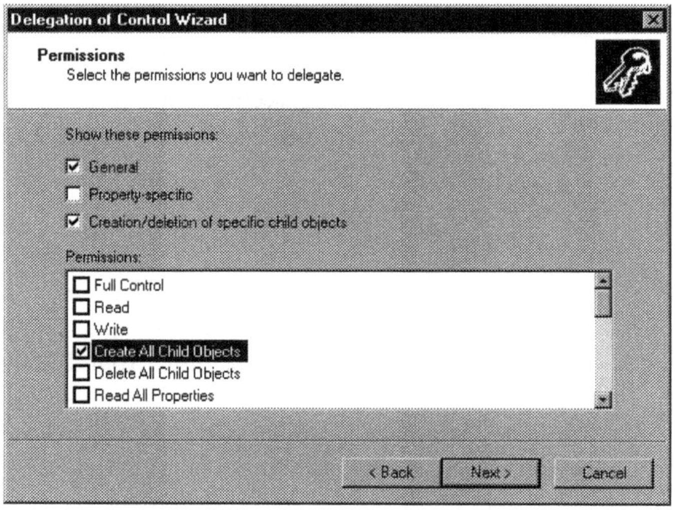

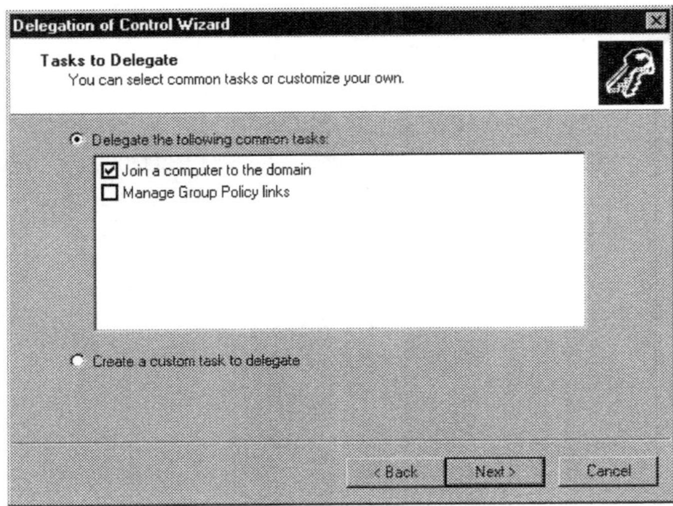

FIGURE 8-21 Specifying the tasks to be delegated

Lab Exercise 8.07

The Windows 2000 Server Resource Kit contains a tool called setupmgr.exe that should ease the management of .sif files.

Start Notepad.

Open **F:\remoteinstall\setup\English\images\win2000.pro\i386**.

Scroll to the [Networking] section (after [Display]). Enter this text:

```
[Components]
freecell = off
solitaire = off
minesweeper = off
pinball = off
```

Save the file in the same folder as nogames.sif. Close Notepad.

Select Start | Programs | Administrative Tools | Active Directory Users and Computers.

Expand the domain controller folder. Right-click CANDCMAIN, and open its properties. Select the Remote Install tab (Figure 8-22).

Select Advanced Settings, and click the Images tab to see the list of available images (Figure 8-23).

Click Add. Choose to associate a new answer file to an existing image, and click Next.

Choose to copy the answer file from an "alternate location," and click Next.

FIGURE 8-22

Properties of the Remote Install Service

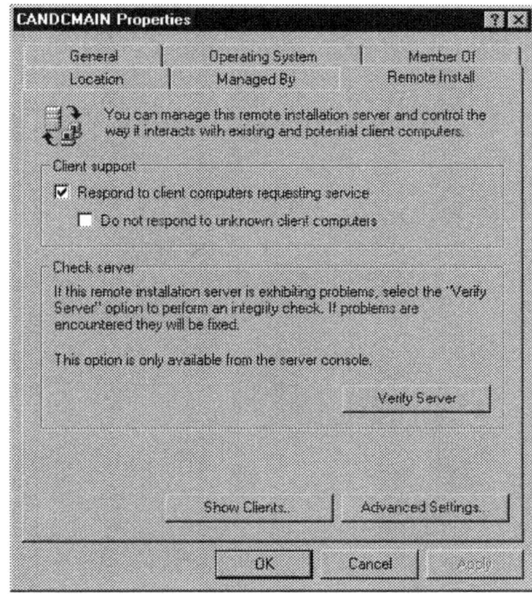

Browse to the location of nogames.sif as shown in Figure 8-24. Select the image to associate, and click Next.

FIGURE 8-23

Opening the list of images

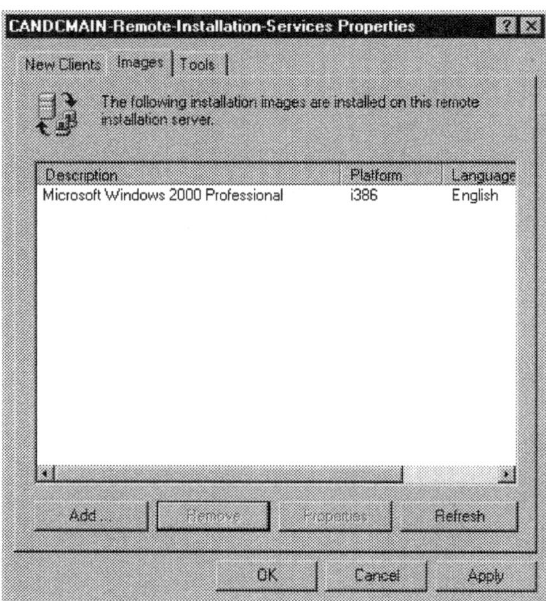

FIGURE 8-24

Specifying the location of the setup information file

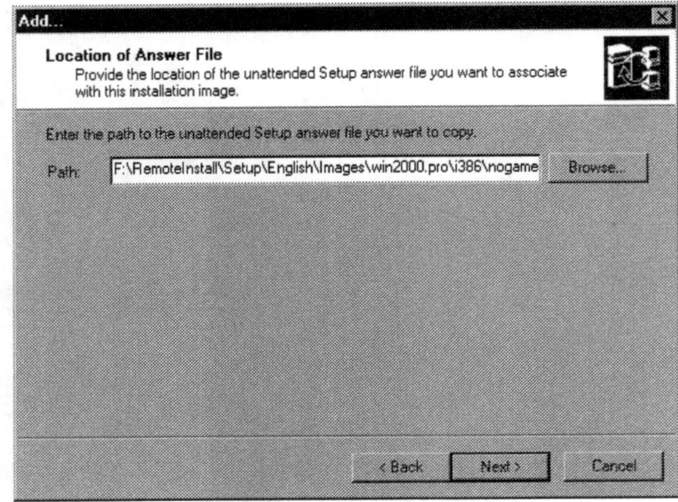

Give the image a relevant title as shown:

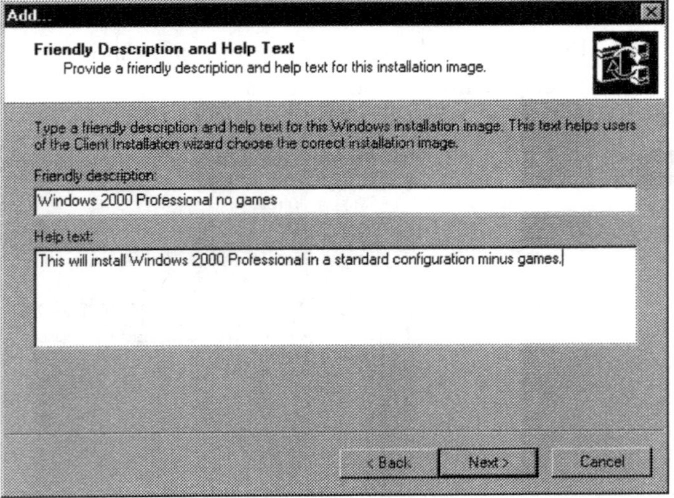

Click Next. When you return to the list of images, select the original image, and select Remove. Click Apply to perform the changes. Afterward, click Close.

Open My Computer, and browse to the location of nogames.sif.

Right-click the file name, and verify that the security permissions are as shown in Figure 8-25.

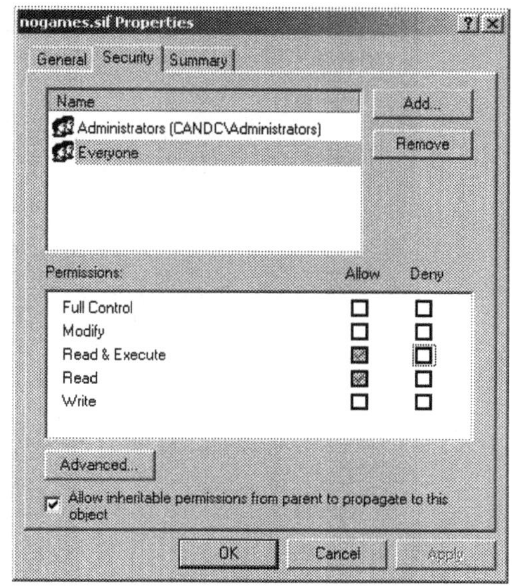

FIGURE 8-25 Verifying the security settings for nogame.sif

Lab Exercise 8.08

Select Start | Programs | Administrative Tools | Active Directory Users and Computers.

Expand the domain controller folder, and right-click CANDCMAIN.

Select the Remote Install tab. Click Verify Server. If all is well, you should see the message shown in Figure 8-26.

Click Finish to restart the RIS server.

Start DHCP by choosing Start | Programs | Administrative Tools | DHCP. Verify that the DHCP is running, and that the scope is active. If possible, run ipconfig on a remote computer to verify that the machine can acquire a lease. Click the Release All button, and then the Renew All button. An IP address should be served.

Start Event Viewer by choosing Start | Programs | Administrative Tools | Event Viewer. Double-click the Information tab for a DHCP server. You will see event properties for the server similar to those shown in Figure 8-27.

Check the other folders for errors on BINSVL, TFTP, DHCP, or DNS. If you find no errors, then RIS should be running well.

FIGURE 8-26

Reviewing a successful verification of remote installation

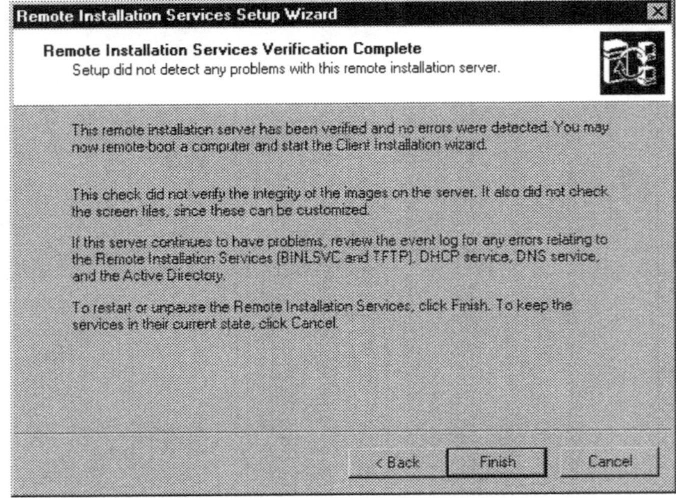

FIGURE 8-27

Viewing event properties for a DHCP server

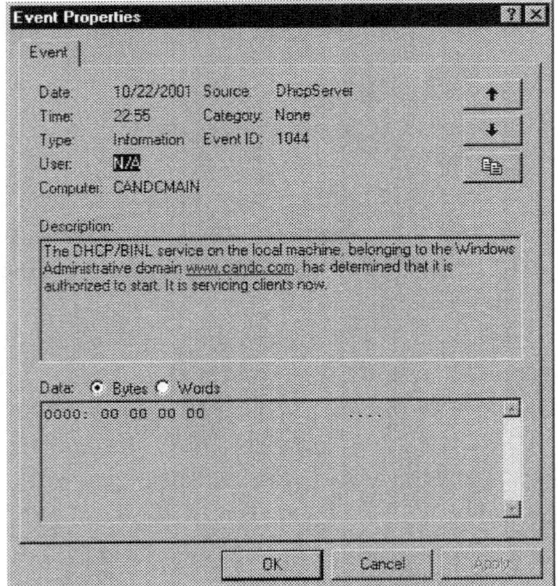

ANSWERS TO LAB ANALYSIS TEST

1. RIS requires a DHCP server so that remote clients can connect. RIS works through the TCP/IP protocol suite. DHCP assigns the IP address to the remote computer. With an IP address, the client can see the RIS server.
2. You might prestage a computer for many reasons. One reason is to avoid giving users the power to create computer accounts. Another is to avoid having rebuilds generate new names in the Active Directory. The down side to prestaging computers is the need to know the GUID for each computer. If you are prestaging several computers, finding out the GUIDs can be tedious.

lab hint ***By default, all user accounts have permission to create 10 computer accounts in a domain!***

3. To identify machines that crash often, try using the MAC address in the computer name. When the computer name is set to %MAC%#, Active Directory creates a new computer icon every time the machine is rebuilt. Computers with higher numbers are the ones that have been rebuilt more often.
4. For you to be able to install RIS, the server must have DHCP, DNS, and Active Directory installed. In addition, the server must have a non-system drive with at least 2GB of available space.
5. Both approaches have advantages. By setting up a dedicated user account, the administrator can remain basically hands-off during the entire rebuild process. The down side is a potential security hole at the image account. On the other hand, by assigning user rights as needed, the administrator can give rebuild ability to people who need it, when they need it. The down side is that the administrator must actually make the switch. The process can be slow if the administrator is busy or hard to find.

ANSWERS TO KEY TERM QUIZ

1. DHCP
2. image, RIPrep
3. GUID
4. answer file
5. PXE

9

Using the Remote Installation Service

LAB EXERCISES

Joanne pulls you into her office for a chat. She has been thinking about the Remote Installation Service (RIS) solution that you implemented. She is concerned that the process leaves a security hole in the organization and that local users will be confused when running the image. She wants some assurances from you that the image can be run only with administrator approval and that the least tech-savvy user can run the image.

You understand her concerns. You tell her that you will apply some permissions to ensure that only administrators and the Image user account can run the image. You will also disable the Image user account so that no unwanted installations are performed. Finally, you will remove choices from the end-user installation screen to reduce confusion.

LAB EXERCISE 9.01

5 Minutes

Setting "Image" as the Allowed User

To increase security in the organization, you plan to set the permissions on the nogames.sif file so that only administrators and the Image user account can read the file. With a dedicated user, the C&C administrators can control who runs the image and when they run it.

Learning Objectives

In this lab, you set permissions on a file. At the end of the lab, you'll be able to:

- Find the nogames.sif file
- Set permissions on a file

Lab Materials and Setup

Setting permissions on a file is a basic network administration task. You need these materials:

- The nogames.sif file created in the Chapter 8
- Administrator account

Getting Down to Business

Here's how you go about finding and adjusting the permissions on a file:

Step 1. Browse or search, and find the file that you associated with the new image.

Step 2. Call up the security screen for the nogames.sif file.

Step 3. Remove Everyone from the list, and add the Image user with "read" and "read and execute" permissions.

LAB EXERCISE 9.02

Setting Install Options

5 Minutes

Joanne is right. Having too many options can scare a user. You want the remote install process to be as painless as possible. Typically, a user who is running an image has had a problem of some sort. Tension is already running high. Making the recovery process more difficult adds to the tension.

Learning Objectives

In this lab, you want to restrict the remote installation choices available to the user. At the end of the lab, you'll be able to do so.

Lab Materials and Setup

Your plan is to restrict access to all but the automatic setup. You need these materials:

- Administrator account
- Group policies configured on the RIS server

Getting Down to Business

You plan to provide one option for the remote installation user. Here are the steps you need:

Step 1. Start Microsoft Management Console (MMC), and open the users.msc file.

If users.msc does not exist, add the Users group policy as instructed in Chapter 6.

Step 2. Under the User settings, set the Remote Installation options to allow automatic installation and to deny all other choices.

Step 3. Save the file, and exit MMC.

LAB EXERCISE 9.03

45 Minutes

Using RIS to Build a Client Machine

After several days, a user has a problem. Mary has a machine that will not boot to Windows. After several troubleshooting steps, she decides that the Windows 2000 software is corrupt and that her computer needs to be rebuilt. She asks you for the install disk and the password for the Image user account.

Learning Objectives

In this lab, you restore the image to a client computer. By the end of the lab, you'll be able to:

- Boot from the network
- Restore the image

Lab Materials and Setup

To build a client computer, you need these materials:

- Client computer
- A network adapter that is PXE (preboot execution environment)–compliant or the remote boot disk generated by Remote Boot Disk Generator (RBFG) and an adapter supported by RBFG.
- The Image user account

Getting Down to Business

You rebuild the computer using RIS and these steps:

lab Warning

If the BIOS has anti-virus capabilities, disable that feature before continuing. The repartitioning and rebuilding will appear to be virus activity, and the anti virus software will respond.

Step 1. Boot the client machine to the network.

Step 2. Follow the on-screen choices, if any.

Step 3. Go to lunch. The install will take some time.

lab Hint

This lab may take less than the indicated time, depending on the number of applications being installed.

LAB EXERCISE 9.04

1 Hour

Using Remote Installation Preparation to Build an Image

Joanne is very happy that RIS worked when needed. Mary did pass on some critiques to Joanne, though. One critique was the number of non-MSI applications that the computer needed, including the anti-virus software and the consulting programs. Installing those after the remote install finished took a considerable time. Joanne would like to know if the process could be speeded up.

You decide to create a new image based on a working client computer. You tell Joanne about Remote Installation Preparation (RIPrep) and the concept of cloning a working computer. Because all of the computers at C&C are of the same type, Joanne tells you to continue.

You must use a clean computer for this process. "Clean" means ensuring that only the applications and data wanted for every computer in the organization are present in the image. Particularly, you want to ensure that no viruses are hiding on the image that you create!

Learning Objectives

In this lab, you run RIPrep to build an image of a client computer. At the end of the lab, you'll be able to:

- Run RIPrep
- Generate a clean image

Lab Materials and Setup

To generate a clean image for C&C, you need these materials:

- A clean client computer with access to the RIS server
- An account with permissions sufficient to log on remotely and modify the RIS images

Getting Down to Business

You will first build a clean computer, and then capture its image on the RIS server. Here's how:

Step 1. Build a clean computer using the Windows 2000 Professional CD or the RIS image.

Step 2. Install the applications wanted on all of the organization's computers.

Including anti-virus software on the image is a good idea.

Step 3. At the client machine, log onto the RIS server as administrator.

Step 4. Using Network Neighborhood, browse to the reminst/admin/i386 folder.

Step 5. Run RIPrep to build the image. Answer all the questions in the wizard.

LAB EXERCISE 9.05

Troubleshooting RIS Installations

10 Minutes

Most administrators have no trouble using RIS. Users are a different story. They tend to skip steps in a series of directions. They also frequently tend to try to fix things themselves—by unplugging media. Those two user problems are quite typical, and you must be prepared for them.

Learning Objectives

In this lab, you see effect and cause for two common RIS-related user problems, and you learn how to resolve those problems. At the end of the lab, you'll be able to:

- Resolve the "press any key to reboot" problem
- Resolve the "no media" error

Lab Materials and Setup

To simulate a user's experience, you need these materials:

- Client computer
- RBFG disk

Getting Down to Business

Two of the most common troubleshooting approaches are:

- Plug in the device
- Read the manual

In the steps that follow, you use those approaches to solve two common user errors.

Step 1. A user with an RBFG disk calls and tells you that his screen says "no media." Apply the approaches listed above to solve the problem.

Step 2. The same user now tells you that his screen says "DHCP, Press any key to reboot." Apply the approaches listed above to solve the problem.

LAB ANALYSIS TEST

The following questions will help you to apply your knowledge in a business setting.

1. One of your users is trying to use RIS to set up his notebook computer—without success. What is the problem, and what is a possible solution?

____

____

____

____

2. What are some of the differences between using the CD image and a RIPrep image?

____

____

____

____

3. What are the minimum system requirements for a client to use RIS?

____

____

____

____

4. A client is having trouble with BINL (boot information negotiation layer). What troubleshooting steps can you perform?

____

____

____

____

5. How does RIPrep reduce disk space requirements for multiple images?

____

____

____

____

KEY TERMS QUIZ

Use the following vocabulary terms to complete the sentences below. Not all of the terms will be used.

- BINL
- DHCP (dynamic host configuration protocol)
- fresh installation
- PC card
- PCI (peripheral component interconnect)
- PXE
- RBFG
- RIPrep
- RIS
- TFTP (trivial file transfer protocol)

1. Newly purchased desktops commonly receive a(n) ____________________ from RIS.
2. The network card in the client computer must be a(n) ____________________- or ____________________-compliant card.
3. The sequence of events on the client computer when starting RIS is ____________________, ____________________, and then ____________________.
4. ____________________ generates an image from a client computer.
5. ____________________ generates a disk for the client computer to use.

LAB WRAP-UP

Congratulations, you have successfully installed a client computer using RIS! That task is performed daily in some organizations. The ability to repair a Windows 2000 installation without spending hours troubleshooting the computer can save organizations millions of dollars. Highly-paid technicians do not need to babysit a rebuild of a computer, nor try to determine what the "problem" with the computer is.

You will find RIS especially useful when your organization purchases several new computers. By having the users run the image for themselves, you are freed from the tedium of babysitting several computers. If that approach is not desirable, then the clients can be configured overnight. When the users arrive at work the next day, their computers are ready to go. Both options make you look like a hero.

LAB SOLUTIONS FOR CHAPTER 9

The sections that follow walk you through the steps to solve the lab exercises. You should avoid looking at these sections unless you are stuck on a particular exercise.

Lab Exercise 9.01

Open My Computer, and browse to the location of nogames.sif. You can find it at **D:\remoteinstall\setup\English\images\win2000.pro\i386**, where D: is the drive on which the remote install is stored.

Right-click the remote install and select Properties.

When the properties dialog opens, click the Security tab.

Select Everyone. Clear the "inherit permissions" check box at the bottom of the form.

Add the Image user, and set the properties as shown in Figure 9-1.

Lab Exercise 9.02

From the Start Button, select Run.

Type **MMC** in the Run box, and click OK.

Open the users.msc file. Browse to the location shown in Figure 9-2.

Double-click the Choice Options icon in the right-hand frame to open the associated properties dialog. Set the properties as shown in Figure 9-3.

FIGURE 9-1 Setting the properties for the Image user

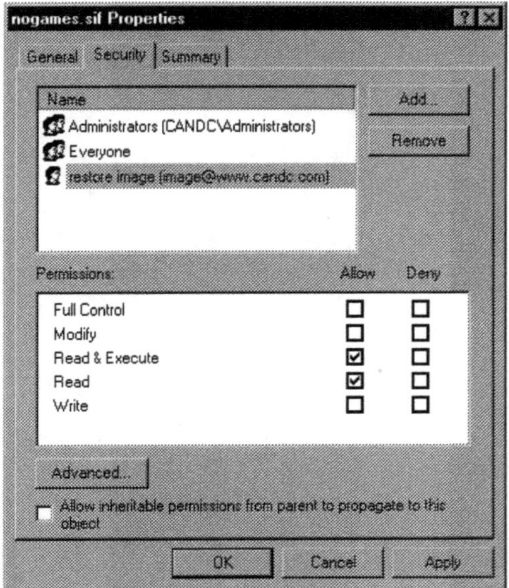

FIGURE 9-2 Browsing to the installation policies

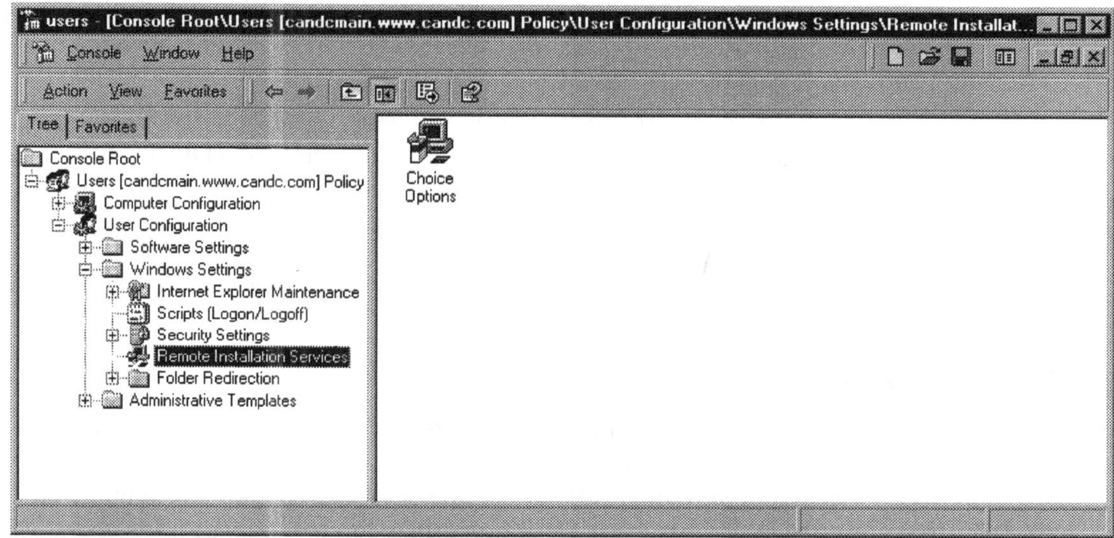

Click Apply, and then OK.
Save the file as users.msc, and close MMC.

FIGURE 9-3

Setting the Choice Options properties for installation

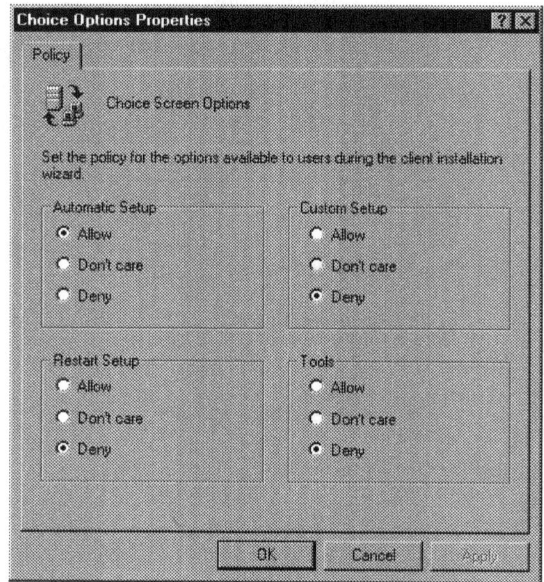

Lab Exercise 9.03

Using the boot disk created in Chapter 8, boot the client machine. When the message indicating a successful boot appears, press F12.

When prompted for the Network Service Boot, press F12.

Press ENTER to bypass the splash screen.

Enter **Image** for the user name, an image password, and **CANDC** for the domain. Press ENTER to accept all defaults, and then take a break. The install will take some time, depending on network traffic and the speed of the client computer.

lab hint

If the image account produces an error, log on as the administrator of the RIS server.

Lab Exercise 9.04

Start with a clean machine. The best method for getting a clean machine is to restore the image as instructed in Lab Exercise 9.03. Once you've reached that point, install all the wanted software packages as suggested by the vendor. Verify that all software and hardware work properly before you proceed further.

Once you are sure that the computer is ready, log on to the machine as the administrator of the RIS server. Open My Network Places from the desktop (Figure 9-4).

Double-click Entire Network, and select Entire Contents.

Double-click Microsoft Windows Network in the right-hand pane. You should see the CANDC domain as shown in Figure 9-5.

FIGURE 9-4

Viewing the contents of My Network Places

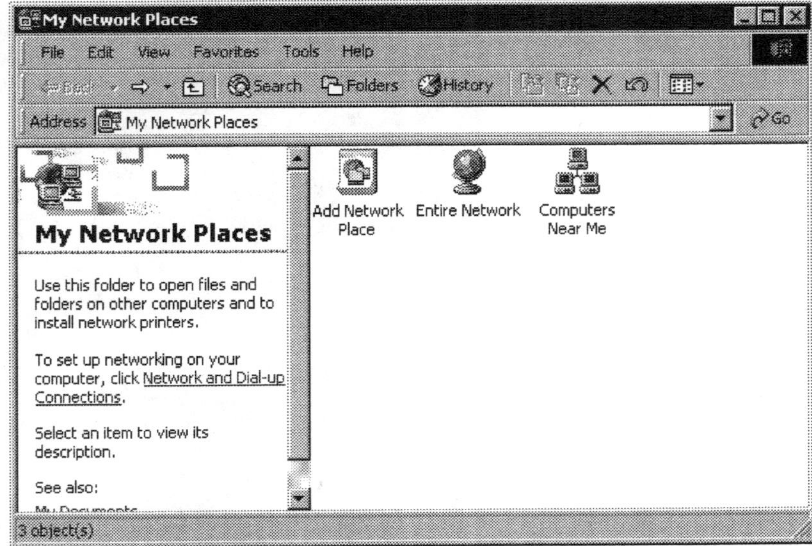

FIGURE 9-5 Viewing the entries in the Microsoft Windows network

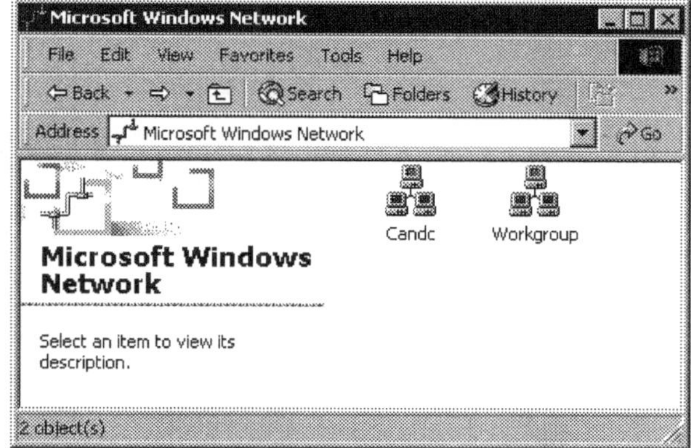

Double-click the CANDC domain to see the CANDCMAIN server. Double-click the server. You may see this prompt:

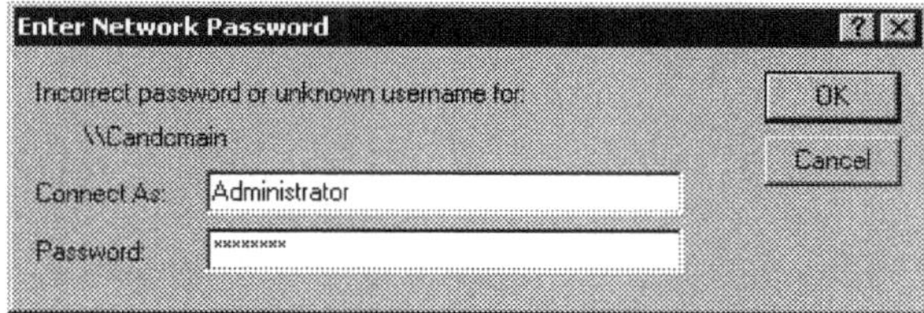

If so, log on as administrator of the RIS server.

Find the reminst share, and double-click it. Open the admin folder, and then i386 folder (Figure 9-6).

Double-click RIPrep to start the Remote Installation Preparation wizard.

Click Next to begin capturing the image of the clean machine with the installed applications. Begin by accepting the default name of the RIS server (Figure 9-7).

FIGURE 9-6 Viewing the contents of the i386 folder

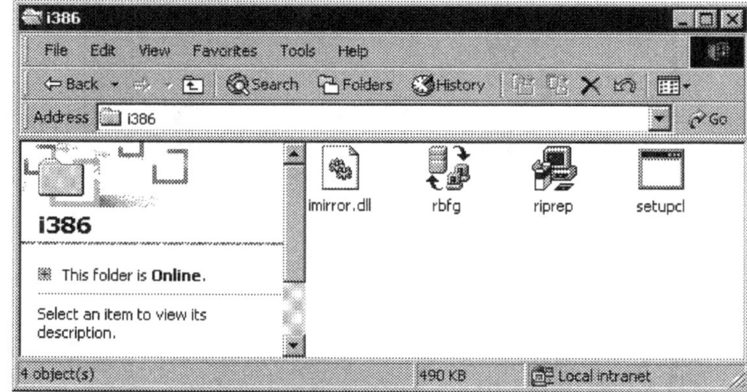

FIGURE 9-7

Specifying the RIS server name

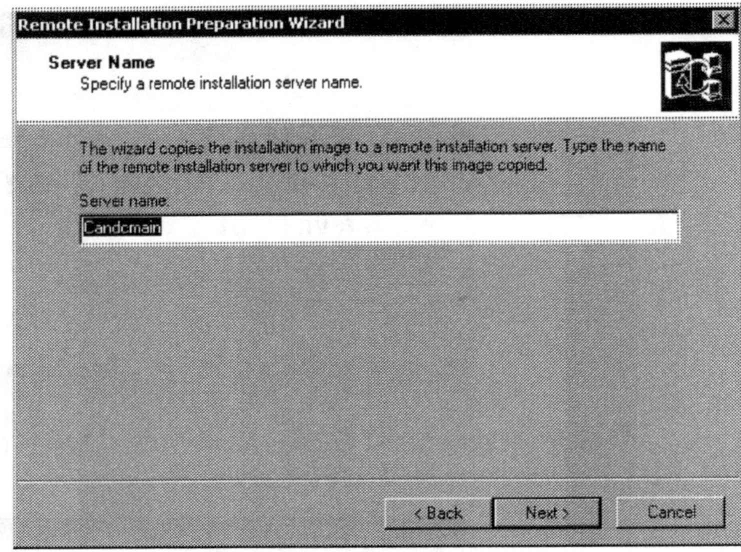

Click Next.
Create a folder called **RIP2000** as shown in Figure 9-8.
Provide a friendly description and help text for the image as shown in Figure 9-9.

FIGURE 9-8

Naming the folder that will hold the image

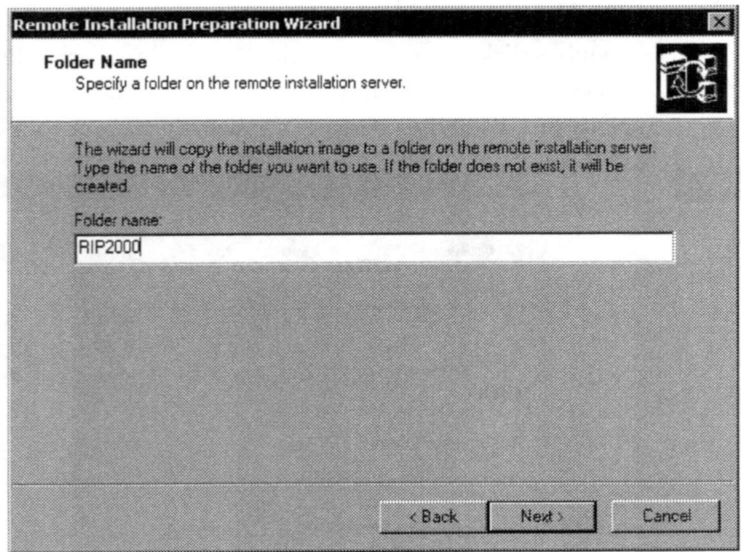

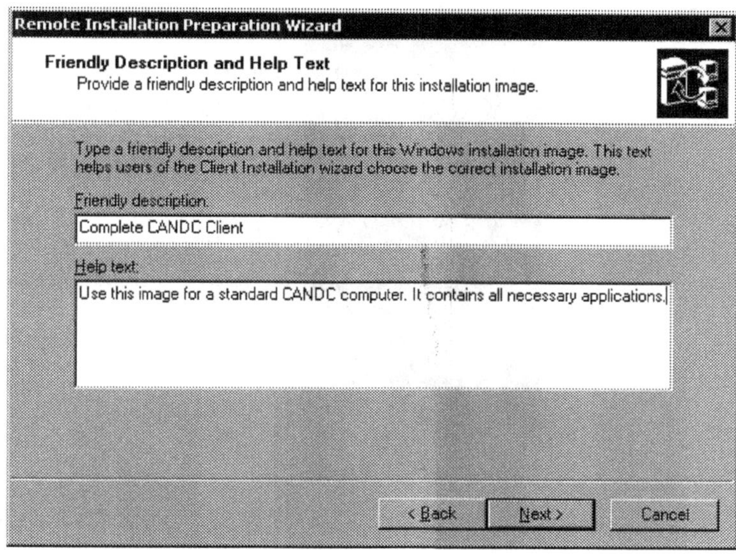

FIGURE 9-9 Entering the friendly description and help text

If so prompted, close any open programs. Then, click Next to review the settings for creation of the image file (Figure 9-10).

Click Next.

Read the messages concerning the image that will be created (Figure 9-11). When you are ready to proceed, click Next.

Remote Installation Preparation Wizard

Review Settings
Verify your settings before you continue.

Before proceeding, review your settings. To change any settings, click Back.

Remote installation server: Candcmain

Folder name: RIP2000

Friendly description:
Complete CANDC Client

Help text:
Use this image for a standard CANDC computer. It contains all necessary applications.

< Back Next > Cancel

FIGURE 9-10 Reviewing the settings before proceeding to create the image

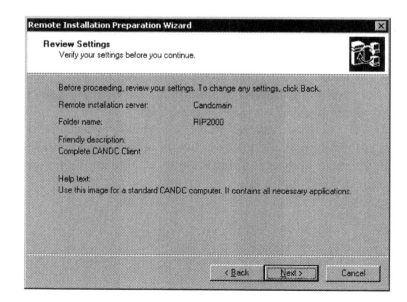

FIGURE 9-11

Taking the final step in creating the image

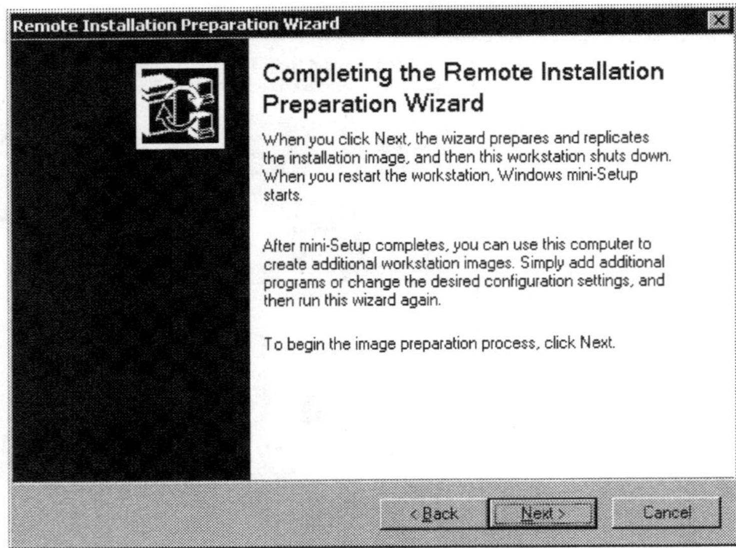

The wizard copies several files to the server, and then shuts the workstation down.

After the workstation reboots, you are prompted to configure the computer. Enter the appropriate information. If in doubt, accept the defaults. When asked for an account so that you can join the computer to the domain, enter **Image** or **Administrator**, and the appropriate password. Finish the setup, and reboot the computer.

Lab Exercise 9.05

The most common hardware problem is a device that is improperly plugged in (or not plugged in at all). In the present case, you should verify that the network interface card (NIC) is plugged into the Ethernet cable. You will find that it is not, and plugging it in solves the problem.

In the second case, the user is not following the directions. When the disk boots, he is not pressing F12 in time, and the network process is failing to start properly. Have the user reboot and press F12 *after* the computer verifies a successful boot from disk.

ANSWERS TO LAB ANALYSIS TEST

1. Notebook computers typically use PC cards, which are not supported under RIS. One solution is to dock the notebook. Many docking stations have built-in PCI network cards that may be supported under RIS. If docking is not an option, then the notebook will need to be built manually or with a third-party imaging tool.

2. CD-based images are only basic installs of Windows 2000. They are best used for new installations or when configurations vary among the client computers. No configuration is required on the client end. RIPrep images can contain a complete PC. "Complete" means that all wanted applications are included. Such images can be restored only to a machine with precisely the same hardware as on the machine used to build the image. For some client configurations, changing the names and addresses may be necessary.

3. The minimum system requirements for the client machine are these: 166 MHz Pentium processor, 32MB RAM (64MB recommended), 800MB hard disk, and either a PCI- or PXE-compliant network adapter.

4. BINL can fail for many reasons. The most common reason is that the computer is not connected to the network. Check the local computer and all hubs to ensure that they are properly connected. Second, ensure that the RIS server is running BINL. Third, ensure that RIS and BINL are authorized in Active Directory. Do any other computers have the same problem? If not, then check that the local computer's network card is compliant. Ensure that routers are not blocking BootP broadcasts. Finally, check the RIS server system logs for DHCP, BINL, or other errors.

5. Unlike third-party imaging software, RIPrep does not keep duplicate copies of installation files. Thus, if your RIS server has four Windows 2000 images, only one copy of the Windows 2000 files is kept. The other images contain pointers to the necessary files.

ANSWERS TO KEY TERM QUIZ

1. fresh installation
2. PCI, PXE
3. DHCP, BINL, TFTP
4. RIPrep
5. RBFG

MCSE

MICROSOFT CERTIFIED SYSTEMS ENGINEER

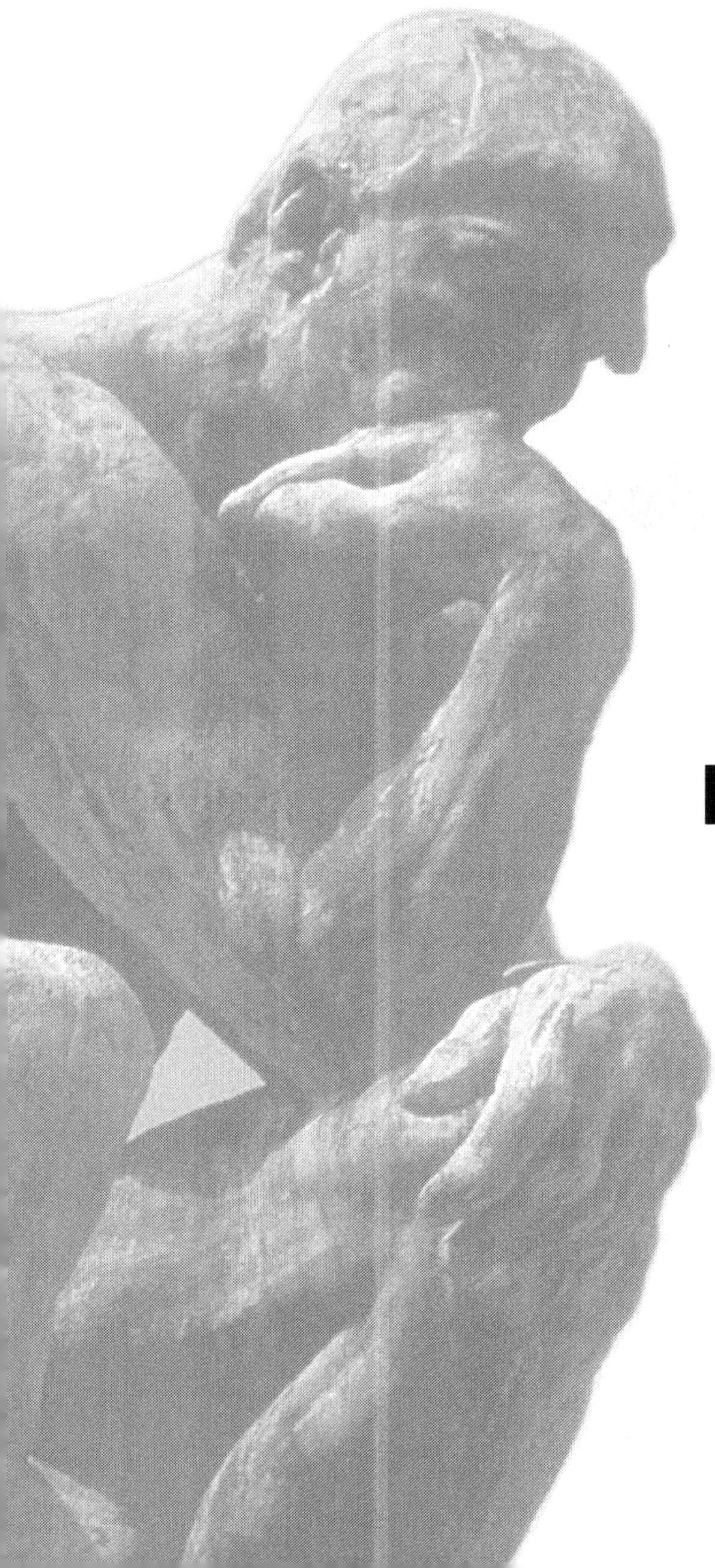

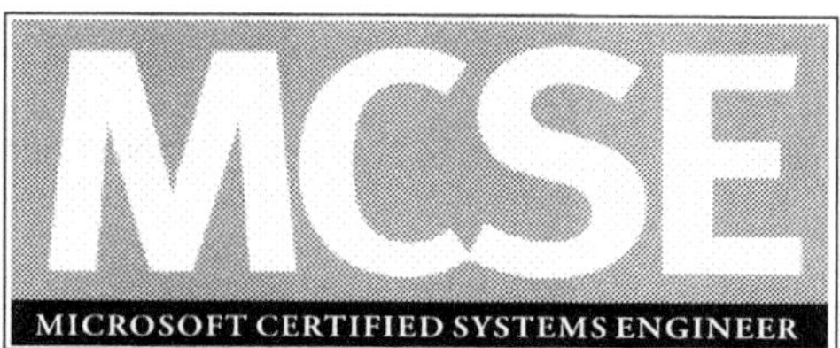

10

Managing Active Directory Objects

LAB EXERCISES

The Active Directory is up and running on C&C's servers. Unfortunately, your job is not complete. Like all network services, Active Directory needs occasional maintenance. Over time, the C&C organization will change and adjustments will be required in the Active Directory setup. Users will come and go. Performance may degrade. Those scenarios all call for Active Directory maintenance. Joanne would like you to perform all of the maintenance tasks.

LAB EXERCISE 10.01

10 Minutes

Removing the Library Site

Your first task is to remove a site from the Active Directory controller. Owing to security concerns and low usage, C&C will no longer host computers in the local library. Patrons will need to stop at their local C&C branch. Joanne would like you to remove the Library site and to move the server to the Main site.

Learning Objectives

In this lab, you learn how to rearrange Active Directory. At the end of the lab, you'll be able to:

- Move an Active Directory object from one site to another
- Remove a site from Active Directory

Lab Materials and Setup

Rearranging the directory is a common activity. You need these materials:

- Administrator password
- At least one server object in the Library site

Getting Down to Business

Here's what you need to do to remove the library site and reposition the server:

Step 1. Start Active Directory Sites and Services.

Step 2. Expand to see both the Library site and the Main site.

Step 3. Move the Library server object from the Library site to the Main site.

Step 4. Move any other objects in Library from there to Main.

Step 5. Remove the Library site.

LAB EXERCISE 10.02

Publishing a Folder

15 Minutes

Joanne needs to give her users access to standard letter templates. Management is concerned that local users not draft their own letters. Templates are provided to ensure that outside correspondence is handled in accordance with C&C's rules and mission. Joanne asks you if Active Directory can handle the requirement.

You decide to publish a shared folder in Active Directory for easy access.

Learning Objectives

This lab shows you how data sharing is simplified by publishing a folder in Active Directory. At the end of the lab, you'll be able to:

- Create a folder in Windows 2000
- Set the rights on the folder
- Share the folder
- Publish the folder in Active Directory

Lab Materials and Setup

Sharing a folder is a common task on a network server. To set up the shared folder, you need administrative access to the server.

Getting Down to Business

You will share and publish a folder in Active Directory. Here's how:

Step 1. On an NTFS drive, create a folder called **Letter Templates**.

Step 2. Share the folder. Allow Everyone to read the folder, and Administrators to have full control.

Step 3. Open Active Directory Users and Computers.

Step 4. Add the new folder to the Main site.

LAB EXERCISE 10.03

Publishing a Printer

20 Minutes

The users are pleased with the simplicity of having letter templates in a folder accessible through the directory. That approach is much simpler than trying to remember the UNC (uniform naming convention) path to the folder.

A group of users have asked that printers be shared through Active Directory as well. They would like the simplicity of finding the printers in the directory, rather than in Network Places. Joanne asks you to show her how to share the main printer; she will then share the other printers in the organization.

You tell her that publishing a printer is much easier than publishing a folder. The printer, when shared, is automatically published in Active Directory.

Learning Objectives

Sharing a printer is another typical network task. At the end of the lab, you'll be able to:

- Share a printer
- Apply rights to the printer

Lab Materials and Setup

To share a printer, you need these materials:

- A printer attached to a Windows 2000 Server
- Administrator account
- Drivers for the printer

Getting Down to Business

To attach a printer to the Windows 2000 server and then share it, use these steps:

Step 1. Install the printer as per the manufacturer's directions.

Step 2. Share the printer, giving the right to print to Everyone.

LAB EXERCISE 10.04

Creating a User Group and Users

15 Minutes

Next week, C&C is going to host several trainers in the facility. The local users are going to learn how to use the newest Office suite and several other applications. The trainers will need access to the system. This particular group of trainers returns every month to introduce other topics to the staff. Joanne would like the trainers to have accounts on the C&C servers, but she wants to be able to turn those accounts off when the trainers leave.

Training is a critical issue in every organization. Security is also important. You decide to create a security group called Trainers. By placing the trainers in that group, you can turn the group off and on as necessary and apply the appropriate rights to each user.

Learning Objectives

Groups are a logical method of organizing users. At the end of the lab, you'll be able to:

- Create a security group
- Create a user
- Add users to a group

Lab Materials and Setup

To create a group you need to be logged on as administrator.

Getting Down to Business

Use these steps to create a security group and several user accounts:

Step 1. Start Active Directory Users and Computers.

Step 2. Under Users, create a group called **Trainers**.

Step 3. Create accounts for these trainers: Eric Donofrio, Jeff Friend, Jeff Hunger, and Zach Wright. Set the password to be changed at next logon. Use the conventional "first letter of first name with full last name" as the logon name (for example, edonofrio).

Step 4. Add the new users to the group.

LAB EXERCISE 10.05

Writing a User Creation Script

40 Minutes

Joanne realizes that you are extremely busy. She would like to remove some of the burden of maintaining Active Directory. Joanne offers to have her assistant Trina create all new users. The task is fairly simple, but time-consuming.

Rather than train the assistant to start Active Directory, you decide to write a script to automate the process. With a script, Trina will be able to create a user while avoiding any potential for accidental damage to other parts of Active Directory.

Learning Objectives

In this lab, you use Visual Basic script (VBScript) to write a script on the Windows scripting host (WSH). At the end of the lab, you'll be able to:

- Create a VBScript
- Execute a script

Lab Materials and Setup

Using scripts to automate processes is a common response to the requirement to keep tasks simple. You need these materials:

- Most current WSH
- A text editor
- Administrator access to the Windows 2000 Server

You can find the most current copy of WSH at msdn.microsoft.com/scripting.

Getting Down to Business

This lab uses a script from the text that you will modify.

See "Scripting the Creation of Accounts" in the study guide for the original script.

Step 1. Create a text file called **builduser.vbs**.

Step 2. Create string variables at the top of the script for last name, first name, user name, client name, and password.

Step 3. Using the InputBox function, ask for and get the last name, first name, and password. For example:

```
firstname = InputBox("What is the user's First Name?")
```

Step 4. Using the string functions left and &, build the user name. The user name should include the first letter of the first name and the full last name. For example, Lee Cottrell's user name would be lcottrell.

Step 5. Write the first three sections of the script as presented in the textbook. Stop at the optional steps. Two lines need to be changed. The line that builds the organizational unit (OU) and the line that creates the user are wrong. Here is the correct code:

```
Set ou = GetObject("LDAP://candc")
temp = "CN=" & uname & ",CN=Users"
Set usr = ou.Create("user", temp)
```

Step 6. Write the last section of the script as presented in the textbook.

Step 7. Test the script.

LAB EXERCISE 10.06

15 Minutes

Monitoring the Performance of Active Directory

Once again, Joanne is concerned with the health of the network. She would like to monitor the performance of the servers. She would also like to log the DNS activity. When she started the performance monitor, the sheer number of counters overwhelmed her. She would like you to set up a performance monitor with the appropriate counters.

Learning Objectives

In this lab, you configure the performance program to watch the network. At the end of the lab, you'll be able to:

- Set counters to be monitored
- Set an alert

Lab Materials and Setup

To monitor the network you need an administrator account.

Getting Down to Business

Monitoring a server is an important but often overlooked task. Use these steps to set up a useful selection of counters.

Step 1. Start Performance from the Start button.

Step 2. Add counters to the performance monitor. If in doubt about making selections, choose the default counters for each object.

Step 3. Save the screen.

Step 4. Build an alert that sends a message to Joanne's computer.

LAB ANALYSIS TEST

The following questions will help you to apply your knowledge in a business setting.

1. Other than removing old sites, what scenarios may require objects in Active Directory to be moved?

2. You shared the letters folder with read-only access. What is a good scenario for a network share that users can write to?

3. How could the user creation script be improved?

4. Logging events is a good way to see what is happening in your network. What are some potential drawbacks to logging?

5. You placed the trainers in a group. What advantages does this bring to the security setup?

KEY TERMS QUIZ

Use the following vocabulary terms to complete the sentences below. Not all of the terms will be used.

alert

counter

Dim

folder

InputBox

log

move

MoveTree

MsgBox

printer

1. The ______________________ object is automatically published when created and shared.
2. The ______________________ function allows the user to type data into a program.
3. The ______________________ statement creates a variable in VBScript.
4. When the performance monitor detects a counter that is too high, it can send a(n) ______________________ to another computer.
5. Rather than delete and recreate an Active Directory object, the administrator should ______________________ the object.

LAB WRAP-UP

Congratulations! You have helped Joanne to monitor, maintain, and manage the C&C Active Directory structure. You removed an obsolete site, published shared objects, wrote a script, and set up a performance monitor. All of those tasks are quite common in the workplace.

The next chapter continues the management process by presenting the methods for handling replication. The knowledge gained in the current chapter and the next will combine to give you the ability to manage any Active Directory structure.

LAB SOLUTIONS FOR CHAPTER 10

The sections that follow walk you through the steps to solve the lab exercises. You should avoid looking at these sections unless you are stuck on a particular exercise.

Lab Exercise 10.01

Start Active Directory Sites and Services from the Start button.

Expand the Library Site to see the CANDCLIBRARY server object.

Right-click the server and select Move to see the Move Server dialog:

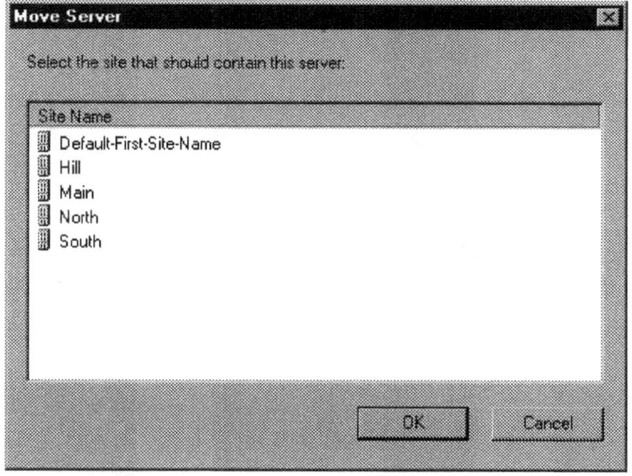

Select Main, and click OK.

Right-click Library, and select Delete. Respond Yes or OK to any message boxes that open.

To verify the move, expand Main, and then Servers. Your screen should look like Figure 10-1.

Close Active Directory Sites and Services.

Lab Exercise 10.02

Open My Computer, and browse to the location where you want to store the templates folder.

Create the folder, and title it **Letter Templates**.

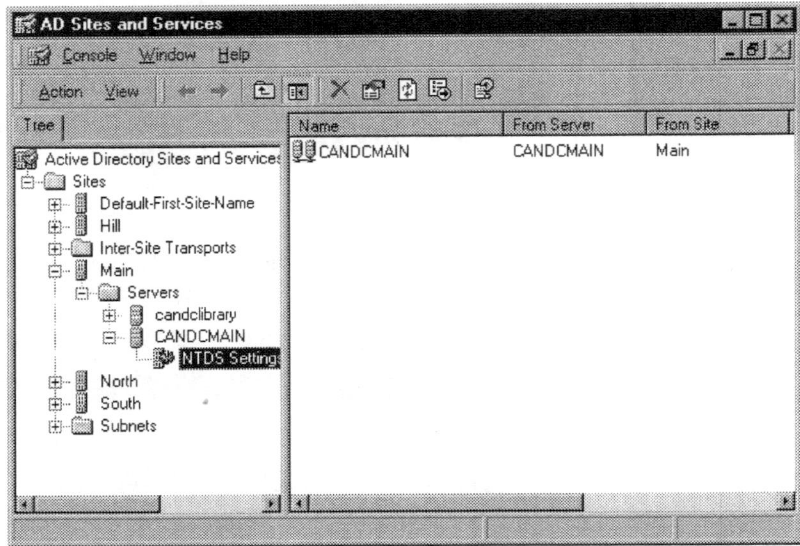

FIGURE 10-1 Verifying that the Library organizational unit is gone

Right-click Letter Templates, and select Properties. In the properties dialog, click the Sharing tab. Set the properties as shown in Figure 10-2.

Select Permissions, and set the rights for Everyone as shown in Figure 10-3.

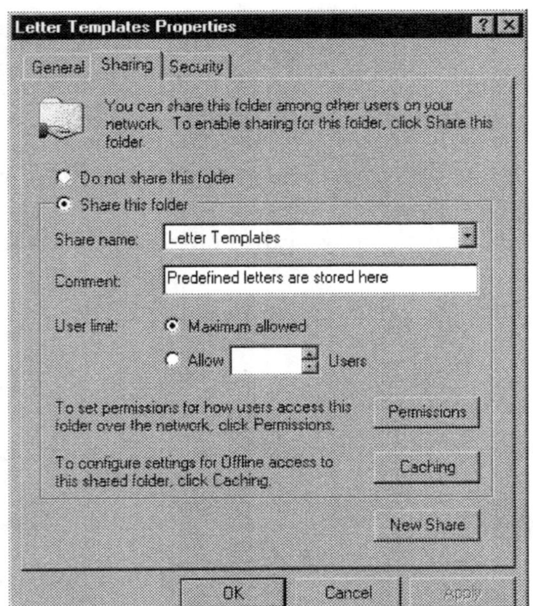

FIGURE 10-2 Setting the sharing properties for the new folder

FIGURE 10-3

Setting the folder permissions for Everyone

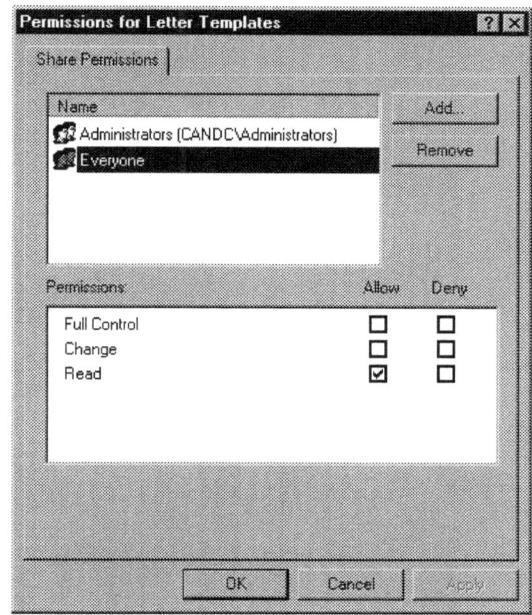

Click Add, and add Administrators. Give Administrators full control over the folder. Click OK to leave the permissions screen.

Click the Security tab. Clear the "Allow inheritable permissions" check box and set the permissions for Everyone as shown in Figure 10-4.

Add Administrators, and give them full control over the folder.

Start Active Directory Users and Computers.

Right-click the domain object in the left-hand pane, and select New | Shared Folder.

Configure the folder as shown in Figure 10-5 by providing the Active Directory name of the folder and the UNC to the folder.

Click OK to return to the Users and Computers screen.

Right-click the Letter Templates object, and select Properties.

When the properties dialog opens, describe the folder as "Letter templates for external correspondence."

Click Keywords and configure the folder as shown in Figure 10-6.

lab hint

The keywords allow for simpler searching in Active Directory.

FIGURE 10-4

Establishing the security settings for Everyone

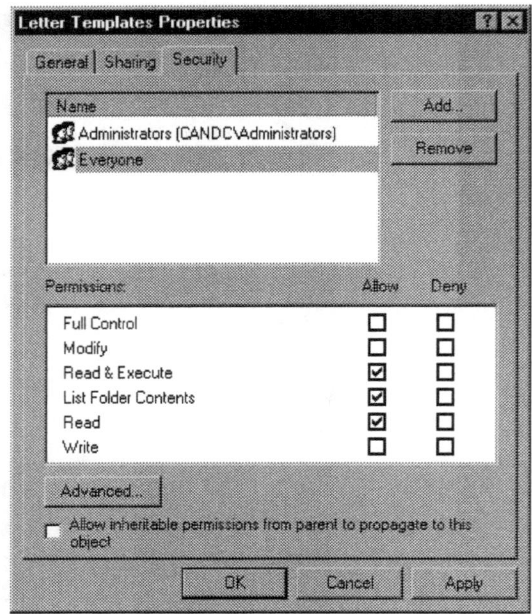

FIGURE 10-5

Setting the properties of a new shared folder

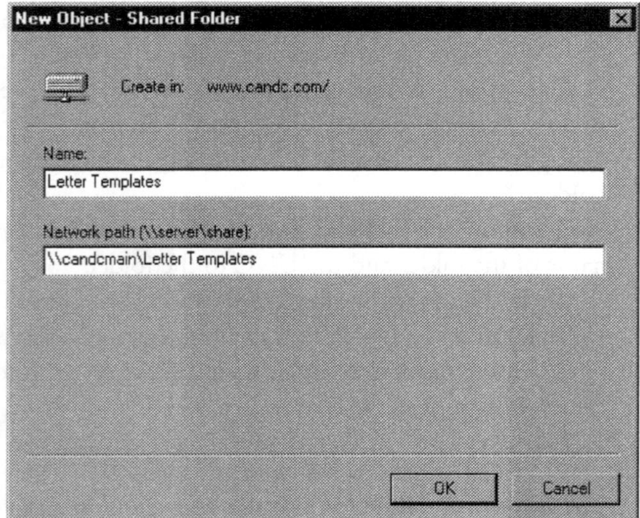

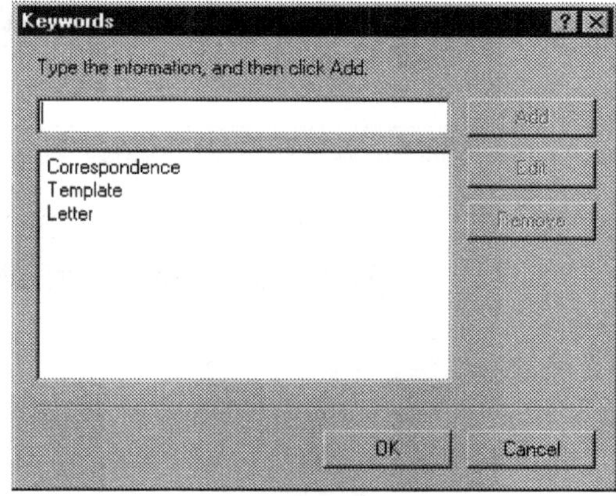

FIGURE 10-6 Adding keywords to the Letter Templates folder

Lab Exercise 10.03

Get the newest Windows 2000 drivers for your printer.

Select Start | Settings | Printers. Double-click Add New Printer. Click Next to begin using the Add Printer Wizard (Figure 10-7).

Clear the "Automatically detect printer" check box, and click Next.

At the next screen (Figure 10-8), select the appropriate port.

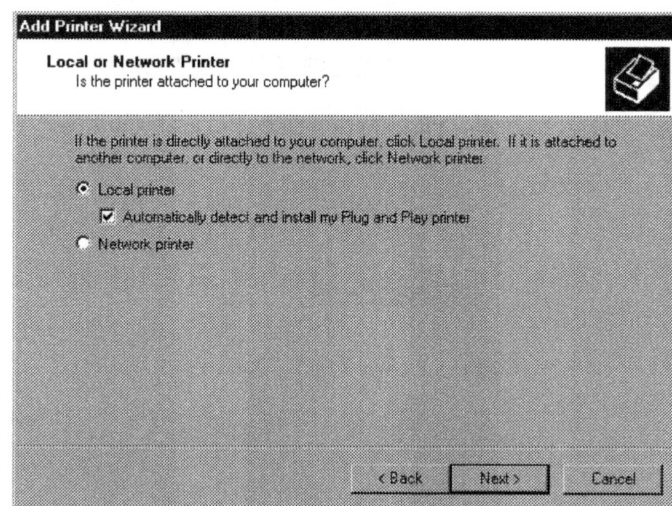

FIGURE 10-7 Specifying the location (local or network) of a printer

FIGURE 10-8

Choosing the printer port

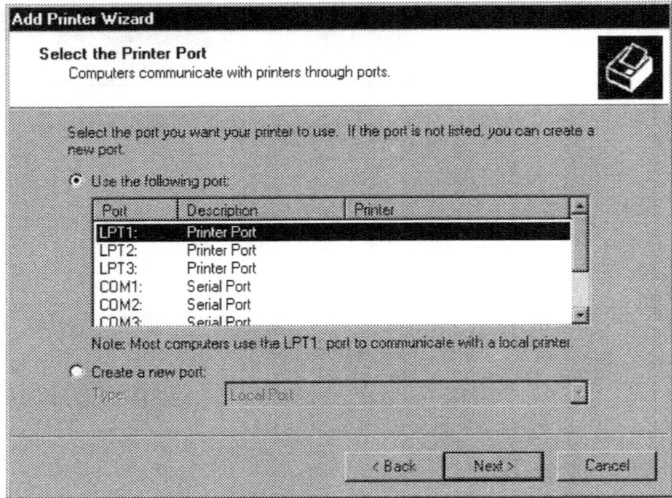

Click Next.

At the printer selection screen, select Have Disk. In the new dialog box that opens, browse to the location of the printer driver. Click OK until you reach the screen for choosing the printer model (Figure 10-9).

Select the appropriate printer model (you may see more than one), and click Next.

Name the printer as shown in Figure 10-10. Click Next.

FIGURE 10-9

Choosing the printer model

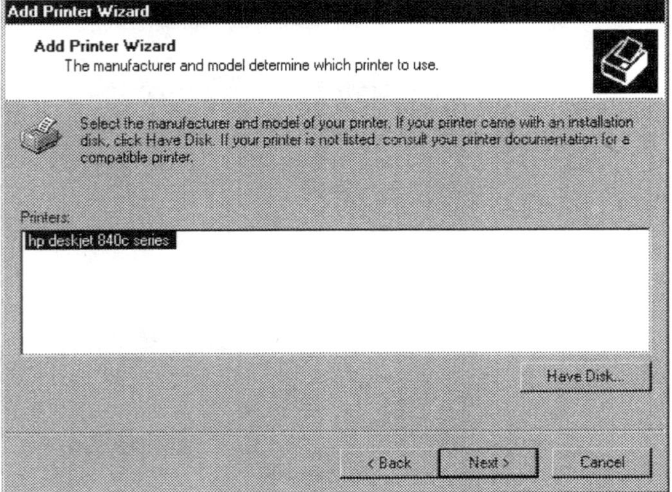

FIGURE 10-10

Giving the printer a name

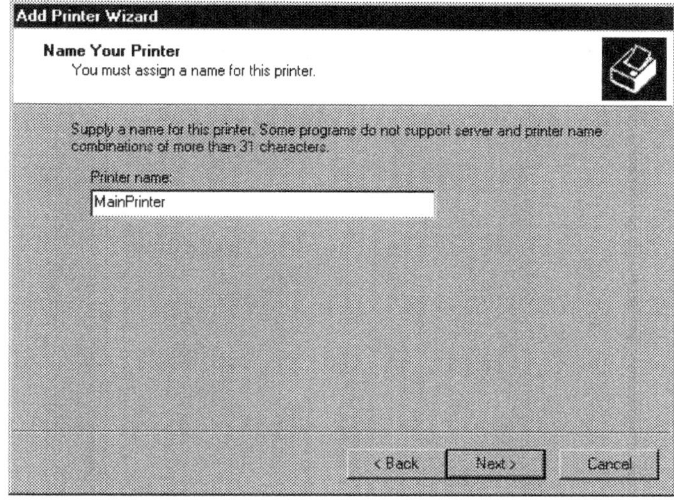

Share the printer as shown in Figure 10-11. Click Next. Print a test page, and then finish the installation.

FIGURE 10-11

Sharing the printer

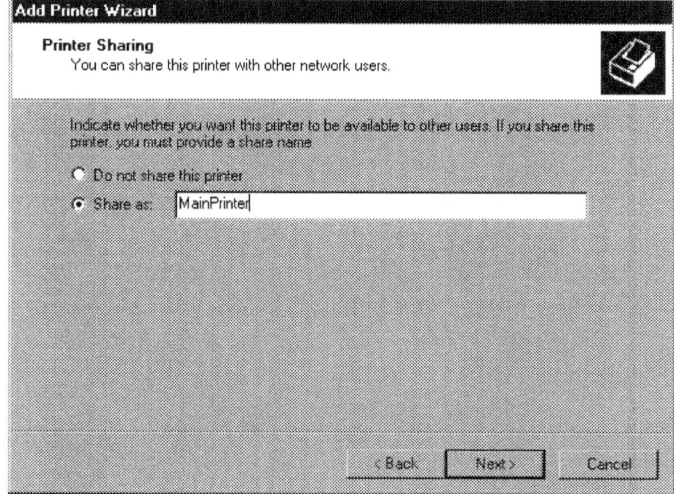

To verify that the printer is installed and shared, start Active Directory Users and Computers from the Start button, and conduct a search for the printer. Select Action | Find, and, as demonstrated here, select Printers from the drop-down box:

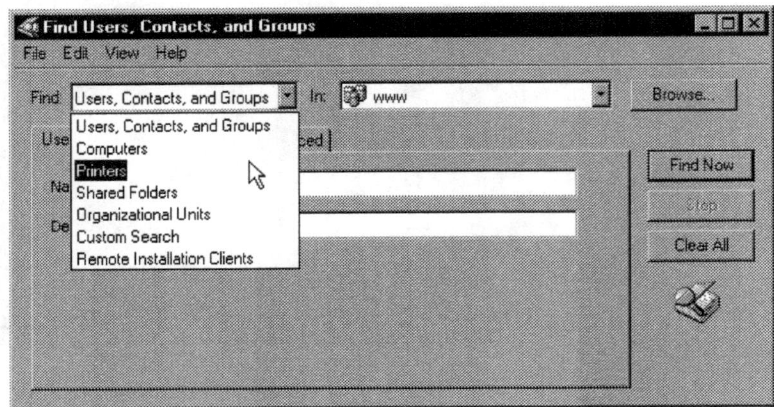

Select Find Now, and you should see the printer.

Lab Exercise 10.04

Start Active Directory Users and Computers.

Expand the Users folder. Right-click Users, and select New | Group.

Create the Trainers group as shown in Figure 10-12.

Right-click Trainers, and create user accounts for Eric Donofrio, Jeff Friend, Jeff Hunger, and Zach Wright. Figure 10-13 shows the first step for **edonofrio**.

Click Next. On the subsequent screen (Figure 10-14), set an initial password of **secret** for the user, and require the user change the password at first logon.

Figure 10-15 shows the final (review) step in creating edonofrio. If you are happy with the information presented about the new account, complete the process by clicking Finish.

Repeat the process for the other users.

Call up the properties for Trainers. Select members for that group by clicking Add, and then adding the new users as shown in Figure 10-16.

Click OK until you return to Users and Computers.

FIGURE 10-12

Adding a new group called Trainers

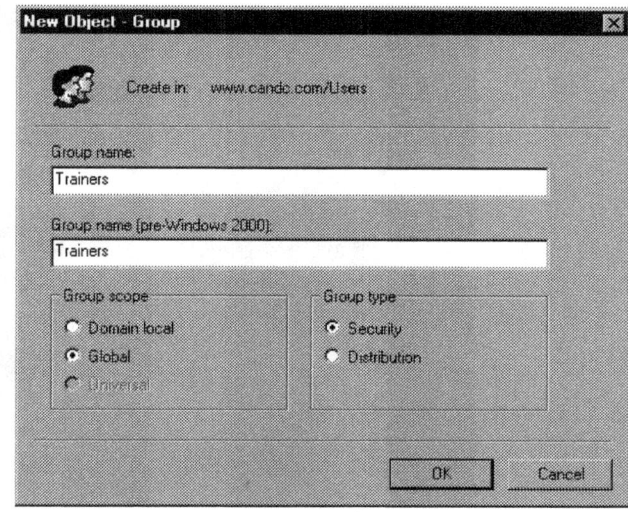

FIGURE 10-13

Creating user edonofrio (Eric Donofrio)

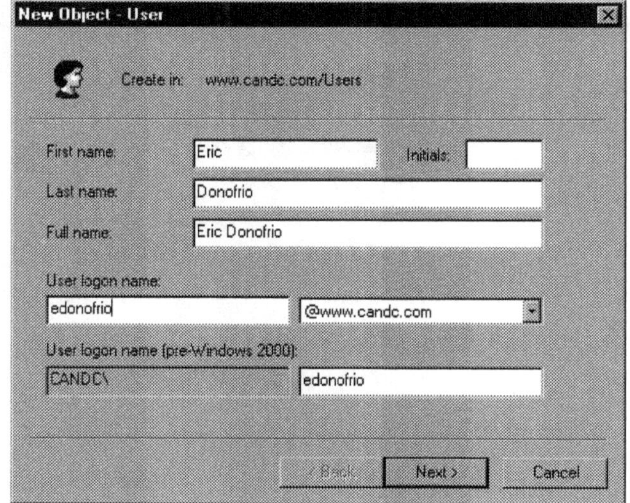

FIGURE 10-14

Setting the password for user edonofrio (Eric Donofrio)

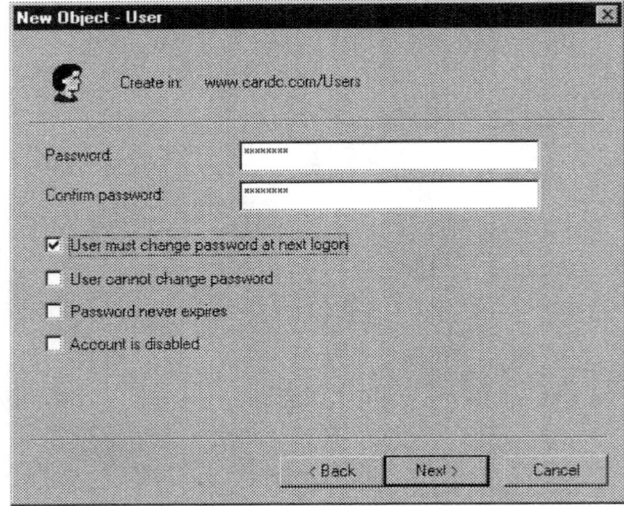

FIGURE 10-15

Reviewing the summary for user edonofrio (Eric Donofrio)

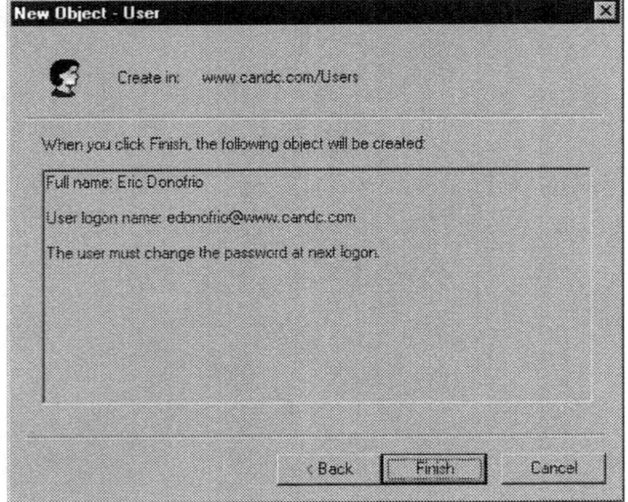

FIGURE 10-16

Adding members to the Trainers group

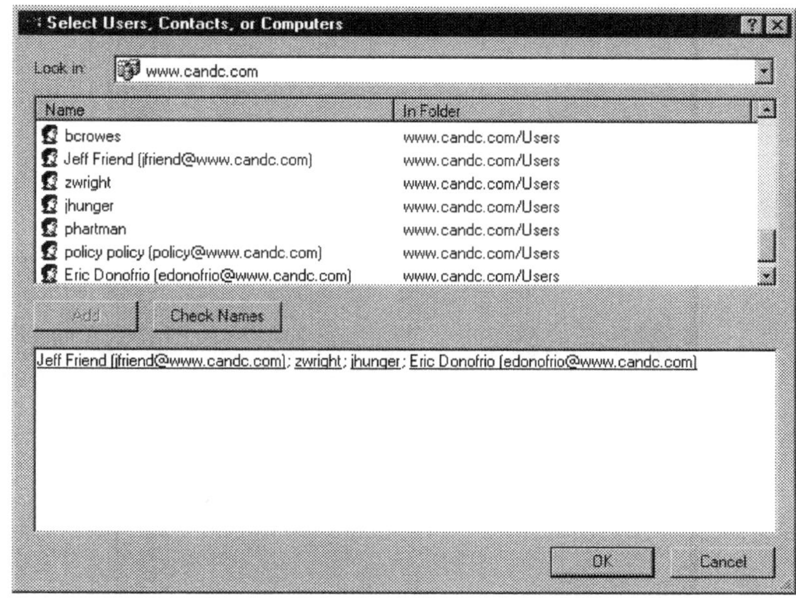

Lab Exercise 10.05

Download and install the latest version of WSH from msdn.microsoft.com.

Start Notepad, and type this script:

```
   'Creates an account based on user input
Dim fname, lname, uname, temp, usr, ou
   'Gets the data
fname = InputBox("Please enter the employee's first name","C and C Domain")
temp = "Please enter " & fname & "'s last name"
lname = InputBox(temp,"C and C Domain")
   'Removes any spaces from beginning or end of string
fname = trim(fname)
lname = trim(lname)
   'Builds the account
uname = Left(fname,1) & lname
uname = lcase(uname)
Set ou = GetObject("LDAP://candc")
temp = "CN=" & uname & ",CN=Users"
Set usr = ou.Create("user", temp)
usr.put "samAccountName", uname
usr.SetInfo
usr.AccountDisabled = "False"
usr.SetPassword "secret"
usr.setinfo
msgbox uname & " is created",,"C and C Domain"
```

Save the script as **createuser.vbs** on the desktop. To test the script, execute it.

More information about scripts can be found at Clarence Washington's scripting site, cwashington.netreach.net.

Lab Exercise 10.06

From the Start button, select Programs | Administrative Tools | Performance.

On the toolbar, click the button labeled with the "+." Set the counters as shown:

Object	Counter	Instance
DNS	Total Query Received	—
FileReplicaConn	Packets Sent in Bytes	—
Memory	Pages/sec	—
NTDS	DRA Inbound Properties Total/Sec	—
NTDS	DRA Outbound Properties Total/Sec	—
NTDS	DS % Searches from LDAP	—
NTDS	DS Directory reads/sec	—
Paging File	% Usage	Total
Server	Bytes Total/sec	—
System	File Data Operations/Sec	—

Most of the counters in this table are the default choices provided by Microsoft.

For example, Figure 10-17 shows the process of adding the DNS counter for Total Query Received.

Figure 10-18 shows the total percentage usage for the paging file.

Figure 10-19 shows the performance monitor in action. The system is fairly inactive, except for the file data counter (some MP3 files were playing on a CD drive).

Right-click the graph area and save the contents as **monitor.htm**.

Expand Performance Logs and Alerts in the left-hand pane. Right-click Alerts, and select New Alert From.

FIGURE 10-17

Setting a performance counter

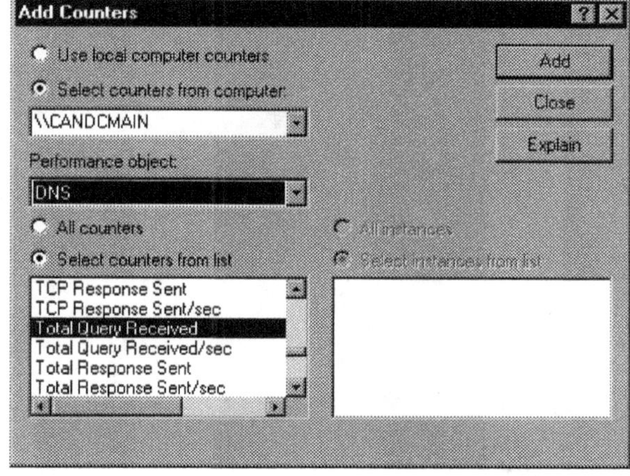

FIGURE 10-18

Setting a performance counter with an instance

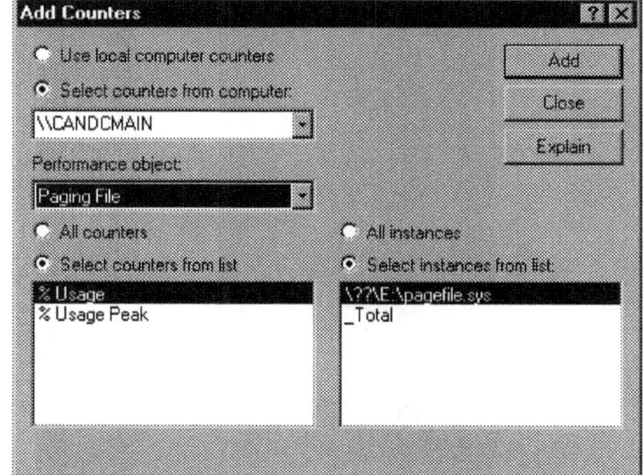

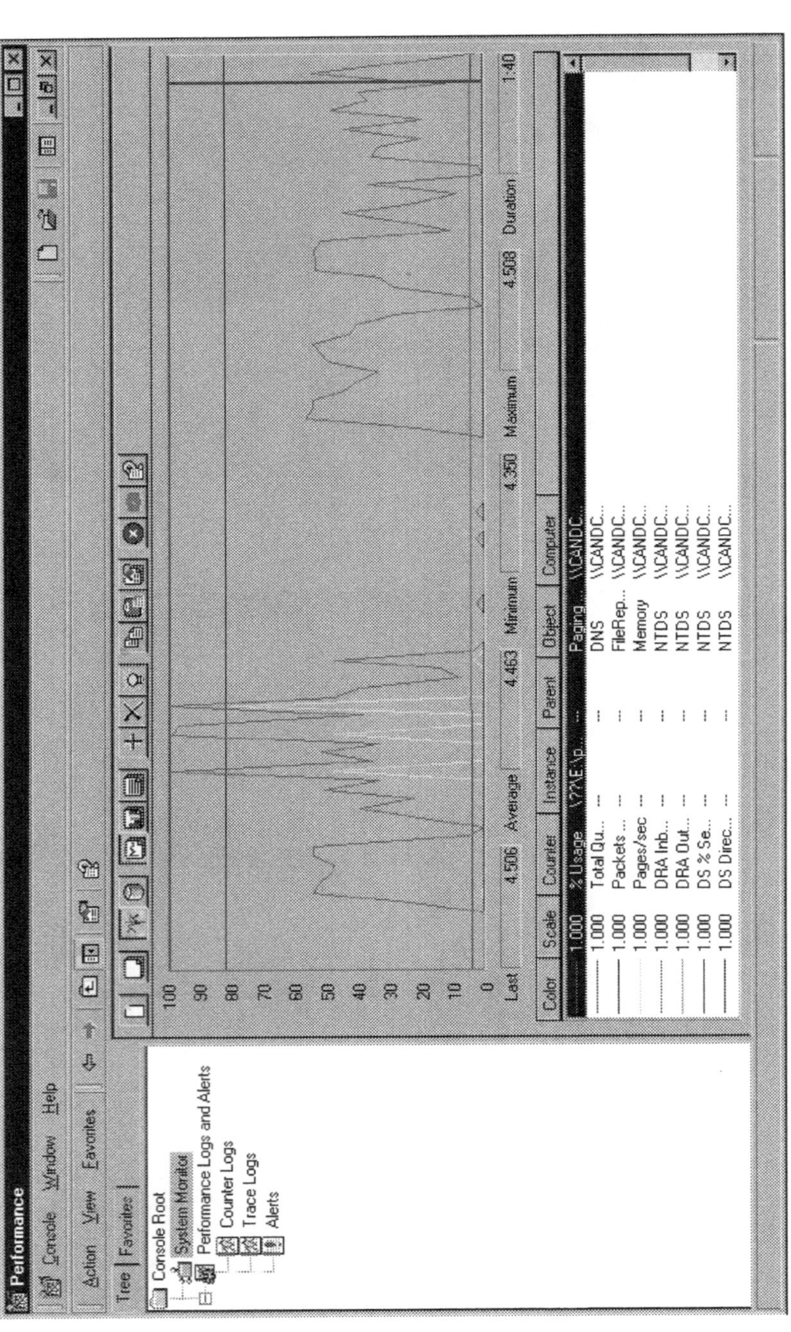

Figure 10-19 Viewing the resulting performance graph

When the File Open dialog box opens, browse to the location of monitor.htm. By default, it should have been stored in C:\documents and settings\administrator\Start Menu\Programs\Administrative Tools. Click Open.

You will see this warning:

Click OK.

Give the name **PagingFile** to the alert. Set the alert by removing all other counters and setting the limit to **85** as shown in Figure 10-20.

Click Apply, and then select the Action tab.

FIGURE 10-20

Changing the settings for an alert

At the Action tab (Figure 10-21), enter the name of the machine that is to receive the alert.

Click OK.

When you return to the performance monitor, select the "paging file" entry. From the Action menu, choose Start. The icon for the paging alert turns green. Close the performance monitor.

The Alerts function uses the NetBIOS name (pre–Windows 2000 name) of a computer, not the Active Directory name! The computer name must therefore adhere to the NetBIOS name parameters(15 characters maximum).

FIGURE 10-21

Establishing the action to be taken by the alert

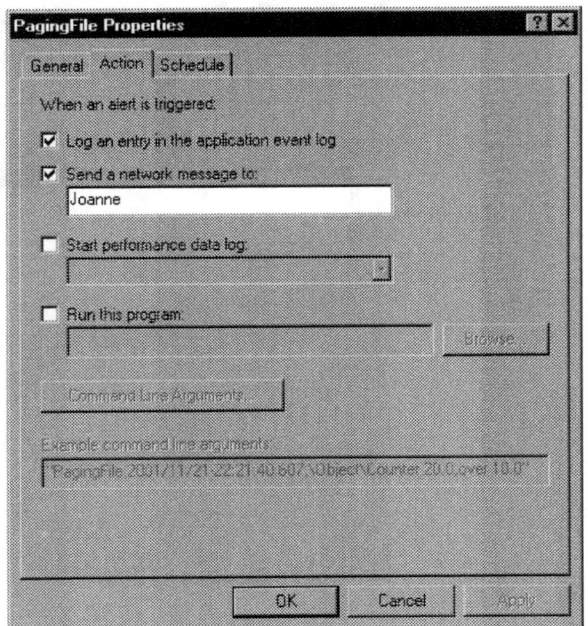

ANSWERS TO LAB ANALYSIS TEST

1. Moves may occur for several reasons. As companies grow or reorganize, the structure of the Active Directory needs to change. Users are promoted and need to be placed into different OUs or groups. Servers may be replaced, requiring a move from the old server to a new server. Finally, basic maintenance may require objects to be moved temporarily.
2. Most network shares are read-only, but some scenarios call for having multiple write access to a folder. One such scenario is the shared database. Typically, many users need to be able to update records in a database. Those users would need permission to change the contents of the folder. Another scenario involves users who need to share files. Providing a folder on the server where users can place files for others to access is quite handy.
3. The "create user" script is pretty neat. It creates a user in the Users OU. It needs some error checking, though. If the script tries to create a user name that already exists in the network, the script will crash. VBScript supports the On Error statement that allows a developer to trap and fix errors that occur. Another improvement would allow the script to read from a file. Often, organizations need to create large numbers of users at the same time (as at a school during the fall). If a text file containing names is created, the script could generate many users at one time.
4. Logging is a good way to see what the network and the users are doing. One potential drawback is the performance drain on the server. Logging many things results in additional disk writes, and slower network response. Network traffic increases and more collisions occur. Another drawback is the wasted disk space. If an administrator fails to set a size limit on a log, that log could grow to fill all the free space on the server, effectively downing the network. When a size limit is placed on a log, the server generates an error message when the log fills up. That error message can reduce network efficiency until the message is taken care of. For example, in one network, I noticed that telnet performance dropped when a server log filled up. When the log message went away, telnet returned to normal.
5. Placing similar objects into a group is a good way to achieve security in a network. By having similar users in one group, assigning permissions to the users is easy. Each user in the group has the same permissions. By grouping, the administrator can avoid worrying about missing a user when setting rights.

ANSWERS TO KEY TERM QUIZ

1. printer
2. InputBox
3. Dim
4. alert
5. move

11

Managing Active Directory and Domain Name Service Replication

LAB EXERCISES

11.01 Scheduling Replication Times

11.02 Troubleshooting Active Directory Replication

11.03 Reducing Latency in Domain Name Service Replication

11.04 Troubleshooting Domain Name Service Replication

- Lab Analysis Test
- Key Term Quiz
- Lab Wrap-Up
- Lab Solutions

Joanne pulls you into her office for a quick meeting. She has noticed excessive WAN traffic during business hours. On-peak WAN costs have risen, and Joanne would like to restrict WAN traffic until after business hours. She remembers from an earlier discussion that the replication can be scheduled, but she cannot remember how.

On a related note, an administrator at the South Side site complained that not all replications seem to work. Joanne believes that the administrator is wrong, but would like to verify that the replication is working.

You tell Joanne that you will reduce her on-peak WAN usage and teach her how to troubleshoot the replication service.

LAB EXERCISE 11.01

10 Minutes

Scheduling Replication Times

One way to reduce WAN costs is to schedule Active Directory updates for after 6:00 P.M., Monday to Friday. You explain to Joanne that a schedule like that will reduce some of the effectiveness of her Active Directory setup. Joanne decides to go ahead anyway, because the costs that are being incurred are much too high.

Learning Objectives

In this lab, you set a schedule for replication. At the end of the lab, you'll be able to:

- List the objects that require a schedule change
- Set the schedule

Lab Materials and Setup

To set a replication schedule, you need these materials:

- Administrator password
- Completed lab exercises from Chapter 2

Getting Down to Business

You will force replications to occur during off-peak WAN hours by using these steps:

Step 1. Start Active Directory Sites and Services.

Step 2. Expand to see the IP folder under the Inter-Site Transports folder.

Step 3. For each link, call up the properties, and set the replication times so that replication does not occur during the hours of 8 A.M. to 6 P.M, Mondays to Fridays.

Step 4. Expand the CANDCMAIN server under the Main site. Expand the NTDS settings, and call up the properties of the connection. Set the replication schedule as described in step 3.

LAB EXERCISE 11.02

10 Minutes

Troubleshooting Active Directory Replication

Without adding new software tools, Joanne would like to know if Active Directory is being replicated properly. You will show her how to use ping, Active Directory Sites and Services, and Event Viewer to verify that the replications are going through.

Learning Objectives

Troubleshooting network problems is a routine task. At the end of the lab, you'll be able to:

- Use ping
- Verify connection objects
- List common replication events

Lab Materials and Setup

To troubleshoot the replication service you need to be logged on as administrator.

Getting Down to Business

You will verify the connection to the remote server and check for bad events. Here's how:

Step 1. From both servers, drop to the command prompt and use ping to verify the connection. The syntax for ping is **ping** *address*. If *address* is alive, you will receive a reply.

Step 2. Start Active Directory Sites and Services on the Main server. Ensure that a connection object exists between the servers.

lab hint

Step 2 is difficult to demonstrate in a classroom that lacks multiple servers.

Step 3. Start Event Viewer on the Main server.

Step 4. Under the File Replication Service object, check for error events. These include 1265 and 13615. Also look for 1013, which indicates a successful replication.

LAB EXERCISE 11.03

5 Minutes

Reducing Latency in Domain Name Service Replication

At C&C, the South Side server is set as a secondary Domain Name Service (DNS) server. It needs to be notified when changes are made to the Main server. By specifying the servers to be notified, less time is spent updating DNS.

Learning Objectives

At the end of the lab, you'll be able to set the notification property for secondary DNS servers.

Lab Materials and Setup

To configure the notification of a secondary DNS server, you need these materials:

- Administrator account
- DNS installed and active

Getting Down to Business

Use these steps to reduce latency in C&C's DNS updates:

Step 1. Start DNS.

Step 2. Call up the properties of the zone.

Step 3. Select the Zone Transfers tab.

Step 4. Click Notify.

Step 5. List the relevant servers, and save the changes.

lab hint

If your learning environment lacks multiple servers, then simply accept the default choices.

LAB EXERCISE 11.04

15 Minutes

Troubleshooting Domain Name Service Replication

Again, Joanne would like to verify that the DNS update occurred.

You will show her how to verify the DNS update. You will use ping, tracert, nslookup, and the event viewer.

Learning Objectives

In this lab, you use several tools to troubleshoot DNS replication. At the end of the lab, you'll be able to:

- Use tracert
- Use nslookup

Lab Materials and Setup

To troubleshoot the DNS replication, you must be logged in as an administrator.

Getting Down to Business

You will verify that DNS replication works. Here's how:

Step 1. Ping the remote machine to ensure communication.

Step 2. Use tracert to verify that a packet gets to the remote computer.

Step 3. Perform an nslookup on both the Main and the remote server.

Step 4. Check the event log for errors.

LAB ANALYSIS TEST

The following questions will help you to apply your knowledge in a business setting.

1. You set the replication to occur only after 6:00 P.M. and before 8:00 A.M. What are some potential problems with that schedule?

2. How do domain controllers track changes?

3. The text suggests using the Internet Protocol (IP) and Remote Procedure Call (RPC) rather than the Simple Mail Transfer Protocol (SMTP). When should SMTP be used in replication?

4. Suppose you have an office that is using a Linux server as a secondary DNS controller. That server is BIND (Berkeley Internet Name Domain)–compliant. What are some potential problems with replicating to that server?

5. Why did Microsoft switch from the single-master domain model to the multi-master domain model?

KEY TERMS QUIZ

Use the following vocabulary terms to complete the sentences below. Not all of the terms will be used.

High Watermark Vector

IP

Knowledge Consistency Checker

nslookup

PDC (Primary Domain Controller)

ping

replication

RPC

tracert

Update Sequence Number

1. ____________________ runs every 15 minutes on each domain controller.
2. The ____________________ is a counter made for each change on a domain controller.
3. The preferred replication protocol is ____________________ .
4. ____________________ provides information about how a packet gets to a site.
5. To determine if a computer is up and running, you can ____________________ it.

LAB WRAP-UP

Congratulations, you have managed and improved the WAN usage at C&C. To reduce WAN times during peak hours, you reset the replication schedule and reduced the latency for DNS updates. In addition to reducing WAN access, you taught Joanne how to troubleshoot replication issues.

Troubleshooting and reducing costs are two very important tasks in every organization. The bottom line affects everybody in an organization. If you, as an administrator, can improve the bottom line, even slightly, then your job position is strengthened.

Troubleshooting is important because things happen to networks. Services that worked last week no longer work—for no apparent reason. Having troubleshooting skills in your repertoire of tools increases your chances of landing and keeping a good job.

The next chapter explores security issues in Active Directory. Security is important in every network. Poor security leads to network downtime or penetration. Neither occurrence is healthy for an organization.

LAB SOLUTIONS FOR CHAPTER 11

The sections that follow walk you through the steps to solve the lab exercises. You should avoid looking at these sections unless you are stuck on a particular exercise.

Lab Exercise 11.01

Start Active Directory Sites and Services from the Start button.

Expand the Inter-Site Transports folder (Figure 11-1).

Right-click the first site link in the right-hand pane, and select Properties. Click Change Schedule.

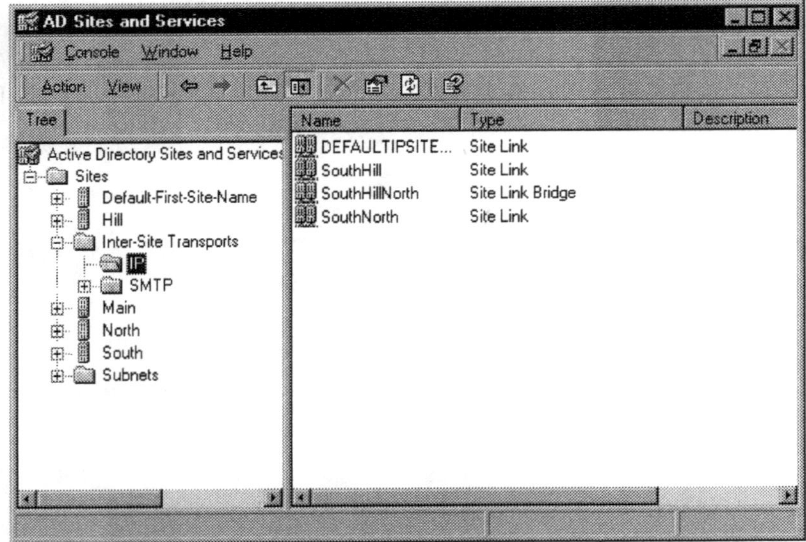

FIGURE 11-1 Expanding the Inter-Site Transports folder

In the scheduling dialog, select the blocks representing Monday to Friday, 8 A.M. to 6 P.M., and select the Replication Not Available radio button:

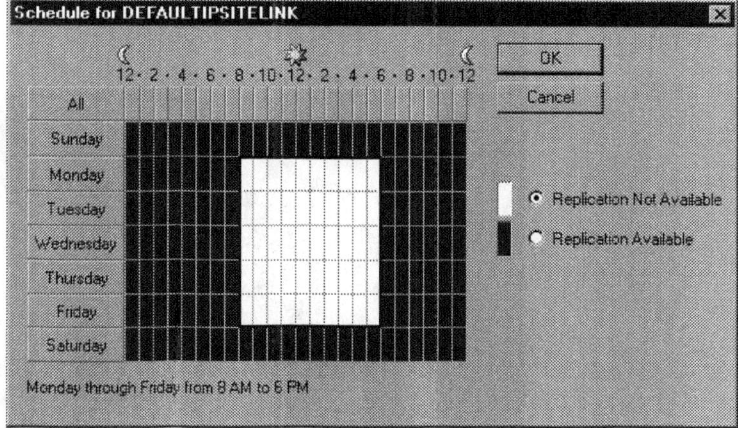

Repeat the process for each site link or site link bridge.

Expand the Main site in the left-hand pane and expand the CANDCMAIN server to see NTDS Settings. Select NTDS Settings.

In the right-hand pane, right-click the connection object, and select Properties. Again, click Change Schedule. Configure the schedule as shown:

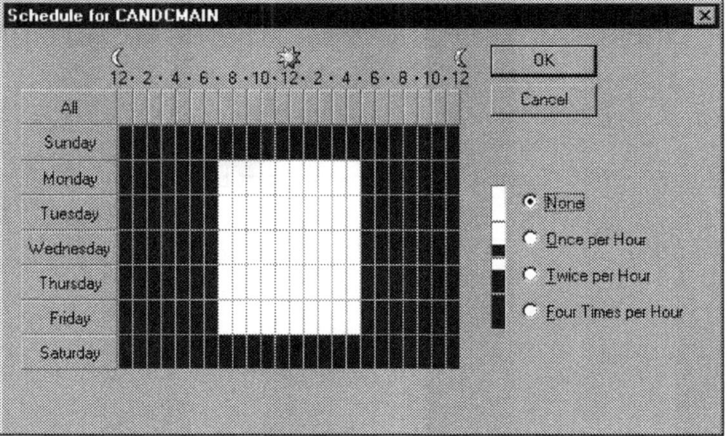

Close Active Directory Sites and Services.

Lab Exercise 11.02

From the Start button, select the Run command. Enter **cmd**, and click OK to open the command prompt. At the prompt (E: in the examples here), enter **ping 192.168.1.1**. For example:

```
E:\WINNT\System32\command.com
Microsoft(R) Windows DOS
(C)Copyright Microsoft Corp 1990-1999.

E:\>ping 192.168.1.1

Pinging 192.168.1.1 with 32 bytes of data:

Reply from 192.168.1.1: bytes=32 time<10ms TTL=128
Reply from 192.168.1.1: bytes=32 time<10ms TTL=128
Reply from 192.168.1.1: bytes=32 time<10ms TTL=128
Reply from 192.168.1.1: bytes=32 time<10ms TTL=128

Ping statistics for 192.168.1.1:
    Packets: Sent = 4, Received = 4, Lost = 0 (0% loss),
Approximate round trip times in milli-seconds:
    Minimum = 0ms, Maximum =  0ms, Average =  0ms
```

Any response from ping other than a "reply from" indicates a problem, either with the machine being pinged or with the connection to that machine.

Type **exit** to leave the command prompt.

Start Active Directory Sites and Services. Expand to NTDS Settings as instructed in Lab Exercise 11.01.

You should see a connection object as shown in Figure 11-2.

Close Sites and Services.

Start Event Viewer from the Start button.

FIGURE 11-2

Finding a connection object under NTDS Settings

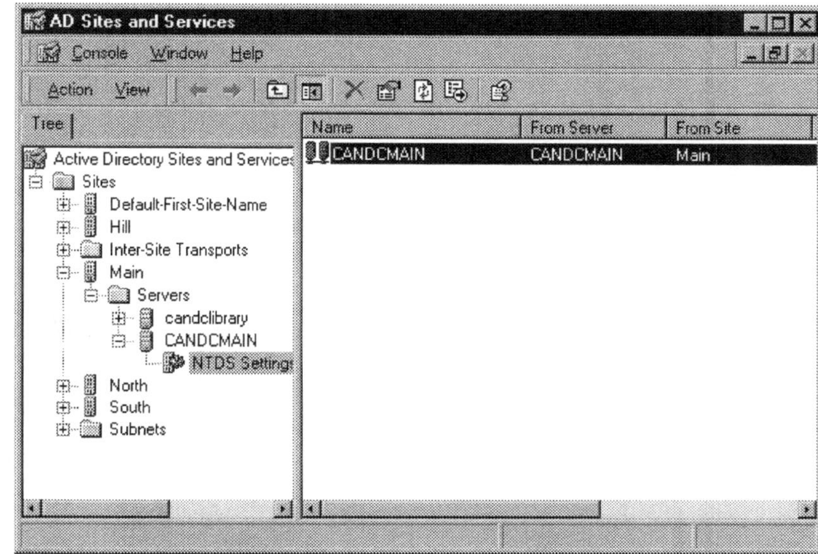

In the left-hand pane, select the File Replication Service tab. A successful replication service will look something like this:

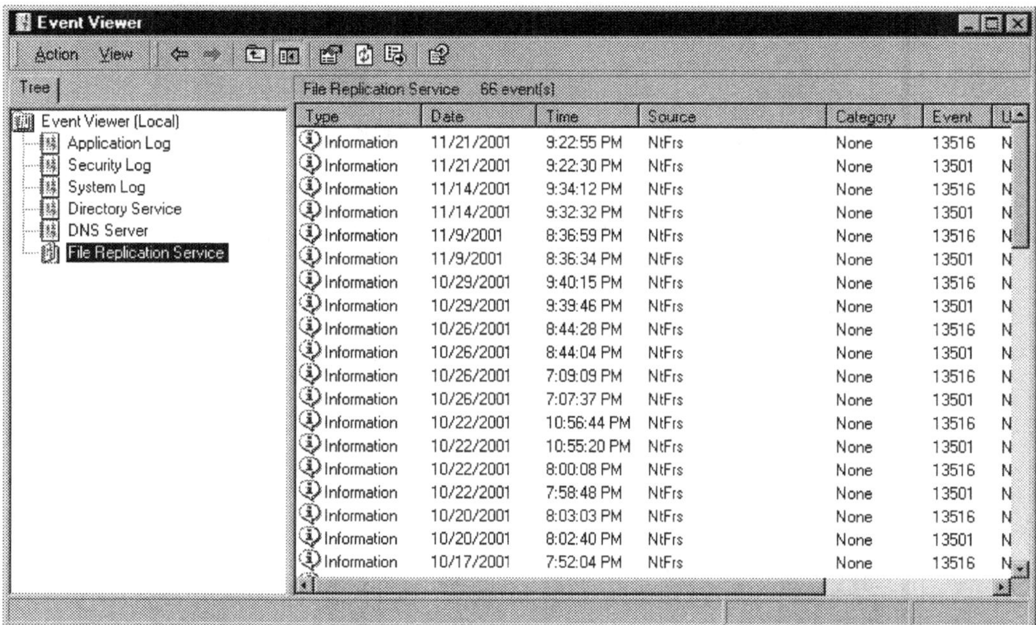

Common events include 13501 and 13516, which together indicate a successful startup of the replication service. Another good event is 1013, which indicates a successful replication. Problem events include 1265 and 13615.

Lab Exercise 11.03

Start DNS from the Start button.

Expand the forward lookup zones as shown:

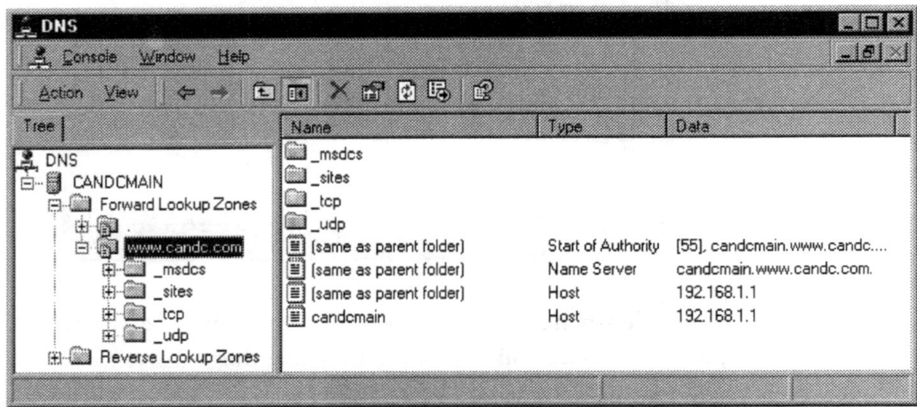

Right-click www.candc.com, and select Properties. When the properties dialog opens, click the Zone Transfers tab (Figure 11-3).

Click Notify. Select the radio button for "The following servers," and list the relevant servers. Figure 11-4 shows an example.

If your learning environment lacks multiple servers, accept the default choices.

Lab Exercise 11.04

From the Start button, select Run. Enter **cmd**, and click OK to open the command prompt.

Ping the remote server as instructed in Lab Exercise 11.02. If the server can be pinged, then enter this command:

```
tracert candcsouth
```

If a problem exists, you will repeatedly see a message similar to that in Figure 11-5.

FIGURE 11-3

Viewing the Zone Transfers properties

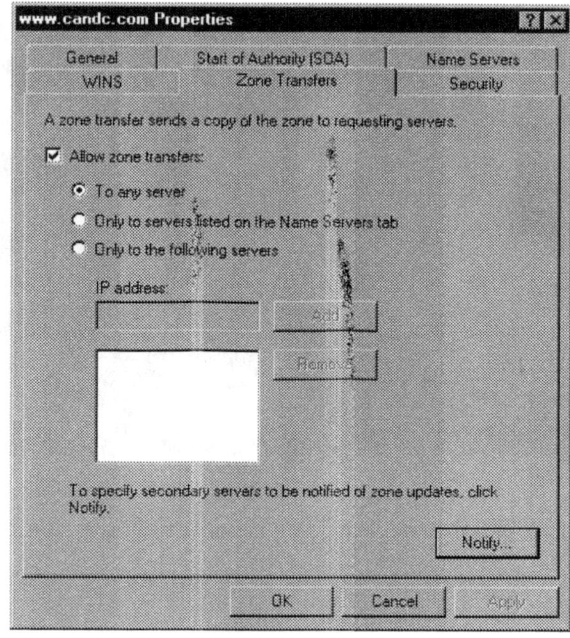

FIGURE 11-4

Adding a notified server

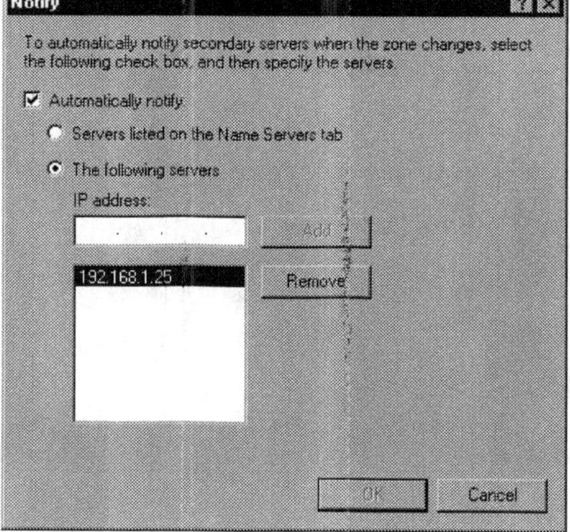

FIGURE 11-5

Finding a typical WAN connection problem

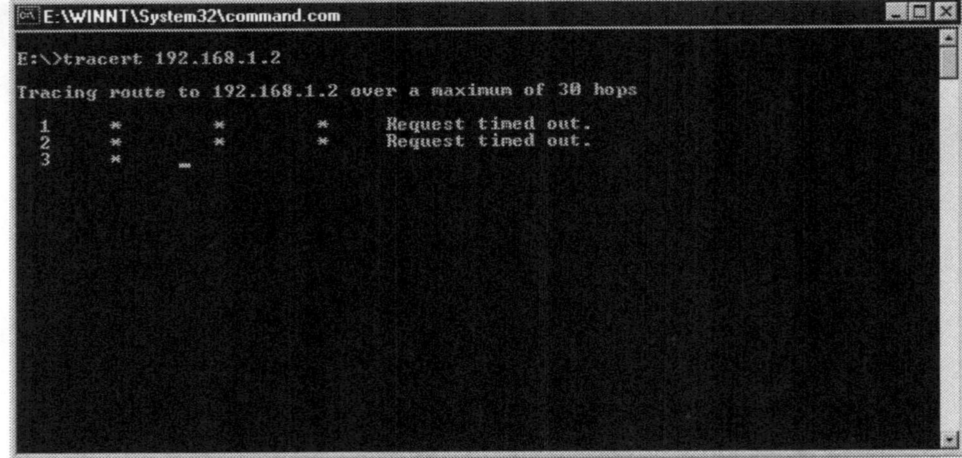

If DNS is not working properly, then the command

```
nslookup www.yahoo.com
```

will produce the error messages shown in Figure 11-6. (Or use another Web site that is active and popular.)

FIGURE 11-6

Finding a typical DNS lookup problem

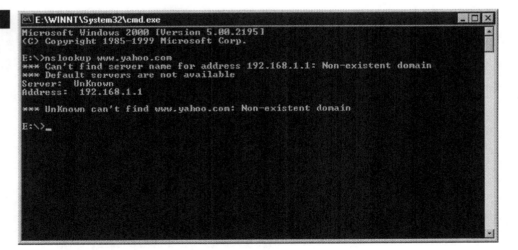

```
E:\WINNT\System32\cmd.exe
Microsoft Windows 2000 [Version 5.00.2195]
(C) Copyright 1985-1999 Microsoft Corp.

E:\>nslookup www.yahoo.com
*** Can't find server name for address 192.168.1.1: Non-existent domain
*** Default servers are not available
Server:  UnKnown
Address:  192.168.1.1

*** UnKnown can't find www.yahoo.com: Non-existent domain

E:\>_
```

ANSWERS TO LAB ANALYSIS TEST

1. The schedule has several problems. One of the major features of Active Directory is quick replication of changes across the network. By restricting changes to after 6 P.M., users will not see the changes until the next business day. Some users will feel slighted and unproductive. Another problem is that administrators may put off Active Directory changes until the end of the day and possibly not test the changes until the subsequent day.
2. Domain controllers track changes to Active Directory using three numbers. The first number, the Update Sequence Number (USN) tracks the version of the change applied to each naming context. The second number is the High Watermark Vector (HWV). That number tracks the highest USN available on the server. The third number is the up-to-dateness vector. That number tracks the most recent USN update for each naming context.
3. SMTP is best used for slow links. SMTP was designed to work over dialup connections, at very low speeds. If your network is connected by modems or slow WAN links, SMTP is a good choice.
4. Non-Microsoft DNS servers are usually very good. Microsoft has added features to its DNS that are not publicly recognized standards. An example is the dynamic update feature of MS DNS. Many BIND servers will not support that feature of Windows 2000.
5. Microsoft switched to the multi-master model to simplify network changes. By using a multi-master model, an Active Directory object can be changed on any domain controller, and replicated out to other domain controllers. Thus, local administrators can make changes for local users, and have those changes affect the entire network. That approach frees the central administrator from having to make small changes to the main controller.

ANSWERS TO KEY TERM QUIZ

1. Knowledge Consistency Checker
2. Update Sequence Number
3. RPC
4. tracert
5. ping

MCSE

MICROSOFT CERTIFIED SYSTEMS ENGINEER

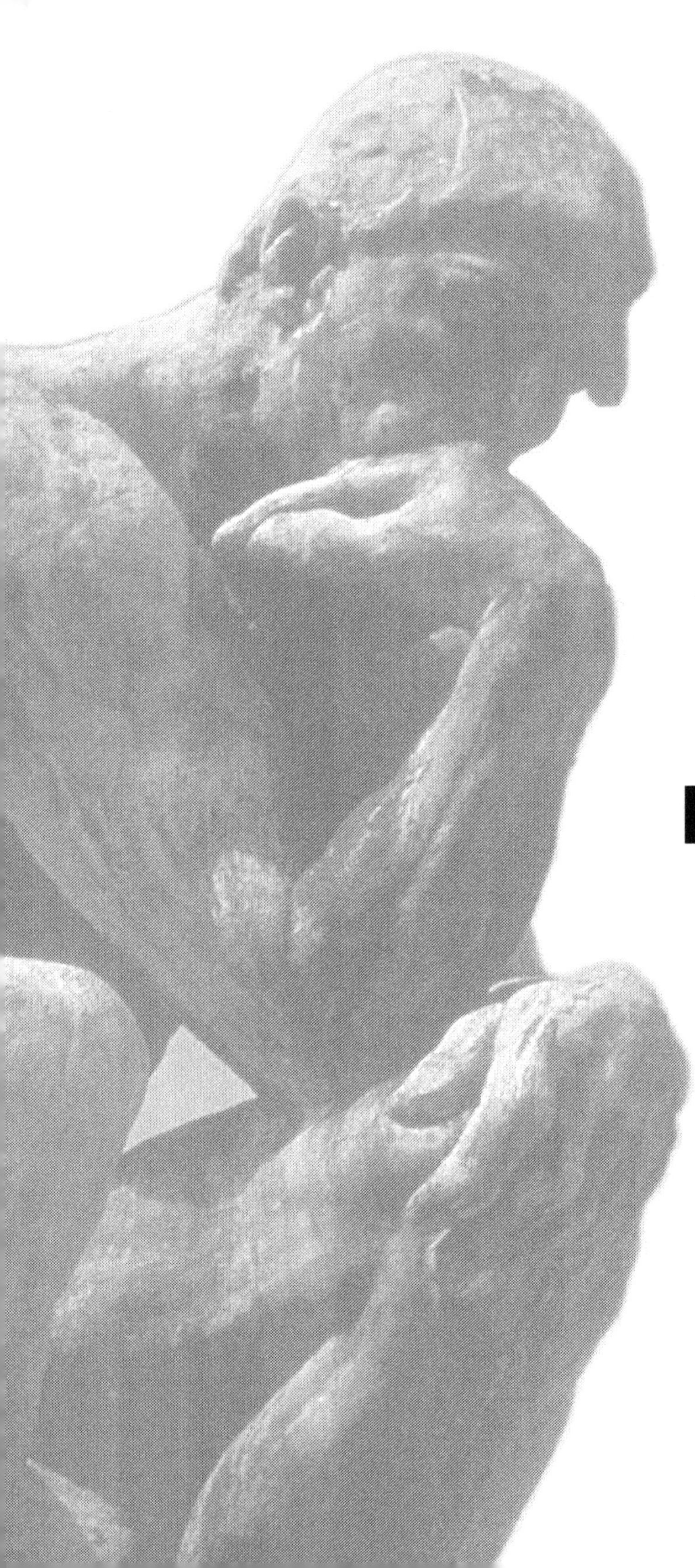

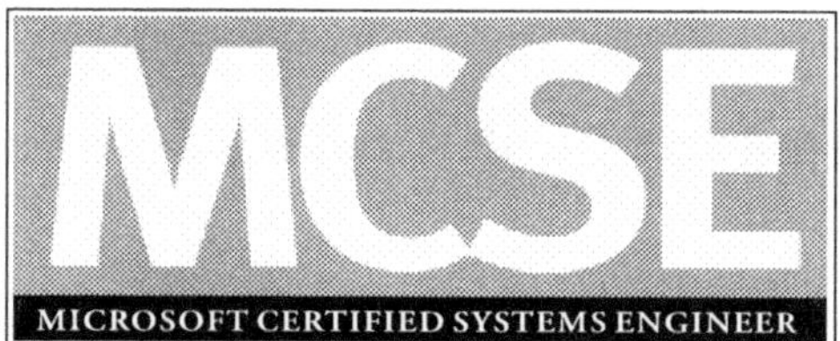

12

Using the Security Features of Active Directory

LAB EXERCISES

12.01 Securing the Workstations

12.02 Performing a Security Analysis

12.03 Improving Server Security

12.04 Auditing Use of the Letter Templates Folder

- Lab Analysis Test
- Key Term Quiz
- Lab Wrap-Up
- Lab Solutions

Joanne is concerned about her network. She recently read an article that suggested that most network intruders are not remote hackers, but internal employees. The article listed several examples of intrusions. She would like to protect her network against intrusion. In addition to the security issue, C&C's directors are worried that the users are not using the letter templates provided on the main server. Joanne asks you to verify if users are accessing the templates.

You tell Joanne that her requests are quite common and valid. You will get to work on them right away.

LAB EXERCISE 12.01

15 Minutes

Securing the Workstations

Joanne is correct: most network hacks come from internal workers. To add insult to injury, most of the hacks can be executed because of simple mistakes or oversights. You believe that the server is relatively secure, but you know that the remote clients are not monitored. You therefore decide to secure the local workstations first, to prevent intentional and unintentional security breaches to the best of your ability.

Learning Objectives

Security is not a simple issue. You know that your security only goes so far, depending on the capabilities of the person trying to break in. Nevertheless, you have to try. At the end of the lab, you'll be able to:

- Apply policies to local computers
- Apply policies to user accounts

Lab Materials and Setup

Applying and maintaining security is a constant task in nearly any network. You need these materials:

- Administrator account
- The Users group policy

Getting Down to Business

In this exercise, you will set some local policies for workstations and for users.

Step 1. Run the Microsoft Management Console (MMC), and open the users.msc file.

Step 2. Expand Computer Configuration until you reach Local Policies. Restrict anything that permits access or shares from the local computer. Also, enable "Automatic timed log off," "Hide the last user to use the workstation," and "Rename the administrator and guest accounts."

Step 3. Expand the Account Policies. Define all password rules and account lockout rules.

Step 4. Save the users.msc file.

LAB EXERCISE 12.02

5 Minutes

Performing a Security Analysis

You believe that the local server is reasonably secure. Physical access to the server is limited to three people. Only what is shared is accessible from remote machines. Despite those truths, you decide to perform a security analysis.

lab hint

Install all service patches as they become available. Microsoft finds most security holes before they are exploited. Take, for example, the Code Red attacks. Code Red exploited a weakness in Internet Information Server (IIS) for which Microsoft had released a patch 2 months earlier.

Learning Objectives

Monitoring security is not an easy job. Most of the time, nothing is happening and you think that you are wasting your time. But when something happens, you will be glad that you were diligent. At the end of the lab, you'll be able to:

- Build a security database
- Perform a security analysis of the server

Lab Materials and Setup

To set up a security database, you must be logged in as administrator.

Getting Down to Business

You will set up a security database for a secure domain controller. Here's how:

Step 1. Start MMC, and add the Security Configuration and Analysis snap-in.

Step 2. Build a new database.

Step 3. Apply the securedc.inf template.

Step 4. Perform an immediate analysis.

Step 5. Expand every tab and look for failed policies.

LAB EXERCISE 12.03

15 Minutes

Improving Server Security

Ouch. You thought that the server was secure. It seems that the default domain controller settings are not overly secure. You need to fix them. You tell Joanne that her server is insecure, but that it will be protected before the end of the day.

Learning Objectives

In this lab, you apply rules to the local machine to make it pass the security analysis. At the end of the lab, you'll be able to apply a template to the security settings.

Lab Materials and Setup

To secure the group policies (GPOs) and the local computer, you need these materials:

- Administrator account
- The users.msc file
- Default domain policy

Getting Down to Business

You will apply policies to GPOs and to the local computer. Here's how:

Step 1. Configure the local computer using the Security Configuration tool.

Step 2. Start MMC, and add the GPO snap-in.

Step 3. Add the local computer, user, and default domain policies.

Step 4. Right-click the security settings for the local machine and import the template securedc.inf.

Step 5. For the users and default domain policy GPOs, import the securews.inf file.

Step 6. After the templates have been imported, restart the server to ensure that all policies are implemented.

In Chapter 12 of the text, see the section titled "Making the Security Policy Changes Effective" for a discussion of alternative methods of applying security policies.

LAB EXERCISE 12.04

5 Minutes

Auditing Use of the Letter Templates Folder

Now that the server is secure, you can tackle the job of auditing the templates folder. You know that a simple audit of the folder provides a list of who is accessing the templates. After a few days, you will be able to tell Joanne if users are accessing the folder.

Learning Objectives

Auditing a shared resource is a common task. At the end of the lab, you will be able to:

- Start an audit log
- Set events to audit

Lab Materials and Setup

To audit a shared resource, you need these materials:

- Administrator account
- A shared folder

Getting Down to Business

You will audit the reads of the Letter Templates folder using these steps:

Step 1. Browse to the Letter Templates folder.

Step 2. Call up the properties of the folder.

Step 3. Go to the advanced security options.

Step 4. Set the audit for Everyone, and watch folder "reads."

LAB ANALYSIS TEST

The following questions will help you to apply your knowledge in a business setting.

1. Why implement security on a network?

2. You imported the secure domain controller template, which is built by Microsoft. Why should you still test your security by trying to hack in?

3. What can an audit file tell you?

4. What should you audit in a network?

5. How can an audit file predict future needs in an organization?

KEY TERMS QUIZ

Use the following vocabulary terms to complete the sentences below. Not all of the terms will be used.

- account policy
- audit
- event ID
- FAT32
- GPO
- local policy
- log
- NTFS
- policy
- template

1. The event ____________________ can be used to check for security breaches.
2. To secure a particular computer, the administrator sets an ____________________ .
3. To simplify the securing of a network, a security ____________________ can be imported.
4. The ____________________ holds policies regarding password requirements.
5. Auditing can be applied only on ____________________ volumes.

LAB WRAP-UP

Congratulations! You have secured C&C's network from most intruders. You understand that the security solutions you implemented are not foolproof, but they are fairly strong nonetheless. You set up an audit to watch the use of a shared folder. Finally, you secured the local workstations from casual hacking.

Additional congratulations are in order for completing this text. Twelve chapters of labs is quite an accomplishment. You should be proud of yourself. The skills that you have practiced and honed here will serve you well in your future career as a network administrator.

LAB SOLUTIONS FOR CHAPTER 12

The sections that follow walk you through the steps to solve the lab exercises. You should avoid looking at these sections unless you are stuck on a particular exercise.

Lab Exercise 12.01

From the Start button, select Run, and enter **MMC** in the run box.

Open the users.msc file. Expand Computer Configuration, Windows Settings, and Security Settings, and then select Password Policy as shown:

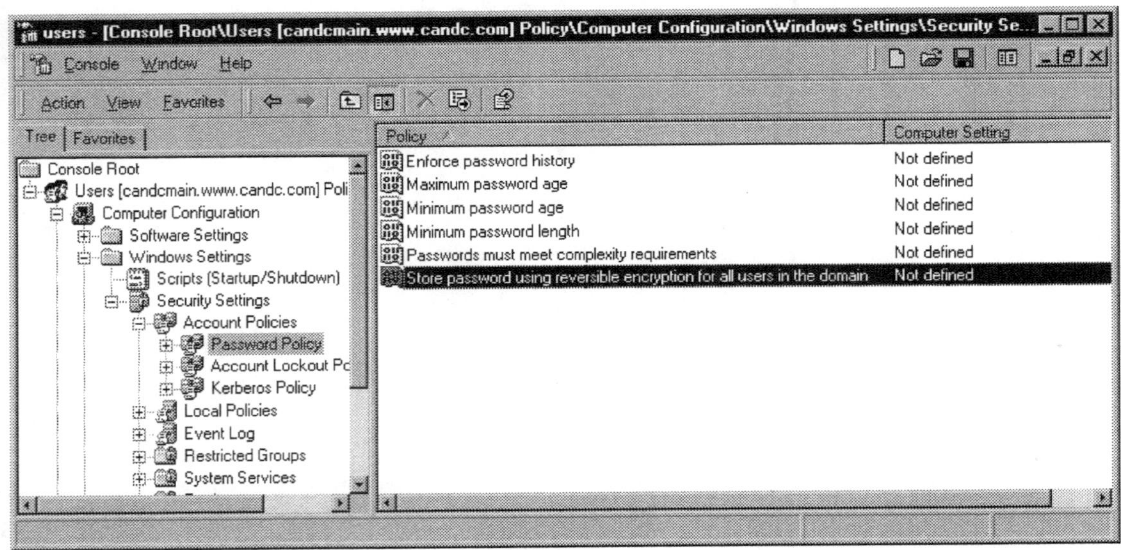

Double-click Enforce Password History and set the dialog as shown here:

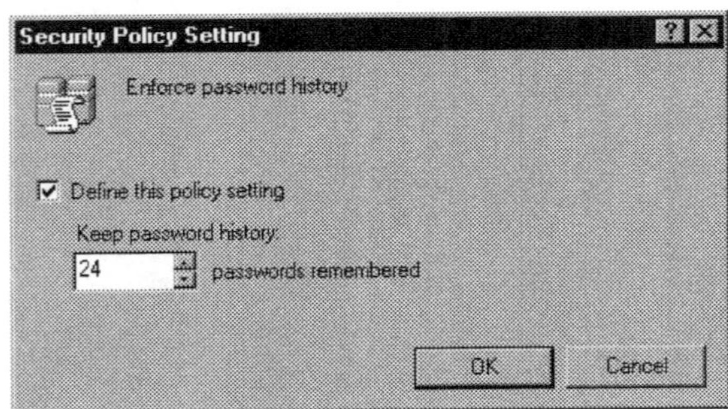

Continue defining all password properties until the screen looks like this:

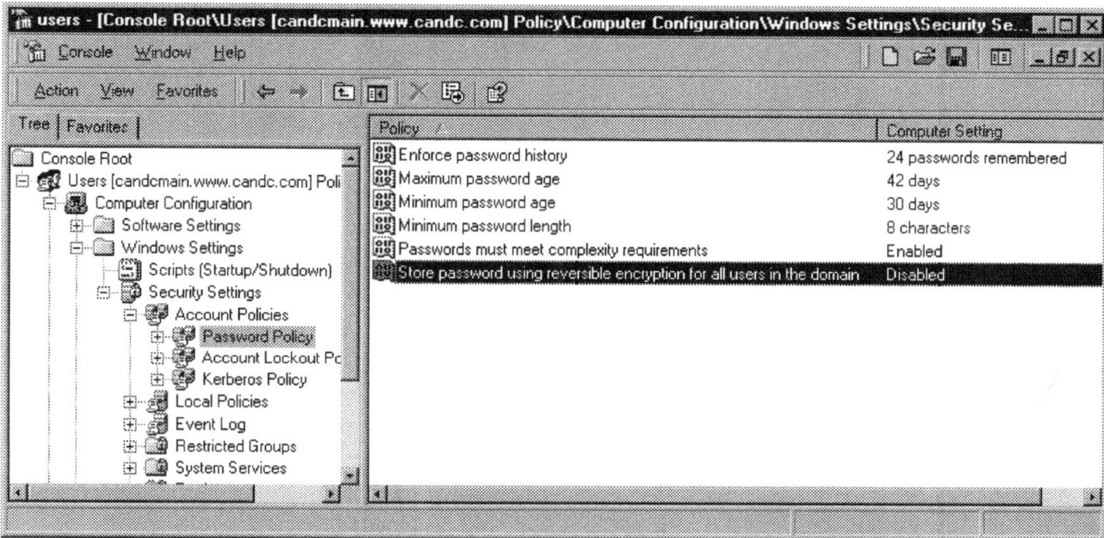

Expand the Account Lockout entry, and define its properties as shown here:

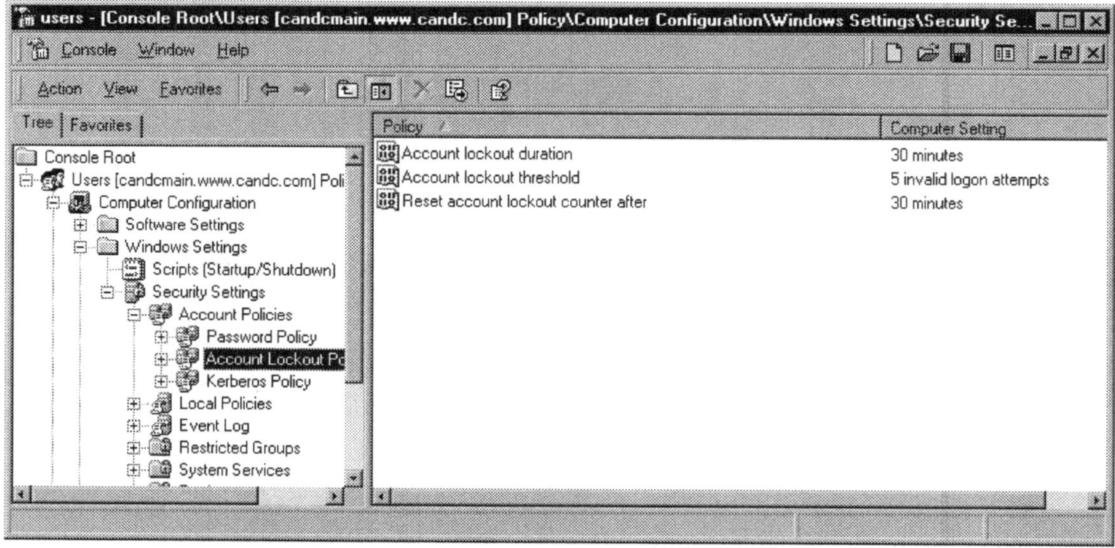

Save the file and close the console.

Lab Exercise 12.02

Using the Run option from the Start button, start MMC.

From the console menu, select Add/Remove snap-in. Click Add, and select Security Configuration and Analysis (Figure 12-1).

Close out of all open dialog boxes, returning to the MMC.

Right-click the Security Configuration icon, and select Open database to start the Security Configuration and Analysis process (Figure 12-2).

Do as the directions on the screen indicate: Right-click the Security Configuration icon, and select an open database. (I have two databases on my system; you probably have none.)

Open the new database file **secureserver.sdb** as shown:

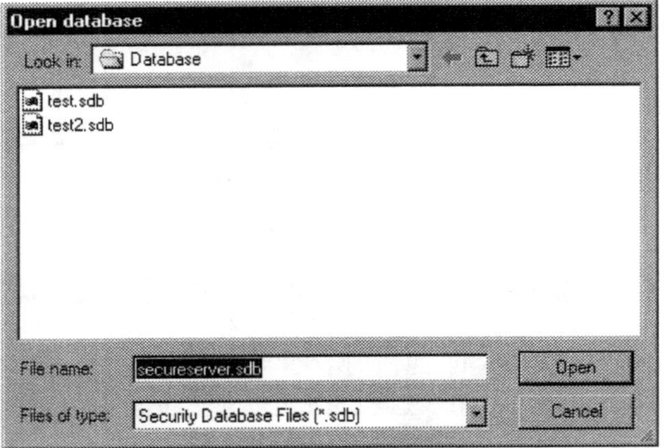

When the Import Template dialog box opens, select securedc.inf as shown:

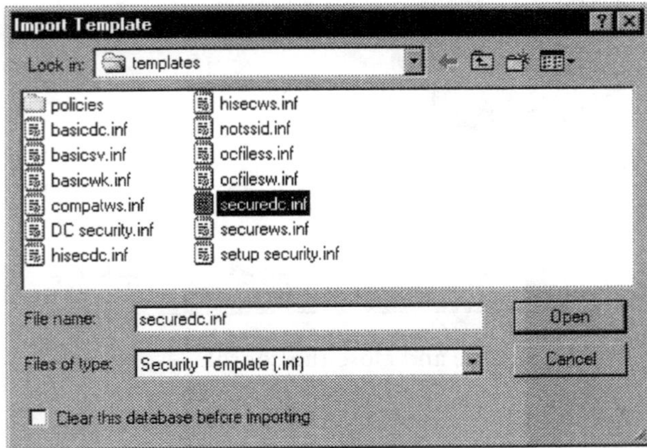

FIGURE 12-1 Selecting the Security Configuration and Analysis snap-in

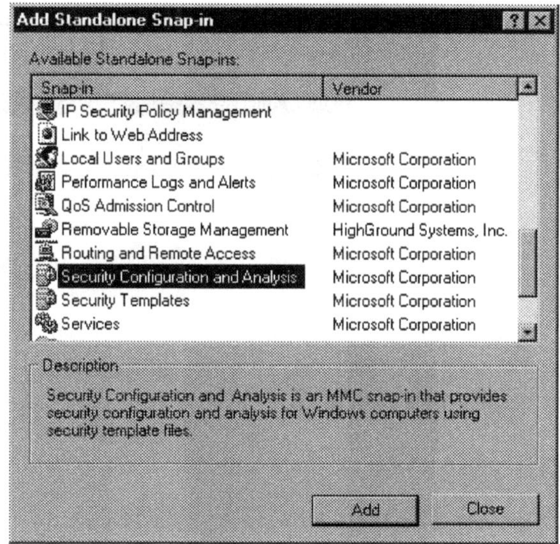

FIGURE 12-2 Starting the process of security configuration

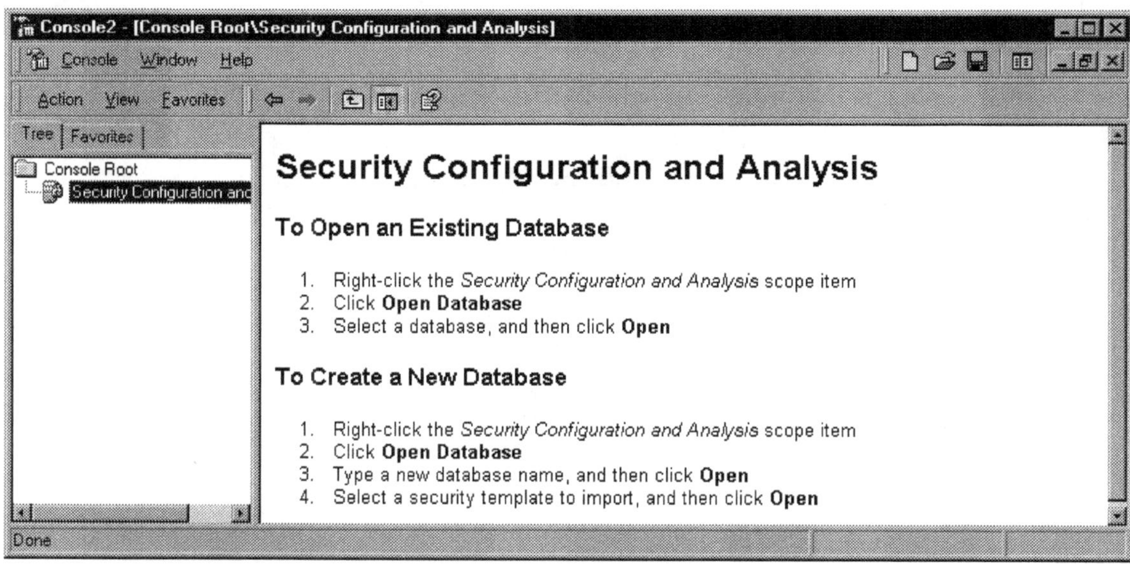

When you return to MMC, right-click the Security Configuration icon, and select Analyze Computer Now. Specify a location for the error log:

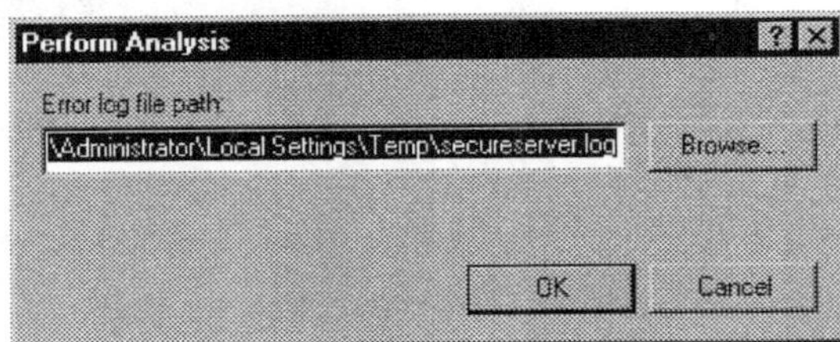

After a pause, you are returned to the MMC screen. Expand Password Policy to see Figure 12-3. The red "x" icons indicate failed policies.

Leave MMC open.

Lab Exercise 12.03

If you left the MMC window open as directed in Lab Exercise 12.02, activate the window containing the Security Configuration and Analysis snap-in. Otherwise, reopen the MMC program, and then activate the snap-in.

Right-click the Security Configuration icon, and select Configure Computer. After a brief pause, the local computer is configured to the secure domain controller standard.

FIGURE 12-3 Reviewing failed audit policies

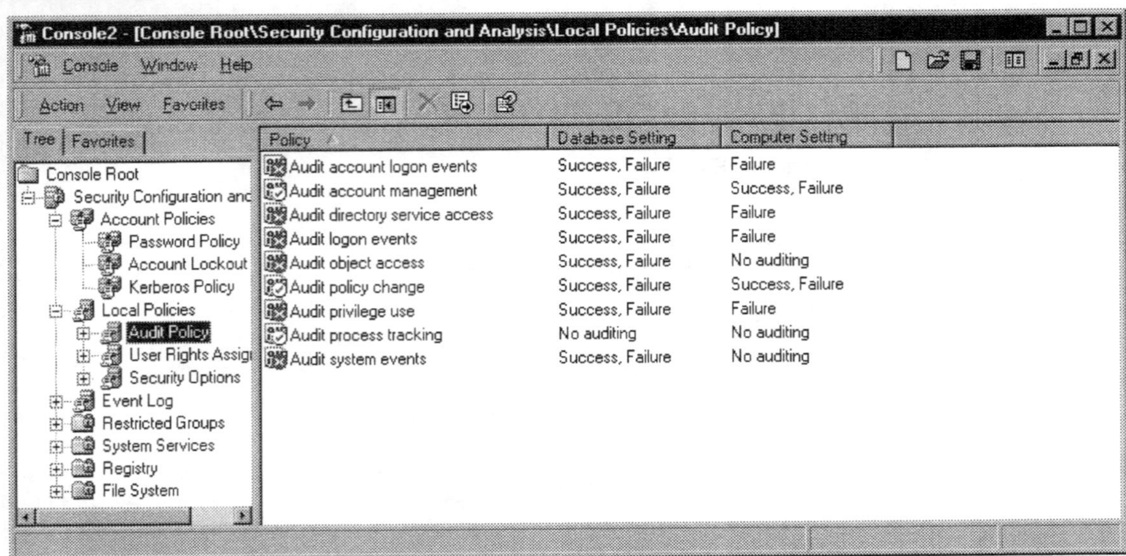

Re-analyze the computer:

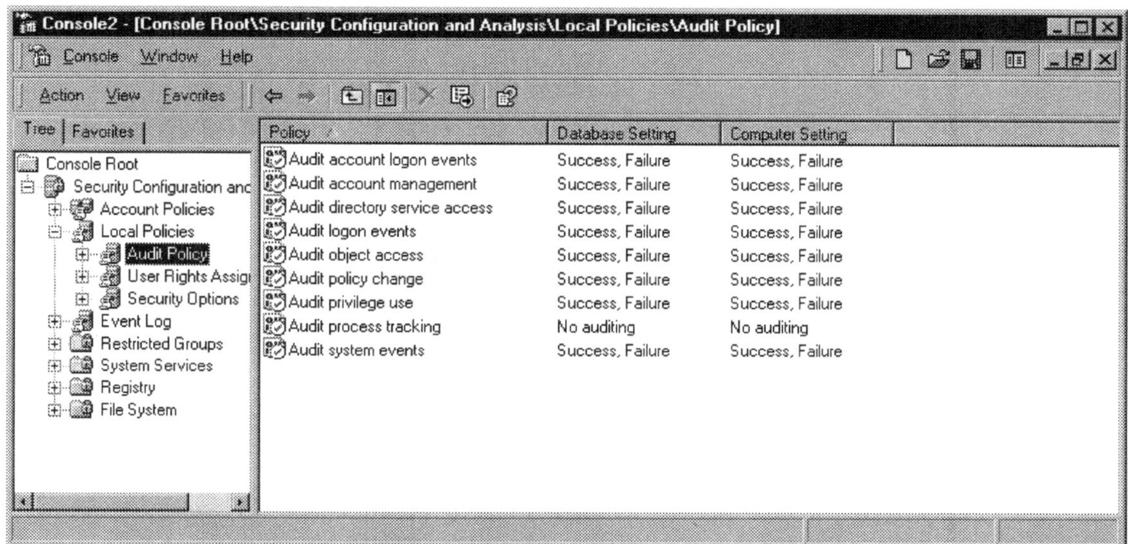

Start a new MMC window. Add the Group Policy snap-in, and add all policies currently on the computer. These include the users, local computer, and default domain policies.

Save the screen as **allpolicies.msc**. The screen will look something like this:

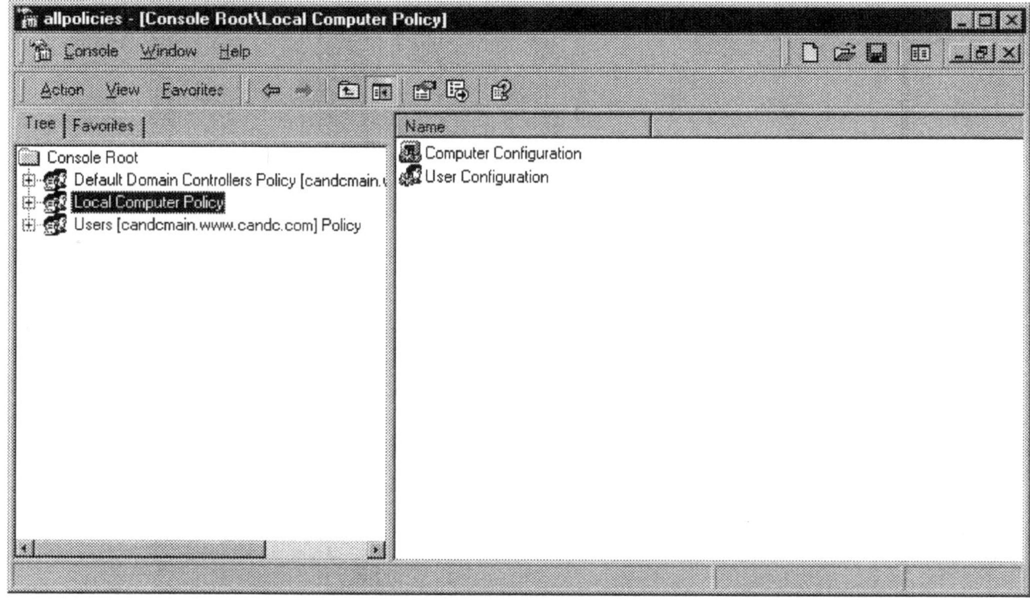

Expand the Local Computer policy to see Security Settings. Right-click Security Settings, and select Import Policy. Select the securedc.inf template as shown:

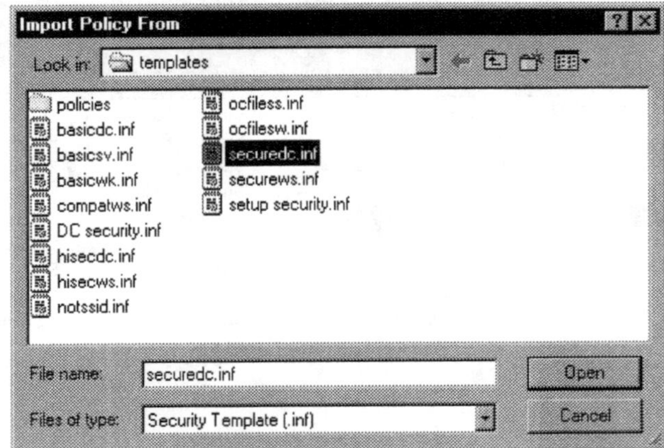

Click Open to apply the template.

Expand the Users policy to Security Settings as shown in Figure 12-4.

FIGURE 12-4 Reviewing the security settings for Users

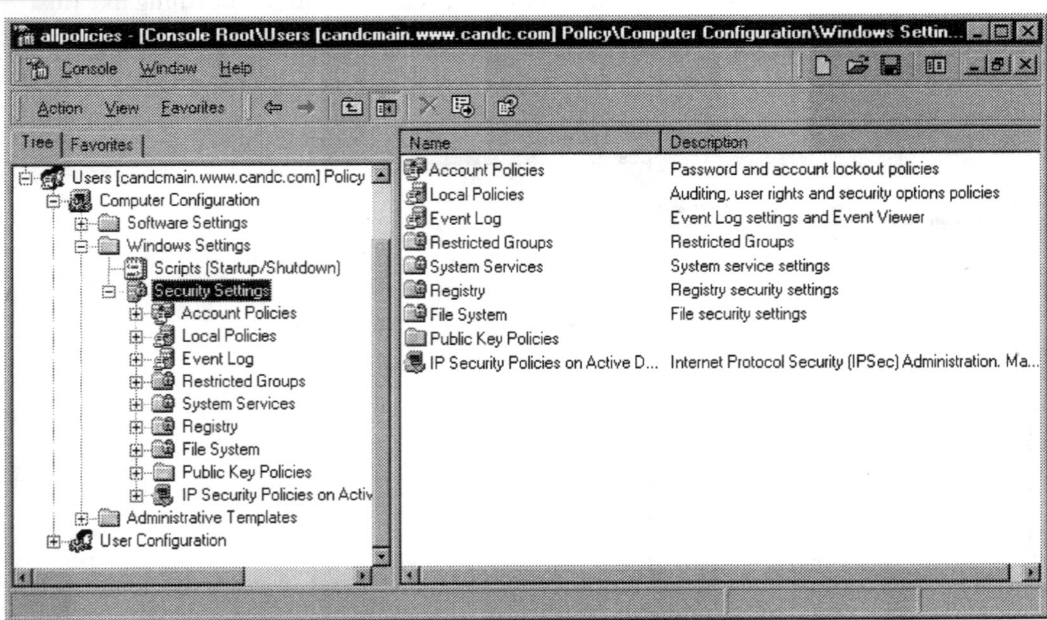

Right-click Security Settings, and import the securews.inf template. Also import the securews.inf template to the security settings for the Default Domain Policy.

Close the screen and, if prompted, save the contents as **allpolicies.msc**.

Reboot to ensure that all settings have been applied.

lab Hint

Applying the securedc.inf template to the local computer and using the configuration tool to apply the template are redundant actions. Redundancy in a security scenario is usually a good idea.

Lab Exercise 12.04

Open My Computer from the desktop. Browse to the location of the Letter Templates folder.

Right-click Letter Templates, and select Properties. In the properties dialog, select the Security tab (Figure 12-5).

Click Advanced, and then select the Auditing tab in the Access Control dialog (Figure 12-6).

Click Add to add an audit event. Find the Everyone group. Double-click it to add it to the auditing entries (Figure 12-7). Set the auditing events as shown in Figure 12-7.

Click OK to select the items for auditing (Figure 12-8).

FIGURE 12-5

Checking the security properties of a folder

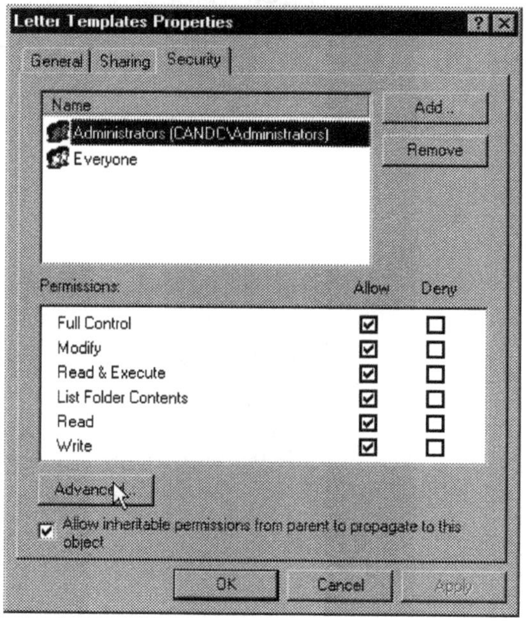

FIGURE 12-6

Opening a blank Auditing tab for a folder

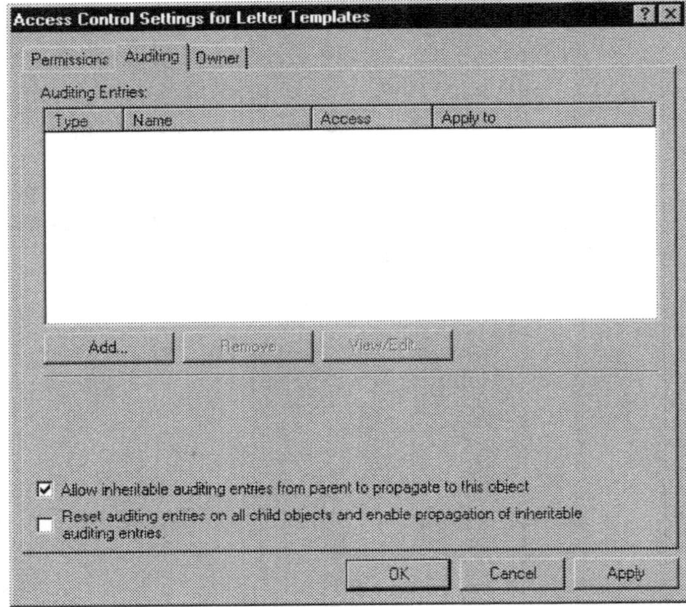

FIGURE 12-7

Adding users to the Auditing entries

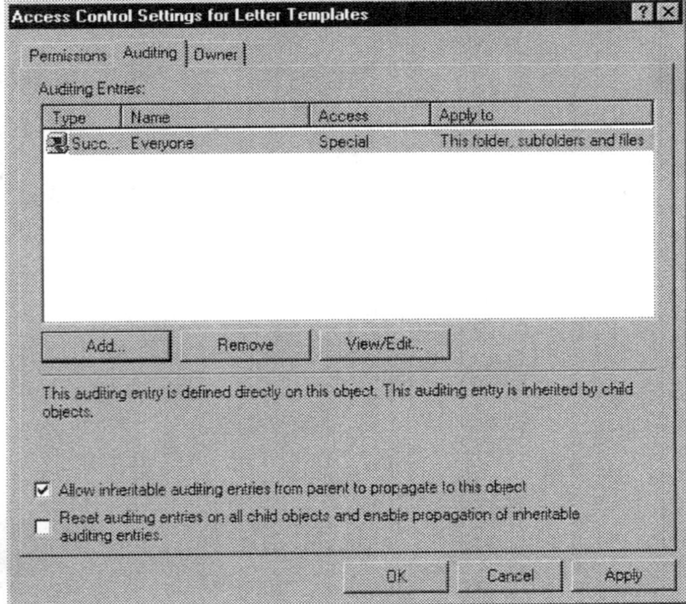

FIGURE 12-8

Selecting items for audit

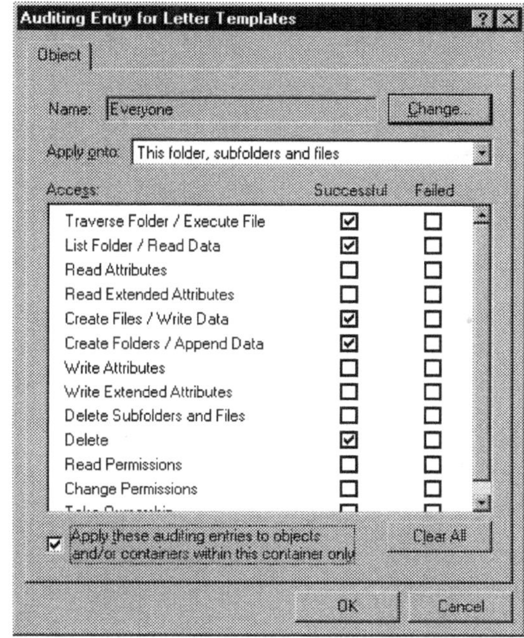

Click Apply, and then close the dialog box.

lab Warning

Audit policy must be switched on in the group policy editor before you can see log events. Audit policy was enabled when you secured the server.

ANSWERS TO LAB ANALYSIS TEST

1. Not implementing security on a network is similar to leaving your car unlocked at the mall. Most likely nothing will happen to the car, but chances are higher that someone will steal it. The difference between the scenario with the car and the scenario with the network is that you can always buy a new car; but you cannot buy new data and customers if those items are lifted from your network. You should take great pains to ensure that your network is secure and safe from intentional or accidental hacking.
2. You should test security because no security policy is foolproof. A determined person could breach security and wreak havoc on your network. By constantly checking the network for problems, you have a chance of finding security loopholes before a hacker does.
3. Audit files tell you what you ask them to tell you. In particular, you can watch for logon attempts, changes to a file, modifications to Active Directory objects, and the frequency of use of an object. An audit file will tell you nothing if you fail to read the file.
4. You should audit anything that is a cause for concern. Good candidates include logon attempts and failures (especially with the administrator account), file permission changes, user permission changes, remote access, and access to secure data. Audit policies vary by organization, but most organizations care about those foregoing items.
5. Audit files can track use of a resource. Consider a printer. An audit file can tell the administrator how often the printer is used. As an organization grows, the use of the printer should grow at the same pace as the organization. If printer use increases faster than the growth of the organization, then an additional printer is probably a future necessity.

ANSWERS TO KEY TERM QUIZ

1. log
2. local policy
3. template
4. account policy
5. NTFS

INDEX

A

C

D

E

F

G

H

I

K

L

M

N

O

P

R

S

T

U

V

W

Z

INTERNATIONAL CONTACT INFORMATION

AUSTRALIA
McGraw-Hill Book Company Australia Pty. Ltd.
TEL +61-2-9417-9899
FAX +61-2-9417-5687
http://www.mcgraw-hill.com.au
books-it_sydney@mcgraw-hill.com

CANADA
McGraw-Hill Ryerson Ltd.
TEL +905-430-5000
FAX +905-430-5020
http://www.mcgrawhill.ca

GREECE, MIDDLE EAST, NORTHERN AFRICA
McGraw-Hill Hellas
TEL +30-1-656-0990-3-4
FAX +30-1-654-5525

MEXICO (Also serving Latin America)
McGraw-Hill Interamericana Editores S.A. de C.V.
TEL +525-117-1583
FAX +525-117-1589
http://www.mcgraw-hill.com.mx
fernando_castellanos@mcgraw-hill.com

SINGAPORE (Serving Asia)
McGraw-Hill Book Company
TEL +65-863-1580
FAX +65-862-3354
http://www.mcgraw-hill.com.sg
mghasia@mcgraw-hill.com

SOUTH AFRICA
McGraw-Hill South Africa
TEL +27-11-622-7512
FAX +27-11-622-9045
robyn_swanepoel@mcgraw-hill.com

UNITED KINGDOM & EUROPE (Excluding Southern Europe)
McGraw-Hill Education Europe
TEL +44-1-628-502500
FAX +44-1-628-770224
http://www.mcgraw-hill.co.uk
computing_neurope@mcgraw-hill.com

ALL OTHER INQUIRIES Contact:
Osborne/McGraw-Hill
TEL +1-510-549-6600
FAX +1-510-883-7600
http://www.osborne.com
omg_international@mcgraw-hill.com

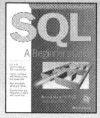

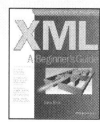

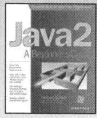

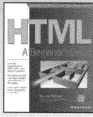

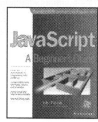

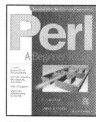

www.ingramcontent.com/pod-product-compliance
Lightning Source LLC
Chambersburg PA
CBHW080151060326
40689CB00018B/3941

* 9 7 8 0 0 7 2 2 2 3 0 3 3 *